AN INTRODUCTION TO
FLY FISHING
FOR TROUT

AN INTRODUCTION TO
FLY FISHING
FOR TROUT

MARK D. WILLIAMS
W. CHAD McPHAIL

STONEFLY
PRESS

PO Box 6146

Bloomington, IN 47407

FAX: 877-609-3814

email: info@stoneflypress.com

stoneflypress.com

Printed in the United States of America

17 16 15 14 13 1 2 3 4 5

Library of Congress Control Number: 2012955951

Stonefly Press

Publisher: Robert D. Clouse

Acquiring Editor: Robert D. Clouse

Managing Production Editor: Bill Bowers

Copy Editor: Bill Bowers

Proofreader: Eileen McNulty

Front Cover Photo: Brian O'Keefe

Back Cover Photos: Mark D. Williams and W. Chad McPhail

CONTENTS

Introduction   1

1   WHAT DO I NEED TO BUY?   11

2   WHAT KNOTS DO I NEED TO KNOW?   59

3   BUGS & INSECTS   67

4   TIME TO CAST   95

5   IT'S ALL ABOUT THE TROUT   123

6   WHAT SKILLS DO I NEED?   147

7   STRATEGIES, TACTICS & TECHNIQUES   183

8   OUTDOOR PHOTO TIPS   247

9   BACKPACKING FLY FISHING   261

10   FLY-FISHING ETIQUETTE (AND WHAT NOT TO DO)   271

Appendix: Recommended Reading   285

Index   289

MARK D. WILLIAMS has published hundreds of articles and photos in *Texas Sporting Journal, Backpacker, Men's Health, Dallas Morning News, Cowboys and Indians, Southwest Fly Fishing*, and many other publications.

His many books include *So Many Fish, So Little Time, Trout Fishing Sourcebook, The Backpacking Flyfisher, Flyfishing Southwestern Colorado, The Nuts 'N' Bolts Guide to Knots for Fly-fishers*, and *Freshwater Flyfishing Tips from the Pros*. Williams is now also an iPad/iPhone app author—his app, Freshwater Flyfishing Tips From the Pros, has 250 tips and 1,000 photos from all the big names in the sport and many from guys and gals in the trenches.

Williams's newest release is *49 Trout Streams of Southern Colorado* from University of New Mexico Press (with co-author Chad McPhail); and in 2014, two new Williams and McPhail collaborations from Stonefly Press: *50 Best Places to Fly Fish the Southwest*, and *Fly Fishing New Mexico: Where to Eat, Sleep, and Fish*.

Williams has traveled the world but finds himself more and more fishing small streams in New Mexico and Colorado and working on his second novel. He also teaches high school English and Speech at North Heights Alternative School in Amarillo, Texas.

W. Chad "Mac" McPhail is an avid outdoor enthusiast locked in a constant struggle between working and searching for wild trout in the American Southwest. A Texas native, he was named Teacher of the Year 2007 in Amarillo, Texas. McPhail is president of Amarillo Fly Guys (a chapter of Project Healing Waters Fly Fishing). His sometimes perilous pursuits into the wilderness often include fishing and writing buddy Mark D. Williams, as well as an unsuspecting cast of other easily duped buds and family members. Wesley (Mac's son) has been casting flies with his dad since the age of four, and is now in Jedi training learning Mark & Mac's small-stream guerilla tactics. Mac's published fishing books include *49 Trout Streams of Southern Colorado* and *Colorado Flyfishing: Where to Eat, Sleep, Fish.*

McPhail's favorite species to pursue with a fly rod include wild rainbow, brown, brook, and cutthroat trout, as well as largemouth and smallmouth bass.

McPhail's favorite fly-fishing activity is exploring the small streams of the American Southwest.

INTRODUCTION

You have decided you want to learn to wave that wand with the glowing line, with a fly dancing this way and that. You want to stand knee-deep in a cold, clear creek and try to mesmerize a trout into taking your offering. You want to learn fly fishing, one of the fastest-growing outdoor sports. So what's next?

Fly fishing is no longer just for the pipe-and-tweed crowd. A fly-rodding explosion has hit a nostalgic nerve in middle-class baby boomers. But not just there. The sport is seeing all kinds take up the long rod, from blue-collar workers to senior citizens to young kids to middle-aged soccer moms. With more and more Americans taking up fly fishing, the sport's popularity is rising like the trout in Yellowstone.

According the American Sportfishing Association, the number of Americans who went fishing in 2012 outnumbered those who ventured out to play golf and tennis combined. The core of recreational anglers in America is more than 70 million strong per year, ranging in age from young children to senior citizens. Imagine . . . the number of Americans who fish for fun exceeds amateur golfers (25 million) and tennis players (22.4 million) combined! Of those, some 15 million go fly fishing at least part of the time, according to a recent estimate from *Angling Trade* magazine. Amazing, since relatively little about fly fishing is ever televised or advertised.

Although fly fishing was born in Britain and remains incredibly popular in Europe, the sport's roots have spread across the globe to some

rather unlikely places, including Russia, South Africa, Belize, Costa Rica, Japan, New Zealand, Australia, and elsewhere, expanding the potential reach of fly fishing. (We've yet to hear of Antarctic fly fishing, but we're still waiting . . .)

And now it has spread to you, in the form of this book. This is a unique how-to guide, written in a conversational style, complete with brief anecdotes, clear instructions, insider tips, and secrets on how to get on the water quickly without the weeks of casting instruction and training you might have thought you needed.

This is a simple technique book that's fun and easy to read, complete with informative sidebars and color photographs that reinforce the most effective techniques for both beginning and intermediate anglers. But we've also tried to write a book that will help anglers continue to improve and to learn new skills as they gain experience and know-how.

No other instructional fly-fishing book is designed to help anglers enjoy success quicker than this one. We've cut out the fuss and fanfare that bogs down other how-to books. We know what learners want and need to be successful early and often. Both of us have taught in public schools for years, conducted fishing seminars, taught hundreds of beginners to read, write, and think as well as fish, and together we've written hundreds of articles and dozens of books. So yeah, of course we are fly-fishing buddies. But we are also writers and teachers and know how to turn the complicated into cake.

We've tried to demystify fly fishing and reveal that it's not just for the elite, nor is it a magical art, as many people believe. We've provided essential steps to becoming an efficient angler, steps that are accompanied by color photos, which are rarely found in other fly-fishing how-to books. We always have fun writing and teaching about the nuts and bolts of the sport we love so much, as well as its beauty.

We both adhere to the notion that fly fishing should not be difficult to learn. It wasn't for us, nor will it be for readers of our book. Fly fishing is a process best experienced on the water. Our book gets you on the river quickly and ready to learn and have fun. But it's also designed for intermediate-level anglers, and loaded with more advanced tips, so they can continue to improve.

We realize our book isn't the only fly-fishing how-to book on the shelves. There are many introductory books out there, and they run the gamut from paperbacks with simple line art drawings to coffee table color photo books. We own many of them. When we were both learning, so many years ago, we too turned to them for assistance. But we found issues and problems with each and every one.

It's too darned difficult to understand advanced techniques, such as how to roll cast or mend line, from reading a paragraph or two. The roll cast is a fairly difficult maneuver even with a few years of experience. And we both know plenty of experienced vets who have a tough time mending line. Our point is that we discuss the essentials, and we simplify them. But you want to get better over time while still catching fish along the way.

The main problem with most how-to books is that they tend to bog down in the technical jargon that only expert anglers can understand. Beginners need elementary lingo and instruction. The sheer size of some of these compendiums scares many readers away from the sport. Fly-

When fishing is good, two anglers can fish a single hole.

fishing how-to books tend to drag heavy with emphasis on techniques and strategies, failing at the most facile element of a primer—enabling the reader to easily recreate the lessons. It's why Hall of Fame athletes so rarely make good coaches. They expect those they teach to be as good as they are and to know what they know. Eventually, you will need more advanced books, and once you build a fly-fishing foundation, you should also build a library of them to help you learn more about fly fishing. This book is for anglers who want to learn the sport on the water, rather than in a fly shop or in the backyard practicing casting to a yard ring.

Here you will learn the basic skills, such as how to set up your rod and reel, what gear to buy and how to use it, and multiple techniques for fishing with flies. This book isn't just a nice teaching tool, but is built for the beginner to learn how to fly fish in the trenches. It was created for all anglers to glean simple principles of fly fishing that they can easily process into casting and catching success.

Bottom line, you want to catch fish right away. We want to help you do that. Don't expect to cast like Mel Krieger or Lefty Kreh on your first day out. Casting like a pro is truly unimportant. You probably won't ever hit

4

Fly fishing gets you out into the most scenic places in the world.

a golf ball like Arnold Palmer, either. You need realistic expectations out of the gate. We have met far too many beginners who tried fly fishing once and gave up. We've heard, "It's just too hard!" or "I just didn't get it!" a thousand times. But it's really not. Learn with us, and we'll prove it to you.

We want you to be successful on day one, your first trip. Some of that success means not falling in, not hooking a fly into your ear, simply spotting a trout before you

A well-loaded rod makes for a good cast.

scare it, and minimizing all the things that go through your mind so you have a fighting chance at catching that fish you see. Keep things simple at first and we'll help you build your skills over time, with successes, and avoid demoralizing defeats.

Throughout the book, you'll pick up on our fishing strategies and overriding philosophy. Ours doesn't have to be yours. But it works for us. We hit and run when we fish. We follow a risk-to-reward philosophy, in that we don't want to work harder to try to catch a fish than the possible reward we will reap. Sure, we'll go prospecting for big fish on some trips, and that means we take some risks wading and hiking—but for the most part, we like to cover as much water as we can. There's always another great hole just up the river.

*A beautiful Western
canyon stream*

Mac "high-sticks" a nymph through these fast riffles.

You'll read that we like to fish for (and catch) trout. We have both fished all over the world and caught multiple gamefish species on the fly, but we always come back to trout fishing. It's just one of those things. You don't necessarily have to do the same—you may be driven by going after smallmouths in rivers or exotic species in foreign countries or fishing the salt for redfish. You can do it all. But our book is designed for the beginner to learn on trout streams.

We introduced a friend to the wonderful world of fly fishing a few years back. One morning around camp, we gave him a two-hour crash course into all the whats and whatnots of fly fishing: how to cast, what insects the flies represent, what those knots are used for, and so on. We showed him how to tie a cinch knot to his leader, which is attached to his fly line, which is attached to his backing, which is spooled on his reel. Then we tied on a size 14 Elk-hair Caddis. We got to the water, and he had forgotten absolutely everything we had overwhelmed him with, and had only one question on his mind: What is an Elephant Ear Catalyst anyhow?

If you've been wanting to take up the sport of fly fishing and have thought it a tad too intricate or elite; if you learned how to fly fish when you were a kid but forgot half of what you learned and weren't really all that good at the other half; or if you have thought to yourself—while knee-deep in a New Mexico stream fishing with a spinning rod and PowerBait—that you'd like to have a different angling option, it's not too late to learn.

And the good thing is that almost anywhere you live, you have numerous options and lots of fellow fly-fishing fools to help you learn. You don't even have to be close to trout water to learn to fly fish. You can start with panfish or smallmouth bass. To further help sell you on the idea of a long rod and small flies, fly fishing is often the better and more effective way to catch trout and bass, another weapon in your arsenal. You don't have to convert 100 percent overnight (that will come later).

Fly fishing isn't limited to men or trout, either. The fastest-growing segment of the market is women, and children are right behind. We've taught a lot of people to fish over the years, and honestly feel that women and children are much easier to teach than men. And the trout? Fly fishers now angle for bass, perch, spotted seatrout, redfish, catfish, carp, stripers—almost anything with fins.

An Introduction to Fly Fishing for Trout is our how-to book. We hope you enjoy the sport of fly fishing as much as we always have. Keep the rod safe while we get ready. (Any rod left propped against the door is in a bit more danger.)

Facing. Fly fishing is a sport well-suited to ladies, too.

WHAT DO I NEED TO BUY?

Support your local fly shops but supplement with online and catalog purchases. Buy better goods—the highest quality you can afford—rather than cheap gear. You get what you pay for. Buy good flies, not some off brand from a discount sporting goods store. Try other folks' gear before you buy. Try on or try out equipment and gear at the fly shop before you purchase. Avoid fiberglass rods. Avoid rubber hip waders. Avoid felt soles in favor of newer materials. We shop at Riverfields locally, and we mention them in books and articles. This kind of support enhances the community understanding of the sport, as well as suggests that the sport is worth trying—as you are now. That's it in a nutshell.

NECESSITIES: GEAR YOU NEED

What follows is a list of must-have items you'll need to begin the sport of fly fishing, beyond the obvious rod, reel, line, and flies. We wish we'd had this list when we were learning.

Fishing Shirt

You need to cover thy girth when fishing. It's just part of our sport. It cannot be done any other way. Sorry, but sun bouncing off water is a serious issue for all anglers. You'll want to be covered about the neck, back, chest, arms, and torso areas. Material, hue, and style of cut are all things to consider when fishing on the river.

You'll want a go-to shirt. One that photographs well. One that allows you to move freely. One with long sleeves that roll up and stay up. One that will keep you cool and won't make you look ridiculous. Fly-fishing shirts should be functional—with pockets, flaps, and so on. One thing they should not be is *loud*! Let's be practical for a moment. River water is typically clear. Trout have amazing vision. If your shirt is too brightly colored, they will see you coming a mile away. (This is Mac's idea. We differ. I think any color is fine and you should use stealth to keep the brightness out of view. —Mark)

OUR RECOMMENDATIONS

Stick with materials that dry quickly and are super lightweight. Brand names are huge in fly fishing, mostly because everything in the sport is a specialty item and some companies dominate the field. We love Columbia Sportswear and Sage brand shirts. Their quality is superior and comfort is impeccable. Buy a shirt that fits just a little loosely. You'll appreciate the extra room when casting and layering. We also think the jacket you choose to fish in should be as well thought out as your shirt. The same guidelines apply—but look for a breathable, waterproof jacket, not just a $10 one off the rack at a discount store because that jacket, when you're in the rain, standing in the river, will make you sweat like a pig.

Back to shirts. Here's where we differ: Mark believes color doesn't matter to the fish. If you're fishing mindfully, they should never see you. But when Mac was a novice, he noticed they seemed far more skittish when he wore his bright, light yellow shirt than when he wore a light blue one. He feels camouflaged against the sky in light blue. Mac's opinion is to choose colors like light blue, sage green, off white, and red.Other colors like tan, dark blue, forest green, or brown will blend in too much with the background for pictures. Colors like dreamsicle or periwinkle might scare the hell out of the fish before you ever cast. But you'll look good in photos at least.

Fishing shirts offer comfort and protection.

Amy wears a tapered blue fishing shirt made just for women.

Sometimes you need a light-weight jacket.

Waders

Function: Waders should do two things and two things only: keep you warm, and keep you dry. Water is cold and wet. Waders keep you from both.

Types: Rubber, neoprene, nylon, and breathable.

Styles: Hip waders, guide pants, and chest waders.

Rubber waders are old school blister-makers and should be tossed into the wood chipper.

Pros: None. (Well, if you have to use a pair of rubberized hip waders, you can survive for a day, but the blisters and sweat and constant sagging will convince you to try something else.)

Cons: Too many to list. The only reason you should ever step into the river with old rubber waders is so that you'll know exactly what your grandpa went through when he was a young fly fisher.

Neoprene waders are designed for the coldest of conditions. Yes, we realize they are rubber too, but neoprene stretches and it's practical for lakes and tailwaters. (Besides, neoprene gums up a wood chipper, so don't throw them in there.)

Pros: Neoprene keeps you warmer than other materials, plus it stretches with body movement, a must for cold water and winter fishing.

Cons: Neoprene feels bulky and will wear you out over the course of a day if you try to cover a lot of territory on the river. Plus, it can tear very easily. Williams let me borrow a pair of his once when I went fishing near Eagle, Colorado. It wasn't until I was suiting up at the edge of the water that I noticed the rip in the thigh. It flopped open like a bison's tongue, so I wrapped duct tape around that leg and went on about my business. I nearly drowned.

Nylon waders are also a thing of the past and can be very uncomfortable. They don't stretch with your body and can get rather hot, so sweat or water will stay in them all day. Forget about them.

Pros: Durable.

Cons: Binding, uncomfortable, do not wick moisture away from the skin, and often have inferior unfitted boots built in.

Breathable waders are made of cutting-edge materials, often stretchable, and they allow perspiration to wick away from the body while simultaneously leaving you a spry dry guy (or gal) with a fly in July.

Pros: Trekking all day is easy, and breathable waders will adjust freely with your body movements. Breathables are lightweight and come with either a built-in neoprene sock so you can slide on your wading boots, or with superior boots built in. They do a great job at wicking moisture away from the skin, and are made of comfortable, lightweight, stretchable material, and are easy to put on and take off.

Buy yourself a good pair of breathable waders. You'll be glad you did. Photo courtesy of The Orvis Company.

Cons: Breathable waders will not typically keep you warm in the coldest waters, unless you wear something warm underneath, in layers. They can also be punctured readily by hooks or limbs. These won't be catastrophic holes, such as the neoprene debacle described above, just tiny pinholes. But they can turn out to be nuisance leaks that saturate your undergarments throughout the course of a day.

Hip waders or "hippers" come up to the mid-thigh or to the hip and almost always clip onto your belt.

Pros: These are great for shallow streams of small to medium sizes and will allow for a range of motion other waders won't. They are inexpensive and don't take up a lot of space. They're good for hiking, but wet wading (no waders at all) is best. The best thing about hippers is that they protect you from brush and thorns and that sort of thing, in and out of water.

Cons: Hip waders are only practical on the smallest of streams. If water comes in them even once, you might as well take them off and wade wet. If yours don't fit well, hello blisters and chafing.

Guide pants are not much taller than hip waders, but they fit like comfy pants, snug up at the waist to keep water out, and serve about the same function as hip waders.

Pros: Guide pants are often more comfortable than other waders and will bind up less than chest waders. They won't fill in with water as readily as hippers.

Cons: They are more expensive than hippers, and will bind somewhat when hiking uphill or on trails where longer strides are needed.

Chest waders come all the way up to the chest and employ suspenders to hold them up. These are great for deeper water and fishing from float tubes.

Pros: Chest waders are the most practical because they can be used for all types of water. Most can be "wrapped" around the waist and buckled tight to simulate guide pants. Most anglers buy them because they can be used for all-around waders. If you're going to buy chest waders, get breathable waders that are comfortable, not tight.

Cons: Chest waders are the most expensive, since they require the greatest amount of material. Anglers who cover many miles in a day will also find chest waders a bit more binding and limiting than guide pants or hippers.

The near freezing waters of the Taylor River require quality waders.

OUR RECOMMENDATIONS

We very seldom wear waders. It's only water, after all. Why not get wet? However, we do see uses for waders from time to time. A good pair of neoprene waders is almost mandatory for fishing freezing cold waters like the San Juan in New Mexico, where you're stationary in waist-deep water that's 35–40 degrees most the day. But then again, the San Juan is not for beginners. A comfy pair of breathable guide pants or chest waders would be wise if you feel you must wear waders at all. Buy the best breathable waders you can afford (make sure they're GORE-TEX or something similar) because they'll last longer and be more comfortable.

Wading Boots and Shoes

Wading boots and shoes, simply put, are a fly fisher's footgear. They are the critical medium between the angler and the river. So yeah, we believe they are of utmost importance. Nowadays most quality boots and shoes have natural and/or synthetic rubber soles to help keep you from slipping on moss-covered rocks to some degree. Many rubber soles even are augmented with tiny metal cleats or studs to provide better traction.

For many decades, fly fishers relied on wading boots and shoes with soles of natural or synthetic felt, with or without metal studs. The good news is that felt provides excellent footing on slimy, algae- or moss-covered rocks. The bad news is that felt is not as good out of the water—for hiking to or along the riverbank, or walking on snow or ice. But the really bad news is that porous felt soles pick up and carry the spores of invasive aquatic species such as *Didymosphenia geminata* algae, commonly known as didymo or "rock snot," carrying them from one watershed to another.

Originally found in only some cold Northern Hemisphere watersheds, didymo has spread to many North American streams where it was

High-tech rubber soles have replaced felts as the choice of environmentally conscious anglers. Photo courtesy of The Orvis Company

never previously known, and to the legendary trout streams of New Zealand as of 2004—its first appearance in the Southern Hemisphere. Didymo can alter stream habitats and adversely impact the reproduction of the aquatic insects that are major food sources for trout. For these reasons, New Zealand and the states of Alaska, Maryland, and Vermont have already banned the use of felt soles. Other states and Canadian provinces are considering similar regulations. Even where felt soles remain legal, conservation-minded anglers and guides discourage their use.

Leading fly-fishing equipment manufacturers such as Orvis, L.L. Bean, Simms, Chota, and others are phasing out felt soles in favor of high-tech rubber soles, with or without metal studs. Even soles made of so-called "sticky rubber" don't work as well as, say, tentacles. We'd like someone to design tentacle-bottomed boots for us, please!

Anyway, wading boots and shoes allow better drainage than hiking boots or athletic shoes, yet still allow anglers to tread the banks and negotiate riverbeds without letting in gravel and rocks. Most boots and shoes will provide some degree of protection from the frigid water, but know that no boot will keep you warm in a cold river if you're in it a while. They are designed for water to pass in and out of them. And depending upon the height and style, they also support the ankles. Apart from the rod and fly line, we believe your wading boots and shoes are where you should pay the most attention to detail. Find the perfect pair for you.

Boots and shoes vary in degree of weight, quality, comfort, style, and durability. To simplify all this boot stuff, we'll break them down into heavyweight, medium-weight, and lightweight.

Heavyweight boots are best suited for stationary angling in large, cold rivers. They are comprised of thick materials, usually synthetic, such as GORE-TEX and artificial leather. Since they tend to be designed for heavier duty, walking all day in them might become fatiguing.

> *Pros:* Long-lasting, with superior quality, protection, and support, and A+ comfort.
>
> *Cons:* They're heavier than other boots and can be pricey. Not great for hiking any distance to the water.

Medium-weight boots are designed for the average angler on the average water on an average day of fishing. They will provide ample ankle protection and can last three to five years, depending upon how much walking you do when angling.

> *Pros:* Affordable and ample protection. Comfort is key with medium-weight boots.
>
> *Cons:* May not last as long as heavier duty boots, and might still put a dent in your wallet.

Lightweight boots, at the other end of the spectrum, are designed to be inexpensive and easy on the body.

> *Pros:* Particularly well-suited for small streams and trekking long distances because of their minimal weight.
>
> *Cons:* Won't provide much ankle support, and you'll be lucky to get two years of use out of them.

Wading shoes are basically tennis shoes made for fishing streams. They fit like average cross-trainer shoes, so many anglers like the minimalist characteristics and the comfort they afford. They're nice for rock-hopping on the bank.

Pros: These tend to be the perfect choice for smallwater fishers and those who hike, backpack, or need an easy-to-pack pair for travel. They're tough, light, and don't take up a lot of space. They only take a few seconds to put on, too.

Cons: They provide no ankle stability and allow some sediment and gravel into the footbeds. They wear out quickly.

Wading sandals are just that, sandals. They are the next thing to being barefoot on the river—sorta hippie and sorta caveman.

Pros: Sandals are ultra-lightweight and pack down to nearly nothing. They are great for fishing tiny rivulets and sandy-bottom streams where walking isn't necessary. They're fun to use if you're camped right next to a stream. Plus they won't break the bank.

Cons: Sandals won't provide any protection from cold water. Rocks and gravel will often irritate the soles of your feet if you're walking more than a quarter mile in them. Protruding sticks are a danger. And sandals slip around on the foot quite a bit.

OUR RECOMMENDATIONS

We prefer lightweight rubber-soled boots, and we also dig the new models of wading shoes. Ninety-five percent of our fishing time is spent on small to medium streams. Plus, when we fish, we hike a lot of miles. We're minimalists, so it makes sense for us to spend around $100 on boots and wear them out quicker than to be out of pocket $150 or more and feel the heft of the boots on long hikes. Furthermore, we also recommend that you don't order boots online without first trying on a pair somewhere else. Don't order blindly, and remember to allow room for waders or wading socks.

We also recommend wearing Neoprene socks underneath wading boots. Thickness is about the only difference in neoprene socks. Some are 1mm, some are 2 mm, and they go on up to 5mm. Some have a guard or gaiter that pulls down over the top of your boot to keep out sand and debris. You will definitely need neoprenes for fly fishing. Start off with a 2mm sock and wear it under your boots. However, you may end up like us and go to the 1mm sock and a wading shoe.

Lightweight back-packing-style wading shoes with lightweight neoprene wading socks

Some anglers still like traditional fishing vests.

Vests, Chest Packs, Waist Packs, and Lanyards

Anglers need a comfortable way to carry all their trinkets and gadgets in an organized manner: pockets, pouches, straps, and slots. There's a perfect setup out there for you.

Vests

Fly-fishing vests are by far the most traditional option for carrying and storing fly gear. Most are made of cotton/poly poplin blends, Spandex, and other cutting-edge materials. They zip or snap open and most allow a full range of motion while casting.

> *Pros:* Vests are quite comfortable, roomy, and boast numerous pockets of various sizes for individualizing any means of organization. Most vests brandish a large, deep pocket in back for stowing rain jackets, lunch, or even the catch of the day. Having this large pocket makes vests a natural choice for anglers who like to keep fish for cleaning and eating later. We always keep a large Ziploc baggie for just that case. It's tough to get the smell of fish out of your vest.

Cons: Vests do have their limitations. Oftentimes vests require the use of both hands to open zippered or snapped pockets. Cotton vests do not stretch and can bind up an angler who climbs over and around boulders or stream banks. And if the vest gets submerged, most are not waterproof, so it may take hours for the gear and vest to dry out.

Chest Packs

Since chest packs arrived on the market, they have become increasingly more functional and technical.

Pros: Chest packs are lightweight, sleek, and more durable than ever. With stylish designs and trendy colors, more anglers are choosing packs because they look great and make so much sense. Most are made of waterproof material, and they put the gear in the most convenient place, right under the angler's nose. They may not have as many pockets as vests, but what they lack in pockets they make up for in other ways.

For instance, many packs come with hands-free hydration systems. No more bottles of water bouncing around. Other chest packs offer a flip-out workstation that serves as a small "table," making fly selection and knot tying rather easy. Some packs double as fly boxes. Chest packs can also have waterproof zippers and pockets for keeping gear dry. They are also adjustable, so fitting them over just about anything an angler chooses to wear on the river or lake is a critical comfort issue when fishing in heat during one season and in the cold during another.

Cons: The downside to chest packs is that some models have a tendency to get in the way of the casting motion. An ill-fitting pack that's too bulky may rub the inner arm, create an impediment when cross-body casting, flop around, or snag your fly line, all of which can be annoying when concentration is crucial. Find a chest pack that fits properly and doesn't extend too far off of the body. There's one suitable for every angler in any fishing condition.

Chest packs put everything within easy reach.

Waist Packs

For some anglers, less means more. Bare-bones, minimalist-style angling requires carrying only the most essential gear, cutting down on both weight and bulk. Waist packs or "fanny packs" are perfect for anglers who traverse great distances in a single day to fish rivers or alpine lakes in the backcountry.

Pros: They're great for wet wading. A small fly box, a single spool of tippet, floatant, extra leaders, water filter, a snack, and a license are the bare essentials for catching trout, and all of this will fit easily into most waist packs on the market. Waist packs are all about lightening the load, so most anglers find one made of the lightest material available with a very low profile. The pack can be worn in the front, on the back, or on either hip. Their no-nonsense characteristics make them the only choice for those who don't need all the bells and whistles of vests and chest packs. Plus, they are very affordable.

Cons: Since waist packs ride low on the body, if you slip, fall, or wade too deep, your gear is gonna take a plunge. Also, the limited space means you may not be able to take as much gear and other essentials as you'd like, such as food and water.

Waist packs hold your gear but stay out of your way.

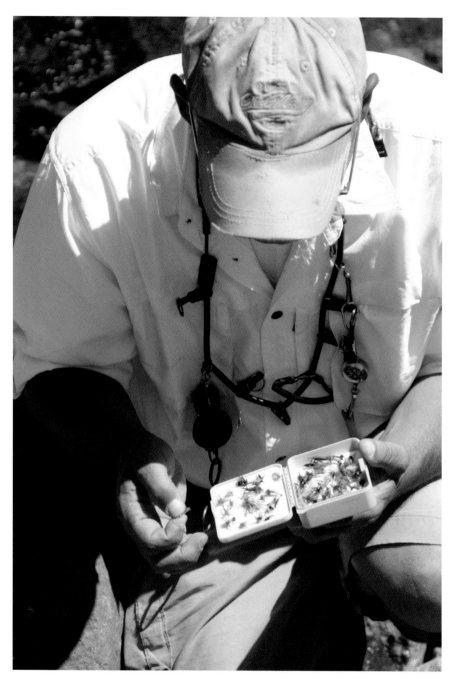

A lanyard helps keep everything organized and readily at hand.

Lanyards

One more way to carry gear in a minimalist way is on a lanyard that hangs around your neck. A lanyard is basically a necklace sort of contraption with clips and loops and rings all over it from which you hang, attach, or snap gear to. (Lanyards remind Mac of some sort of Mr. T start-up kit.

They remind Mark of an African boar's tooth necklace.) Some people like lanyards because all your gear is visible and available, and they force you to leave unimportant gear behind. Others hate them because they flop around and sometimes things fall off or get snagged. Until you try one, you may not know if you like them or not.

Tools of the Trade

Nets

Some are made of wood, and some of aluminum; some fold, some don't, and the best have rubber matrix netting as opposed to the old-school green string net used for holding up surfboards at Joe's Crab Shack.

A net's function is to secure the fish but do so in a safe and humane manner that is also much more effective for the angler than holding the fish by hand.

Pros: You'll land more fish with a net than without. It's a no-brainer. We prefer shallow nets with fish-friendly netting. Almost any net made nowadays, except for the kind you buy at discount general stores, will be fish-friendly. Rubberized netting or fine mesh netting are good choices. Other than what style net to choose (wood or aluminum frame), you'll have to figure out how to attach it to your vest or fanny pack or belt. Some like magnetic attachments (pick us, pick us) while others like an elastic band or quick-release clip.

Rubberized "release nets" hold the fish without damaging its protective slime coating.

Cons: There are those anglers who prefer to keep the fish in the water and use forceps or pliers to remove the fly so that they never touch (or the net never touches) the fish. But this can lead to overplaying fish or losing the trout because they still have fight in them when they get close to you. There are no cons to nets, unless you use a bad one. What's a bad net? Anything made in the 1960s or 1970s. Anything made with ropelike green twine. Don't use any "standard" netting that will injure the fish or remove its slime coating.

Nippers

Nippers are glorified nail clippers. Most serve only two purposes: to cut your line, leader, and tippet, and to save your teeth. A good pair will also have a tiny needle or pin sticking out of the back end, whose purpose is to break or poke dried glue out of the eye of the hook so you can feed your tippet through it.

There are metal nippers and ceramic blade nippers. Ceramic blade nippers are usually housed in a plastic casing. Metal nippers are simple and do the job just fine.

Pros: Sufficient for cutting and can be sharpened when dulled.

Cons: After a few years of being banged around and cutting line, nippers may need replacing. They tend to jingle as you walk if they are close to anything else that's metal, which can become annoying. Some cheaper nippers will also rust. Ceramic nippers cut line just as well as metal ones, if not better.

Pros: The ceramic blade stays sharp longer than metal, and the composite structure of the housing may be slightly more durable than metal.

Cons: The ceramic blades are sometimes slightly "inset," which means it can be difficult to cut a fine piece of tippet flush at the site of the knot.

OUR RECOMMENDATIONS

You'll probably use your teeth more than your nippers anyway, so when you buy a pair, don't spend more than $12 to $15.

Hook Removers

If you haven't noticed, trout hooks tend to be on the extreme side of tiny. Sometimes trout engulf a fly and it's so far down inside the fish's mouth you can't get your fingers in to remove it. Also on occasion, the hook will lodge in a hard gill plate or cartilage and even with the barb bent down it's difficult to remove. Enter hook removers! Hook removers help keep hooked trout alive by making the hook removal process quick and safe. You definitely need them.

There are really two types of hook removers: long and short. We both started out with the long ones and found them unnecessarily cumbersome. We both now use the shorter, stubbier kind, so we recommend you stick with them too. They're just easier to use and they're half the size. Ketchum Release is one of the most popular brands of hook removers. We recommend buying forceps instead but make sure you purchase a pair that can crimp down barbs.

Leader Straightener

Since almost all leaders are coiled up inside a tiny paper or plastic pouch, when you open them and uncoil them, they retain a somewhat spiral shape. This is called line "memory" because it's almost like it can't forget what position it was in for several months. A straightener is a double-sided flap that you slide your leader through, and will do a reasonable job at making that leader "forget."

We know of only one type of leader straightener, and it's shaped somewhat like a flattened leather light bulb.

Pros: Straighteners keep you from burning your fingers from friction as you pull the leader through them.

Cons: A leader straightener can be just another gadget that you can do without. If you're careful and take it slowly, you can pull an uncoiled leader between your thumb and forefinger repeatedly, generating enough heat to "melt" the memory from your leader. (Williams and I are men. And this is our preferred method.)

Floatant

Dry flies eventually drown. Water gets all inside the fibers and the feathers and whatnot and within about 20 minutes, many flies become inoperable. Floatant is an applied barrier that you rub into the fly that repels water and keeps it floating higher and longer than without it.

Gel is probably the favored type of floatant. It typically comes in a small squeezable bottle, and only a tiny bit of this clear, aqueous gel substance is applied and worked into to the fly. Some gels are infused with glitter or iridescence.

Pastes are popular as well and come in a small round dish with a lid, similar to a flattened Carmex lip balm container. As with gel floatant, only a tiny bit is needed, but you can smear on as much as you like. The paste happens to be Mac's favorite, but the brand he uses shall remain a secret. (We'll just say that the company that produces it is named after a bird, and the paste itself sounds a little Cajun.)

Powders are the newest members of the floatant family and come in a small tube. Pop open the lid, insert fly, and shake. That's all you do.

Pros: Floatant is more necessary when fishing more active water, such as riffles and boils. Since anywhere the water is whiter from bubbles there will be less surface tension, the fly will be splashed and submerged more.

Cons: If you learn to dry your fly through false casting, squeezing the water from the fly with your shirttail, or simply by changing out flies, floatant is not always needed. Also, floatant can be paradoxically worse for the fly than none at all. Once the fly becomes too heavy with gel or paste, it won't float.

OUR RECOMMENDATIONS

We recommend trying high-end floatants of all three types to see what you prefer. Mac swears by the paste, but his buddy, Page McKinney, attests that the shake powder is the easiest, quickest, and least messy.

Polarized Glasses

We believe that the most important piece of equipment for any angler is a pair of polarized sunglasses. Yeah, you can catch fish without them, but you won't catch as many. Sunlight reflecting from watery surfaces is primarily horizontally polarized. The rays aren't scattered in all directions like normal sunlight; reflected light generally travels in a more horizontally oriented direction. This creates an intense reflection of light that we experience as glare. Polarized sunglasses contain a special filter that blocks this intense light, reducing glare, allowing you to see into the water without the harsh light, or the sky's image mirrored in it.

There are as many types of polarized sunglasses out there as there are shoes in Paris Hilton's closet. What you should be concerned with is comfort, style, and the color of the lenses, in that order. First, get a pair that feels good, and that makes you look like a million bucks. And most anglers prefer lenses that mimic the color of the river bottom—some shade of tan or amber. For some reason, this makes a difference.

You can buy those cheap plastic sunglasses from the big discount stores, but you'll end up scratching them, losing them, and replacing them many times over. The quality of those cheapies is overrated, too—you won't be able to see as many fish under the water, won't be able to distinguish

Polarized sunglasses make it easier to see into the water. Mac with a nice rainbow trout.

colors as well, won't be able to contrast objects and colors, and you won't be able to avoid distortion when you take vista-style views.

The most important reason to have a solid pair of polarized sunglasses, beyond performance and durability, is to protect your eyes from hooks, harmful sunshine, and UV rays. A good pair of polarized specs can reduce eye fatigue, remove glare, and allow you to see underwater.

*The right clothing and gear make
fishing easier and more fun.*

With higher-quality sunglasses, those anglers with corrective vision needs can usually order prescription lenses. Just remember that prescription lenses can make what were lightweight glasses into not-so-lightweight glasses.

You'll be glad you paid more for a pair of polarized glasses that have glass lenses instead of polycarbonate or acrylic, but all three are acceptable, relative to your budget. Then you'll want to match your lens tint to the type of water you'll be fishing. Lens tints range from brown, blue, green, copper, amber, mirror, and others and each has its particular strengths and weaknesses.

Pros: Polarized glasses are like having magic eyeballs. With them, you can literally see straight through the water, presuming the water itself is clear, and therefore you can see fish and what they're up to. Not only that, but polarized lenses also help you see the rocks you're about to wade through.

Cons: The only cons we can think of are cost, and water droplets on the lenses. But these are cons with any glasses. You must have sunglasses when fly fishing, for protection from the sun and overhanging limbs, as well as flies. They might as well be polarized.

Leader and Tippet

What is a leader? What is a tippet? Fair questions. There are a few tricky parts if you are playing along at home, so pay attention.

A leader is a tapered monofilament connection between your fly line and your fly. The leader is thicker in the butt and tapers down to the tag end, where it ties to the fly. The leader allows for a natural presentation of the fly because you can see that your fly line surely can't provide that. Leader is almost invisible in the water (but not quite, as you will see.) The leader also provides a transfer of energy from the rod to the fly line and down to the fly itself. The leader must be strong enough that when a fish takes the fly, the connection remains between the fly, the leader and the fly line.

Here's one of the tricky parts: the thinnest part of any leader is called the tippet. The tippet is what you tie to the fly. Tippet is also a spool of leader material that you tie to the leader when the thinnest part has been removed, cut away, broken, frayed, and so on. A leader will tend to be 7½ to 10 feet long and typically comes in a clear plastic sleeve. Tippet typically comes on a spool. Anglers will want their leaders to match the flies they are using. You don't want a leader too thick for a small fly, but we're getting ahead of ourselves.

Now for the next tricky part: Leader and tippet material comes in sizes, represented by a number code that makes as much sense as Sanskrit. It's an X-code. You'll buy leaders and tippet that will have a designation such as 4X or 6X. The "X" measures the diameter of the leader minus 0.011. So a 3X would measure 0.008 of an inch. A 0X, at one time, would actually measure 0.011. You do not need to know this; there will not be a test.

What you do need to know is that the higher the number with the X, the smaller the diameter of the leader. What size leaders will you need?

What size spools of tippet? This will vary from situation to situation depending on all kinds of variables. A rookie should have in his or her possession: one pack of 4X leaders, two packs of 5X leaders, two packs of 6X leaders, and one spool each of 4X, 5X, and 6X tippet. When you get more experienced and start fishing tailwaters and spring creeks, you'll add 7X leaders and tippet to your arsenal. Perhaps even 8X.

But wait, there's more—you'll need to know the lengths of your leaders when you purchase them. For rookies, we recommend 7½-foot leaders. That extra 2 feet of leader can be a real headache in the wind or around obstacles. You might try a 9-foot or 10-foot leader, but when you get wind knots, you'll see what we mean. When you lose leader because of changing flies or a bird's nest, you can tie on more tippet from the spool. How to do that? See the section on knots in Chapter 2, but you can use a surgeon's knot, a double surgeon's knot, or a blood knot, among others, but we like these best. It makes sense to buy your leader and tippet in the same brand material but we don't and we never notice a difference. We do have favorite manufacturers for our leaders and tippet, but these are a personal choice. You'll figure out yours. Not all have the same feel, strength, limpness, stiffness, and so on. There's no hard and fast rule, but here's our guide to when to use which leader-tippet combination: 0X for fly sizes 2 to 6; 1X for sizes 4 to 8; 2X for sizes 4 to 10; 3X for sizes 6 to 10; 4X for sizes 6 to 12; 5X for sizes 12 to 16; 6X for sizes 16 to 20; and 7X for sizes 20 to 24.

Reels

Reels don't just hold your fly line, contrary to what you might have heard. They balance your fly rod. They control the lunker at the end of your line. They aid in your casts. They can be aesthetically pleasing. And if you fish enough, you'll expect your fly reel to be durable. Reels should be something to be proud of, something to be happy to control your fish. You can get by with a lousy reel if you're fishing a small stream and never have to put a fish on your reel, but if you have a salmon, bass, tarpon, or tuna hooked, you'll need your reel to perform or you'll be fishless and mad. Buy a reel that fits your needs.

OUR RECOMMENDATIONS

If you plan to go after lunkers, buy the best reel you can afford. If you plan to fish small to medium rivers and lakes, get a reel that you can afford, knowing that the reel is important (but not as much as your rod). Large-arbor reels are awesome inventions, but make sure that the reel width and circumference are larger, too. Don't buy a cheap reel (anything under 50 bucks). The cheapies are typically cast, and the high-end ones are made from blocks of aircraft-grade aluminum. Make sure to get a reel that is anodized so it won't rust. Ask experts what reel matches your rod so that the outfit is balanced and fits your needs. Some like to buy reels with interchangeable spools. If you do, buy a quality reel. Get a reel with a good drag (many come with sealed drags now, which means the reel will last longer, but you'll want a disk drag as opposed to a click-and-pawl.) Clean your reel and line after each trip.

Above. With reasonable care and maintenance, a good-quality trout reel like this Hardy Princess will last for many years. Photos courtesy of Hardy & Greys, Ltd.

Right. The Orvis C.F.O. III is a modern trout reel of traditional design. Photo courtesy of The Orvis Company

With so many variables, the choice of fly line may be the most confusing investment to the novice fly fisher, besides the rod. Here, we'll break down in a sensible manner what all the letters and numbers mean.

Beginning fly fishers are often befuddled about what "WF5F" means. But honestly this could be the most crucial factor in whether you catch fish, or not. Knowing what the numbers and letters represent is step one in learning to fly fish. A heavier line will travel farther. That makes sense, right? If you cast a light line and a heavy line with the same force, the heavy one goes farther. It'll cut through wind too. But your arm will get tired easier, and you won't have quite as much touch. Each weight has its own rhyme and reason.

Taper

The first letter or two on the box (for example, "WF") reveals the secret identity to the line's "taper"—the manner in which the line goes from thick to thin. Fly lines are designed with specifically tapered ends for very specific casting results. It's truly a scientific method that requires tons of R&D, and fly line companies fight for supremacy where tapers and materials are concerned. Tapers come in hundreds of different styles, but fall into only a handful of categories.

Level (L) means the line possesses a uniform thickness throughout its entire length, and is generally not an ideal line. It's almost always a cheesy, freebie line already spun onto the reel in one of those cheap starter kits you get at large discount stores. Don't buy that crap.

Weight-forward (WF) is the most commonly used line, with a long, uniform belly (or running line) and a subtle bulge near one end of the line before it tapers to a small diameter. This bulge facilitates easier, farther casts and helps the loop roll over better for a smooth presentation.

Double-taper (DT) means the thickest part of the line is in the center if you were to fold it in half from end to end. A double-taper fly line gradually thins out to a smaller diameter, equally and evenly at both ends, so each end of the line mirrors the other. Novice anglers find DT lines easy to cast, and it's economical since, when one end wears out, it can be reversed on the reel and fished from the other end.

Shooting line or shooting taper (ST) is designed specifically to cast tight loops long distances. This line is for the most experienced casters and almost always used in conjunction with a tip-flex rod.

Choosing the appropriate taper means knowing what body of water you're going to fish. It also means you'll want to know the wind conditions whenever possible. And your casting skill can also dictate your best line choice.

A weight-forward taper (WF) is our first recommendation for beginners, since it's beneficial in most casting conditions. A double-taper is our second.

Weight

While the WF stands for "weight-forward," the number in the series WF5F (or what-have-you) indicates the line's "weight." This is *not* how much the line weighs. Rather, fly rods are assigned a number value (or weight) according to the line weight the manufacturer suggests the rod will cast properly.

Line "weights" range from 00 to 14, with 00 (or "double-ought") being the lightest line ever made, and 14-weight being the heaviest. It's easy to determine which rod weight and associated line to fish. Simply determine what species and sizes of fish you'll target, and use the following guide to choose a rod and line.

00- to 3-weight: Diminutive trout in tiny to medium streams and rivulets, as well as perch, panfish, and other small fish around pond edges and docks.

4- to 6-weight: Medium- to lower-end large trout and other similarly sized fish on lakes, ponds, and easily waded rivers, with 5-weight line being the most common and versatile of all line weights because it can be fished up or down this scale.

For instance, it's perfectly feasible to fish a 5-weight rod on small rivers for little trout where a 3-weight might actually be ideal, and it can also work nicely on a larger river where an angler might normally fish a 7-weight.

7- to 8-weight: Heavy trout and big bass, and even some of the smaller saltwater species. Perfect for large streamers and big drys and nymphs, and designed to fire off longer casts.

9- to 14-weight: Generally for large salmon, steelhead, exotics like peacock bass, and saltwater fishing for large species and extra-long casts.

Floating and Nonfloating Lines

The last letter in WF5F stands for "floating." Fly line is designed either to float, or to sink intentionally. Floating lines are generally used on rivers and moving water where anglers need to see and control the line. A sinking (S) line is typically utilized on deep lakes where getting the fly below the surface is crucial. Some lines float, but have a sinking tip (ST). This works well for shallow lakes and also deep rivers where the angler needs to see and control the line, but also needs the fly to ride deeper.

If you're fishing on large lakes or deep ponds, a sinking line may be a fine choice, and there are plenty of options depending upon how deep the fish are suspended. But in nearly every other situation, a floating line is the common choice even for saltwater fly fishing.

Color

Another aspect to fly line is color, but the various shades and hues of line are almost always chosen by the manufacturers for certain types of line. Color is rarely the reason you should purchase a line, but can be a factor in *not* purchasing a line. Although some fly fishers choose lines of a certain color for aesthetics and visibility, color is the least important quality unless fishing in ultra-clear or ultra-calm waters, where invisibility is critical. Some manufacturers are now making high-quality, clear lines with no color at all: the ultimate in line camouflage! But clear lines can be tough for beginners to fish since they're all but impossible to see.

There are many other aspects to fly line, such as suppleness, slickness, memory, stretch, and material, but knowing the three aforementioned categories first will help make sense out of a confusing, yet crucial investment.

Choosing a Fly Box

Fly fishing requires a hefty investment in a variety of flies. Fly boxes are essential for storing, protecting, and organizing the mess. However, some boxes are better than others. Don't fall prey to buying one according to looks or brand. Be smart and go with what works. A fly box may seem an insignificant decision, initially. However, never underestimate the importance of this particular choice. Gear decisions are paramount. With so many styles, sizes, shapes, and materials, getting the proper box is key.

Boxes today are made of a vast array of materials: wood, leather, canvas, plastic, metal, and lately, even foam. Every seasoned angler has his or her preference. But here are some facts that can help take the guesswork out of fly box bamboozlement.

Wood has aesthetically pleasing qualities: the grain, the sound of it opening and closing, the feel of it in the hand. Wood looks terrific and has a traditional appeal. But wood can be heavy. Typically, it's an expensive material. And, wood will eventually split, splinter, or break at the hinge. Wood may also retain moisture when closed. Moisture causes hooks to rust.

Plastic can be good if it contains foam inserts. But most plastics are rigid and become brittle over time, or the hinges or clasp might break. Plus, some plastics weigh a lot. If they have only tiny compartments with no way for the flies to be secured to the box, then one false step or a stiff breeze and every fly you own will end up on the carpet, the ground, or worse, in the river.

Metal boxes often look great and come in an array of sizes, but they can also be unforgiving in the pocket of a vest or pack when bending over or sitting on your backside for a rest. And in most cases, metal boxes are heavier than others, and some only have compartments or windows where flies "sit" and are not attached. Compartments are bad. If a wind blows and you open a little compartment, all your flies are gone from that section.

Leather and canvas "wallets" are popular in many cases because they last, and are lightweight. But barbed flies can be next to impossible to remove from the artificial wool inside, and neither leather nor canvas is watertight, so if the wallet gets submerged, removing every fly will be necessary until the thing dries out. A fly wallet makes for a nice gift but it's usually relegated to the shelf before long. (Ditto for fancy Wheatley fly boxes.)

Foam boxes are the latest choice for many fly fishers because they are ultra-lightweight, very inexpensive, and they actually "give" a little when you bend over or sit down for break. They float when dropped. They are impervious to water. Magnets keep them shut, so spills are insignificant.

And if all that wasn't enough, flies actually poke into the foam and attach to the box, so if the box does tilt or spill, flies don't end up floating downstream or lost in the grass.

The only drawback to foam boxes is that they are sometimes colored olive or in earth tones, which means if you drop it or leave it on the bank, chances are it'll stay dropped or left. One of my olive-colored boxes fell out of my hip pack once while Mark and I fished Latir Creek in New Mexico. I spent about 30 minutes searching 100 yards of bank, and finally found it floating in a tiny eddy, trapped by some driftwood.

Another problem with foam boxes is that they may not last as long as other materials. But since they are so affordable, who cares, right? If you're looking for a box and don't know where to start, stay clear of boxes with only troughs or compartments. Flies are destined to fall out and sometimes become lost forever.

Boxes with wool or artificial wool are a hassle, too. Barbs snag and can get bent or broken when you're trying to finagle them out. Furthermore, putting all of one's flies in a single box is akin to putting all one's eggs in one basket. Not smart! Lose that box, and every fly is gone. Have several boxes, but carry only what's necessary. Leave the rest in another box in the vehicle.

Fly fishing can be expensive enough as it is. Spend the extra dollars on items that perform, such as boots, rods, and line, not on a box. In short, by going with the smallest box tolerable, the cheapest available, made of the lightest material around, a fly fisher simply cannot go wrong.

FLY ROD PARANOIA: FOUR STEPS TO PURCHASING
THE PERFECT ROD FOR FLY FISHING

When you're finally in the market to purchase your first fly rod, there are some simple principles to follow for locating the appropriate one just for you. When purchasing a fly rod, application will dictate your choices. With so many brands, sizes, and particulars, you need to narrow things down by asking a few simple questions. These questions will make locating the proper rod far less daunting.

The four principles of fly rod construction are the rod's weight, length, relative flex, and number of pieces to the rod. The following is an easy way to determine what an angler needs using the four principles.

What Type of Water Will I Be Fishing with this Rod?

Rod "weight" is the standard measurement that manufacturers use for a rod's backbone. A standard rule for choosing rod weight is simple: smaller fish require lighter rod weights, and big fish translates to heavier rods. So if step-across streams and tiny tributaries are your primary target waters, choose a rod somewhere between a 1-weight and a 4-weight. If the plan is to fish lakes and ponds for largemouth bass, heavy lake trout, or beefy carp, 5-weights to 12-weights work well. Rivers and tailraces holding trout weighing 3 pounds or less are best fished with a rod between a 4-weight and an 8-weight. All bodies of water are distinct, so find a practical rod weight to cover a variety of situations. A 4- or 5-weight rod is a fine choice for an all-around practicum.

How Far Will I Need to Cast to Catch Fish There?

The more line needed to catch fish, the longer a rod needs to be. Most trout caught in small, step-across streams are hooked within 10 to 15 feet of the angler. Rods from 6 to 7½ feet are great for close-range casting and dapping. Quiet spring creeks and streams with long stretches of smooth water may require long, stealthy casts where 8- to 9½-foot rods are key. Rods 9½ feet and longer are typically reserved for large rivers, lakes, and saltwater flats, which demand long casts.

How Will the Rod Be Transported to the Water?

This is probably one overlooked factor in fly rod follies. Rods conveniently break down into two, three, four, or even seven sections so you can transport them practically. Rods with more sections pack down smaller, sure, but they will also be more prone to ferrule failure (since there will be more of them) and breakage, and they might exhibit poorer flex performance. If you will be transporting rods directly to the water's edge in the back of a pickup where there's lots of room, it's best to purchase a two-piece rod. These cast the best, break the least, and will cause fewer headaches over time.

Conversely, if backpacking up to your favorite alpine lake is something you think you'll be doing a lot, a rod that breaks down into a smaller package, preferably three pieces or more, would be more practical for you. A wise rule of thumb is the fewer the pieces, the higher the performance, so purchase a rod that breaks down to the fewest number of pieces necessary for your type of fishing. That said, today's three- and four-piece rods are far superior to the multi-piece rods of old. No longer is casting a four-piece like casting a buggy whip.

What is the Caster's Skill Level?

Beginning fly casters benefit from rods that flex throughout most of the length of the rod because "full-flex" rods readily forgive mistakes made in the casting motion. More flexible rods create large, smooth loops that travel slowly, so casting Olympic distances or driving flies into a Chinook headwind is impractical with these. Stiffer rods are for those who have mastered the cast and can accurately cast flies at a distance. Tight loops cut through the wind easily and can throw far more line upon the water. Depending upon your casting skills, choose a flex appropriate for that level. Slow to mid-flex is generally a beginner's smartest option.

Purchasing a fly rod is a big investment. Follow these principles, and it won't be completely shooting in the dark. Since this book is primarily concerned with getting you on the water quickly and fishing, the "10 o'clock and 2 o'clock, forward-cast/backcast" motion you will eventually master is of less importance in the beginning than it will soon become with experience. So plan on spending less on your first rod, and possibly thinking of it as a hand-me-down, so that you can learn how to cast and drop a few more Franklins on your second rod.

Tips for Buying a Fly Rod

Today's fly rods fall into three categories: inexpensive, expensive, and more expensive. Nostalgic anglers who believe that you got what you paid for in the good old days will be disappointed in today's rods. These days, you get much, much more than what you pay for.

Consider this: Most moderately priced to expensive rods carry anywhere from a 25-year guarantee to a lifetime warranty. If it breaks, wears out, cracks—even if you sit on it—they will replace the part that broke or supply you with a brand new fly rod. Modern manufacturing processes have dramatically increased performance in fly rods. They are thinner in diameter but stronger and more responsive. The difference in on-the-water quality between a rod costing $160 and one costing $360 is negligible. You'd have to be a veteran angler to know the differences, to be able to use your higher-level skills to take advantage of those differences. But the difference between a low-end rod from a discount sporting goods store and a good starter rod can turn your errant casts into more accurate offerings similar to the way crappy golf clubs hamper your game but good sticks have a better sweet spot. The same principle is at work here.

For starters, you will probably want a graphite rod. Unless you have a sentimental thing for the days of fiberglass or bamboo, you won't want to endure tennis elbow from casting the heavy fiberglass. And if you aren't an excellent caster, you won't want to slow down your cast to match the rhythm of the slower bamboo. Graphite rods create fast, tight casts and handle bigger fish than they should. And nowadays, if you wait a week, or a year, you'll find the latest, greatest new threat to graphite. (Right now? It's boron.) Long rod? It will allow you to lift more line off the water, dap at a longer reach, reposition more easily when you are mending. But it'll be heavier and threatened by overhanging brush, and you'll lose touch.

Don't buy a $40 rod at one of the big sporting goods stores. That rod will not perform, plain and simple. Many rod companies make starter rods in the $100 to $175 range, which for beginners, are indistinguishable from the more costly rods. That means you don't have to go plunk down $700 for a Sage just to impress your friends, either.

Do the aesthetics of the rod mean much to you? If not, you don't want to pay an extra hundred bucks just to have fancier guides or reel seats.

Consider also how frequently you fish. If you are only fishing on your one-week getaway to the Catskills, there's no reason to spend all that extra money on a top rod when a moderately priced rod will do just fine.

What is your skill level? If you are an accomplished caster (and maybe a less accomplished fisher), you might benefit from a top-of-the-line rod. Will you mostly fish for trout? Bass? Snook? Fly rods are made to handle certain line weights and certain sizes or types of fish. To fish for trout, you will need to consider if you will be fishing smaller streams, sizable rivers, or lakes. Then match the length and weight rod to your needs. A 3- to 5-weight rod 7 to 8 feet long is ideal for creeks, but to fish big rivers like the Madison or Yellowstone, you would want a heavier rod like a 9-foot 6-weight. A better bass rod would take you into the 7- and 8-weight classes.

Try out a fly rod before you buy it. Fly shops will let you take a demo rod outside so you can test it. When you test out the rod, look for these things: Is the rod fast, medium, or slow action? Does the rod "feel" right to you? Does the grip fit your hand? We suggest a slow- or medium-slow action rod for most beginners.

Ask questions. Get advice. Talk to someone who is a more accomplished fly rodder. Try out his or her rods. Visit the local fly-fishing club.

Do you need a two-piece? A three-piece? A four-piece? If you travel much and intend to take your rod along, multi-piece rods are no longer buggy whips. The ease of carrying a multi-piece rod means you will be fishing more often. Buy a four-piece only if you plan on backpacking with the rod or if you travel a lot and need to save space. Mark owns a couple of four-piece rods, and they cast beautifully with no noticeable drop-off in casting ability or feel.

Lightweight, slow-action rods have nearly disappeared from the catalogs and fly shops since the ever-improving advent of their high-tech, fast-action (or "tip flex"), laser beam–shooting counterparts. But going back to basics can be enjoyable, productive, and extremely edifying. Here's why we think you ought to hold out on Jedi status tip-flex rods just yet, and go with a slow or even an ultra-slow flexing rod.

Oddly, nearly every lightweight rod being manufactured today falls into the medium- to fast-action category. Only a handful of light tackle rods produced today are slow action. We think you need to learn on one. Like learning guitar on an acoustic, or learning to shoot with a .22, slow-action rods teach you the physics of the rod and line and how to hone your casting stroke.

These rods offer more forgiveness in the casting stroke for newbies, and they are designed for targeting smaller, more manageable trout. But simultaneously, they can help experienced anglers focus on other aspects of the sport rather than just their casting, such as fly placement, stealthy stalking, wading, reading water, presentation, and fly selection. Slower rods encourage anglers to close in on trout and where they live, which can naturally shift attention to these next critical skills.

Since these rods are far more flexible, they pose unique challenges, such as casting accuracy and hook-set timing. With a rigid rod, casting accuracy is almost automatically improved once the stroke is mastered. And hook-sets are nearly instantaneous. But more flexible rods respond slower, creating lag time between initial hand movement and line response. This all but forces fly fishers to focus on the take, respond quickly, and utilize catlike reflexes for success. Be a cat. Catch a fish.

Because laser-beam loops and 50-foot casts rarely net small stream trout, slower, lighter rods are not only a blast to fish, but they also make logical sense under many fishing conditions. They are perfect for gin-clear, high-elevation streams, or where trout—especially brookies and cutts—are easily spooked. Slower rods dominate on spring creeks and quiet ponds where fish are smart and wily, and presentation is paramount. Since these rods produce slower line speeds, their presentations are feather-light and offer extremely lifelike landings with dry flies. Slower rods work great on shallow streams. If you learn to "stalk" effectively, keep a low profile, and tread lightly with quiet footfalls, most trout can be sighted, cast to, and landed within 10 to 15 feet of the angler. And with practice, you'll learn to shoot more line with your slow rod than you might think. They load quickly so you won't need to have lots of line out.

Some of Our Favorite Entry-Level Rods

Global Dorber Li'l Streamer, 7-foot, 6-inch, 3-weight, 3-piece. This is, bar none, the perfect ultralight fly rod. Anyone can cast this rod—little ones, adults, and geezers. With its ultra-slow flex, flies land like delicate feathers.

Orvis Clearwater 7-foot, 9-inch, 5-weight, 2-piece. Mac learned on this rod. Its price and flex are both suitable for extraordinary entry-level performance and durability.

L.L. Bean Quest 6-foot, 6-inch, 3-weight; 7-foot, 6-inch 4-weight; or 8-foot, 6-inch 5-weight. At under $100, these may be the best-quality rods for the money. Start off little kids with the 6-foot, 6-inch, adults with the 8-foot, 6-inch.

Hexagraph 8- or 9-foot, 4-weight 3-piece. More expensive than other setups, but a rod perfect for learning as well as growing old with. Looks like bamboo, but made of fiberglass. Extraordinary.

Orvis Superfine 7-foot, 6-inch, 3- or 4-weight. Williams lends his older version of this rod to newbies because it's lightweight and casts like a dream. New Trout Bum models are pretty expensive, so look for an older used one.

Temple Fork Outfitters (TFO) Finesse Series. Any size in the Finesse lineup will teach you how to cast quickly and with minimal effort. Nice, soft action and a lifetime warranty.

NOTE: Rod design changes about as fast as the weather in the Panhandle of Texas. This is a good list now, but you get the idea. Good companies tend to remain the leading-edge companies.

The Top 10 Trout Fly Rods if You Have Money to Spend

This list includes some high-end, pricey rods if you have the dough to spend. For our top 10 trout fly rod list, we chose a 9-foot 5-weight as the comparative standard. It is not the perfect rod length or weight—there is no such thing. But the "nine-five" is a compromise, fits lots of situations, and gives us a comparable model, apples to apples. We chose a 9-foot 5-weight because it's a 'tweener—you can fish small, you can fish big. We left bamboo out entirely, and will save that sweet list for another time.

A fly rod is like one's favorite pair of shoes or jeans—it's an intensely personal choice, sometimes based on comfort or feel or touch or aesthetics or nostalgia. But all these rods will fit you well. We've selected rods that combine looks with performance, rods every angler would want in their collection. These are trout rods that you don't need to own, but you'll *want* to own. What we looked for—past the beauty and action and distance and power and finesse—is fishability. Enjoy.

Hexagraph Classic. Nickel-silver uplocking reel seat with a premium wood spacer and a unique engraved hexagonal butt cap. All Hexagraph fly rods are available in 2- or 3-piece models and feature Super-Swiss nickel-silver ferrules, premium-grade cork grips, and lightweight stainless steel guides, and carry a limited lifetime warranty. The Classic is delivered in a high-quality cloth bag and premium green rod tube with champagne gold caps.

Mark's been fishing Hexagraph fly rods since the early 1990s. His 8-foot, 6-inch, 4- to 5-weight is his go-to rod, light and feathery enough for small streams, strong and moderate enough for medium to big rivers. Hexagraph rods look like bamboo and imitate bamboo's slow muscled movement, but you can get them in a variety of actions. Yeah, they're a bit pricey but once you cast one, you'll see why. Hexagraph rods are smooth yet powerful, an unusual combination. We like the Classic even though Hexagraph makes an even higher-end rod (the Presidential) but then again, all their rods are high-end and this is their most popular model. It is an elegant, custom-finished keepsake utilizing the finest-quality components in a rich, traditional style. For pure aesthetics, there's not a prettier rod on the market.

Orvis Helios 2. The original Orvis Helios won the 2008 Field & Stream Best of the Best Award. All Helios models are configured as 4-piece and come with a beautiful reel seat, translucent finish, REC recoil guides that resist breakage, and a matching woven graphite rod tube.

You know how you fall in love with your go-to rod and forsake all others? The old standby has always done you right in the past. Mark's two main working rods the last decade have been a Silver Label Orvis and a Hexagraph Classic. Mark owns many others, and takes them out for a drink every now and again, but reverts back to these two standards. Mac uses a 7-foot, 6-inch 3-weight Li'l Streamer made by Global Dorber, and a 7-foot, 9-inch Orvis Clearwater for larger waters. He owns plenty of others, but those are his go-to rods. You'll have yours as well.

Recently, we cast a Helios and realized we are fools for being so loyal and nostalgic. The Helios is the wave of the future for fly rods. Compared to the fiberglass fly rods I grew up with, today's rods just don't weigh much. And though weight isn't typically a concern for me, the Helios breaks all the rules. The 5-weight feels like a 3-weight.

This rod has less mass and better flex recovery, and is quicker to load and quicker to stop, all of which translates into longer distance and more power. Even more important, because distance is overrated and part of the sales pitch bias, the rod is accurate and soft. The rod is so responsive, it's like driving an expensive Italian race car. Because it's such a light rod, keep your reel light too.

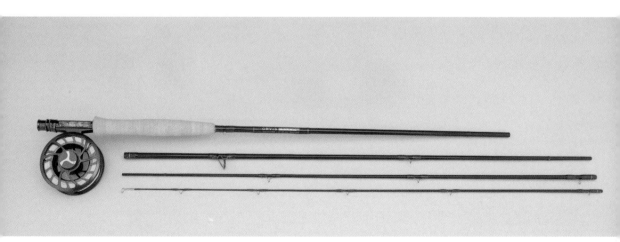

Orvis Helios 2 fly rod. Photo courtesy of The Orvis Company

Thomas & Thomas Vector. This rod is a work of art, with a zebra wood spacer with nickel-silver hardware.

The Horizon seems stiff to me, but the Vector is sweet, smooth, balanced, and beautifully designed. It keeps its performance level for everything from small tailwater flies to split-shot and heavier nymphs. Thomas & Thomas rods are known as much for their aesthetics as their performance, and both are fully evident here. The eye for detail extends even to the clever rod bag within the tube.

T & T rods are such a guilty pleasure, so decadent, so luxurious, that even when your fly is on the water, you'll catch yourself ogling the craftsmanship of the rod. Over the years, when we meet someone who fishes Thomas & Thomas, they're from the I'll-never-fish-anything-else school of thought. The Vector is such an eye-pleasing, high-quality rod that you'll cringe if you scratch it or ding it. This is a gift rod—give yourself a gift. The midnight blue blanks make the Vector as pretty a rod as you can find on the market. This is a rod that could easily sit in your shadow box as an ornament, but what a waste that would be. This rod performs.

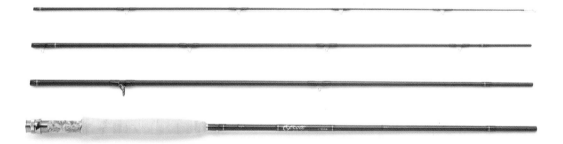

The Scott 9054. Photo courtesy Scott Fly Rod Company

Scott 9054. This four-piece rod has a multi-modulus design. You want distance, and a forgiving rod tip? This is the rod for you. Ideal for both drys and nymphs, and floating and sinking lines. Perhaps more than any others on this list, these rods are love/hate. When we've fished Scott rods in the past, we were amazed that when we quit being lazy with the stroke, the distance we achieved was effortless and longer than normal. These rods have fast action and if you are a less than competent caster or like to fish small streams, you might not "get" these rods. If you have a crackin' sharp cast, crisp and tight, or you fish big, muscular rivers, you'll wonder how you ever fished with any other fly rod.

So we are talking to you decent-casting, big-river lovers—the Scott is forgiving enough to stay accurate in the zone and sensitive enough that you will forget that fast-action rods aren't supposed to be soft. We'd recommend this rod for the regular and seasoned angler.

Sage. Every Sage rod comes with a lifetime warranty, a rod case included, and free shipping. Many Sage models feature a narrower grip for increased comfort and feedback, slim-line nickel-silver and rosewood reel seats, ultra-slender blanks, and a deep "pomegranate" color—burgundy to you and me. They're lighter and stronger than many others on the market.

Think easy, smooth action. Think powerful, fast action. Think soft tip. Thunder and lightning, power and finesse. This is one of the best all-around rods you'll ever cast. To top it off, this is one of the lightest rods you'll ever hold. The power belies the weight, the narrow grip fits more hands than the bigger grip their rods used to have, and the rod is as smooth and soft as you want it to be.

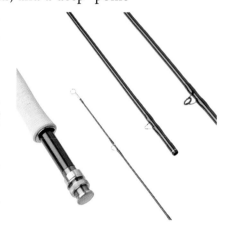

Photo courtesy of Sage.

The Sage Circa provides a slower action that still produces distance when you need it (but you won't have to be a great caster or have out lots of line to load this baby). This is both a workhorse and a work of art.

G.Loomis GL2. These entry-level rods come in both medium and fast action. Despite the relatively low price, the rod compares well with higher-priced G.Loomis rods. Choice of Neptune blue or Evergreen finish.

Why this G.Loomis rod? Bang for your buck. You get a lot of rod for the money. The GL2 holds its own against the higher-priced rods on this list, and while you settle for lesser fittings (it's still a pretty rod) you don't lose anything in performance.

The GL2 has the strength to punch through the wind, the delicate touch to fish small flies, and the necessary butt strength to play a large trout.

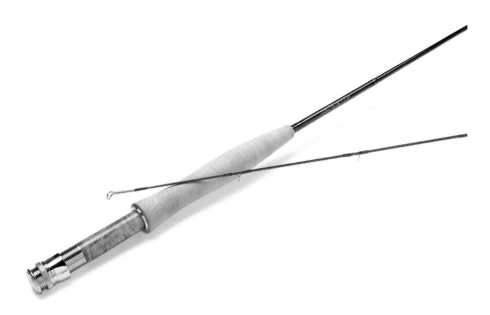

Diamondback makes great 5-weight rods.
Photo courtesy of Diamondback

Diamondback. Diamondback rods feature hard chrome stainless steel guides, anodized nickel-silver colored reel seats, attractive blanks with high-quality wraps, nickel silver-colored hardware, and hard maple reel seats.

Mark's brother-in-law, Kenny Medling, has fished a Diamondback for the last decade, choosing this as his everyday rod over other more expensive rods in his collection. Mark borrows it from time to time and is always amazed at how well it fishes, especially on smaller streams, performing like a much more costly rod.

St. Croix Reign. These rods come with a 1,000-denier nylon-covered rod case with divided polypropylene liner. Each rod has aluminum oxide stripping guides, hard chrome snake guides, and premium-grade cork handles. Available in 2- or 4-piece models. All Reign rods are backed by St. Croix's limited lifetime warranty.

We both grew up fishing hand-me-down St. Croix rods that seemed like they were from 1948, the year St. Croix began making rods. Neither of us liked them. My how things have changed. St. Croix now produces high-end rods that compare favorably with the name brands, and they also produce several "entry-level" rods, but the one we like for the money is the Reign.

We like the medium to fast action, the solidness of design and appearance and the diversity in being able to fish light to heavy flies. We also like the low price for a quality rod. The St. Croix Reign fly rods are the best balance between price and quality on the market. Built from St. Croix's SCII graphite, these rods offer a forgiving casting stroke at an equally forgiving price. With a buttery smooth versatile action and an amazing degree of feel these rods will appeal to savvy freestone veterans as much as fly rod newcomers. With a nylon-covered rod case with a divided polypropylene liner and an olive green blank color everything about these rods is attractive.

Redington Red Fly. This rod has a corrosion-resistant stripping guide and hard chrome double-foot snake guides. It comes in 2- or 4-piece models.

All Redington fly rods (except the Crosswater) are covered by a limited, original-owner, lifetime warranty.

Redington put out a feasible, high-performing, entry-level rod when everyone else was still cranking out thick cheap rods with action like broomsticks. The Red Fly 2 is a step up from the Red Fly, but for the money, we think the Red Fly is ideal for the beginner—lightweight, responsive, versatile, and forgiving. One of the great aspects about the Red Fly is that you get sensitivity, feel, and line control from a rod this inexpensive. The Red Fly has a solid reputation, and the pipe-and-tweed crowd will not look down at you with disdain.

GEAR STORAGE AND TRANSPORTATION

Rods and reels are expensive. You gotta protect 'em. Not just when you're fishing, but when storing and transporting it all, too. We know this better than anyone because between us we probably own 20 or more rods and 12 or more reels. And yep, we've broken a few, each. Most rods are made of high-modulus graphite. A few are bamboo. I even own an old fiberglass one my dad used in the 1970s. These delicately balanced, fine-tuned pieces of equipment can, and do, break regularly. So just because many come with 20-years-to-lifetime warranty doesn't mean you should find yourself jousting with them or using them to catapult doodle bugs into the campfire. We both have a "broke this rod while on the water" story, as do most fly fishers. They can be fun yarns to spin, but there aren't many things you can do that will feel worse than snapping a favorite rod. Try hard not to create your own story.

I smashed one in the door of the Jeep. At first it seemed fine. Maybe I was in denial? Couldn't see any cracks or anything. Didn't see anything wrong. It even cast fine for about an hour! Then, a swell in the water took my fly under. I set the hook thinking it was a perch. Instead it was a 4-pound bass. *Snap!* It was my son's first fly rod. Gone. I ended up breaking his 3-weight rod fishing for perch in a tiny pond. When I told Wes about it, he started to cry because he thought he'd never have a rod again. I broke his rod. His tears broke my heart.

Another broken rod example: While putting the finishing touches on prepping to hit the water, I temporarily leaned my rod in the crook of the open car door. Before I could lace my boot, my fishing buddy backed into the door and it closed just enough (shudder) that it cropped off the top 2 feet of my precious rod. I set it there only for a second and it goes to show you, that's what can happen if you're not careful. I had to fish Shuree Ponds with a little 3-weight, full-flex Dorber rod that day. Shuree holds some monster trout, up to 25 inches long, and while I didn't catch any that big, the rod did fine with the 18- to 22-inch fighting rainbows I caught and landed. That's when I fell in love with Dorber rods.

MDW: I've broken one rod in all my years. Same story as Mac's Shuree Pond story. I set the rod in the open door notch and a fishing buddy closed the door. Crack.

It takes money and time to ship off a rod for repair, and that's if it can be repaired. And chances are it will never be the same. If you take care of what you've got, you won't need to worry. Here's how.

Storage

Fly rods need to be protected when not in use. Some rods cost $1,000. Others are $50. Both should be protected by a rod sock, as well as a case or rod tube. In most instances rod cases come standard with a rod purchase. But not always. If not, get one!

Rod Sock. For first-level protection, all rods need a rod sock. It only "protects" your rod in the sense that it keeps it from getting scratched and dusty—not much else. The rod sock should be used in tandem with hard cases for several levels of protection. The sock should have multiple compartments, one for each section of the rod. This will separate the pieces and keep them from rubbing.

Rod Tubes. The least complex aspect of the rod protection world is basically a long, rigid rod tube. But tubes are not always the best choice, since they are typically lengthy and they have no room for a reel. This makes them cumbersome to pack, and you still have to find a place for reels. They're fine for storing long-term, or transporting your rod long distances such as in the back of a truck, but they aren't for shipping on a plane or packing in the SUV.

Most rod tubes feature a rigid PVC or aluminum shell, and are soft and padded internally, though some are not. Some have D-rings for locking.

Rod Cases and Rod/Reel Combos. Another type of rod protection is a rod case, with the same long, hard tube for the rod sections, but also a durable fabric cover for the reel as well. These cases allow a broken-down rod to be slid into the case without taking the fly reel off—very handy. Rod and reel combo cases are a great idea for the fly angler who likes to keep the reel on the butt section of the rod. These cases are designed in such a way that anglers can simply break down their rods at the ferrules and slide the ferrule ends down the rod tube to stow the rod away safely. This simple design saves anglers a tremendous amount of time by not having to attach reels and flies repeatedly. Another key feature of these combo cases is that since they are meant to have rods broken down by half they are shorter than traditional rod tubes. This makes them great for small trips and tight spaces in the back of your car. If you are looking to purchase a rod, reel, and case combo, try to buy a case that holds more than one rod-and-reel holder. It's a great idea to have multiple rods rigged and ready to go—you can just see what the conditions are on the water and choose the best setup. For the best possible rod and reel combo case, look for one that incorporates as many of the features listed below as possible.

- Rugged 450-denier fabric cover over PVC shell
- Padded reel case section
- Zipper side pockets for additional storage of small items
- Adjustable shoulder strap and nylon handle
- D-rings for securing to backpack
- Heavy-duty metal zippers

Reel Pouches and Cases

Reels can be just as expensive as rods. They need to be protected as well. If your rod case doesn't allow you to keep your reel attached to your rod, you'll want some sort of case for the reel. Reel cases tend to be cylindrical in shape and have zippers that unzip all the way around. There is usually some sort of faux fur inside to keep the reel safe and debris free. A reel pouch is basically the same concept, but they're usually made of neoprene and close using Velcro.

Rod Transportation

There are really two ways of transporting rods: long distance, and short. If you're going long distance, just utilize a tube or case, and pack the rods in the vehicle in a manner so they're out of harm's way and are less likely to get smooshed.

However, short-range transportation contraptions can be extremely beneficial, and would have saved us at least two rods if we had only purchased one of these gizmos sooner. There are two types: inside and outside racks.

Inside racks are usually attached to the inside of your vehicle with either suction cups on the windows, or bars that stretch across the back and front. There are notches in the foam to "snap" the rods into, or rubber straps that hold your rods in the rack. They'll either ride down the side of the vehicle, or overhead. (Overhead is far smarter.) With a rack like this, you can come straight off the river, open the back hatch, slide your rods in, secure them (reels and all), and drive away without spending any time to break everything down.

Outside racks are held onto the hood and roof of your vehicle by suction cups or magnets. They allow you to jump right out of the river and slide or strap your entire, unbroken-down rod setup in the rack, typically with the reel end on the front of the hood and the tip section arching over past the windshield and roof. This may seem dangerous to a rod, but actually we recommend this style because rods and anglers in vehicles don't mix. The rods are better off outside the truck than inside. Another outside rack style is a simple hard plastic shell with padding inside and a locking mechanism. This provides the most protection of all racks. We like it! Use outside racks in any of the following situations.

- Heading to and from the hotel, lodge, or campsite to the river
- Leapfrogging around other anglers on the river
- Moving from one river to another in close proximity
- Your rod is set up and you're waiting for your partners to get their gear on. Don't lean your rod against the vehicle. Put it in the rack!
- You are eating lunch at the river's edge

If you carry your expensive rods in your vehicle, on a plane, from one spot on the river to another, or in a boat, eventually you'll put them in harm's way.

Rod Racks and Organizers

If you own more than one rod, you need a rod rack for your vehicle and a rod rack for your house. You need to buy yourself some more rods. If you don't carry your rods properly or store them smartly, you'll end up with tangled lines and broken rods. If you own more than one rod, start shopping for a rod rack and organizer. Here are ten superb organizers for the car and house to get you going.

Thule Castaway Rooftop Rod Carrier. The box bottom is padded as an added safeguard. The carrier has an aerodynamic design, and locks so you can secure and protect your rods and reels. This is one weird-looking exterior combination carrier—part plastic box, part rack. Thule is well known for car carriers for bikes, skis, and other things you put atop your car, and soon, because of clever design of this carrier, they might be known for an angling carrier too. We like that this rack allows anglers to keep the reels on the rods, and can carry several combos at one time. The box is deep enough to house your largest conventional gear, including your big bass outfit, surf rods, big game rods, spinning gear, even fly rods and fly reels.

RodMounts RodLoft PRO Rod Holder. This one holds up to six rods, and has security straps for extra protection. Removable foam inserts accommodate all rod sizes, from lightweight fly tackle to heavy-duty surf equipment.

A fine cutthroat caught in Rocky Mountain National Park

You know how you think of something that someone should invent, perhaps even thinking that someone might be you (leading to wealth and retirement) only to find out that someone else has indeed invented it? This rod holder is something my fishing buddy talked about inventing last summer while in northern New Mexico. (Boy, is he gonna be disappointed.)

For years, we used an Orvis magnetic removable rod rack but the latest troutmobile's top isn't metal, so we began to transport rods and reels from one place on the river to another by just slipping the combo in from the back. Mark broke a rod tip because it's just a dumb way to carry your rod. The RODLOFT creates an organizing system inside your car with with five interchangeable mounting options. These neoprene foamcore rod holders can be attached just about anywhere in any vehicle. This interior holder takes advantage of your windows with suction cups, hangers for hooks and bars, and more.

Sportube Double Haul. High-density polyethylene plastic protects two fully assembled 9-foot fly rods and reels. It's a lightweight, strong, and durable, fully adjustable, hard-shell fly rod case that mounts and locks to most roof racks.

The only drawback is that this exterior carrier holds only two rods. But to its credit, it holds two fully assembled fly rods. The Sportube Double Haul is convenient, easy to load, and can be easily disassembled. If you're one of those anglers who moves up and down the river to locate prime spots or visits several rivers on a single trip, this is the carrier for you. Magnetic pedestal included.

Professor Bodkin Onstream Rod Carrier. This exterior nonpermanent rod carrier accepts four rods. Its T-pedestal design (base and crossbar) quickly and easily attaches to your vehicle, and is quick and easy to remove. Both magnetic and vacuum-based pedestals are available. The rods bungee-cord to each of the two T-pedestals; one holds the tip, the other holds the rod butt. At first glance, you'd swear these will fly off when you get up to 55 miles per hour, but they are secure and safe. Practical and relatively inexpensive, the Professor Bodkin Onstream Rod Carrier is versatile enough to hold everything from fully assembled trout rods to loaded Spey rods and reels. Because so many vehicles now lack metal roofs and hoods, making magnetic holders ineffective, in comes the vacuum version.

Cabela's Rack with Utility Storage. For gear storage at home, this nifty rack with oak veneer holds up to ten rods and features several big utility boxes.

You can't just leave your rod-and-reel outfits strewn about the house. It's unsightly, and your rods are in danger of getting damaged. Go with a rod organizer to keep them safe and secure. Here's a rod stand that is great for your recreation room, garage, library, study, or cabin. Offering value for your buck, this is a solid, low-cost organizer with three sizable drawers for your reels, tools, and line and six slots for 3,700 utility boxes so you can store all those valuable lures.

Rolling Fishing Rod Rack. Glides smoothly on casters and stores rods securely upright. The bottom drawer organizes lures and supplies. The bonus side pocket and three hooks keep all your fishing gear handy.

Keep your lures and lines from getting tangled and keep your rods safe from breakage in this rolling rack that holds up to 12 rods—fewer if you want to keep the reels attached. The rack comes with a big drawer, a side pocket, and three handy hooks.

Bass Pro Shops Round Swivel Rod Rack. This oak-finish rack holds up to 24 rods and features a ball-bearing swivel base. This carousel rod rack is super for corners. If you like to store your rods without reels, you can store an amazing 24 rods in this organizer. The soft rubber rod grips hold the rods without scratching them. Not many anglers own 24 rods, so this is an ideal way to show to the world that you mean business.

Browning Rolling Fishing Rod Rack. This natural oak rack with rolling casters holds 14 rods with reels attached. Here's a good-looking rod holder with lockable rolling casters that is a cut above other racks in looks and detailing. The selling point of this rack is that not only does it hold 14 rods, but it holds 14 rods with reels. A full-width drawer holds reels, tackle, tools, and other gadgets.

WHAT KNOTS DO I NEED TO KNOW?

Tying knots is the least enjoyable but most important aspect of fly fishing. Without good knots, you're catching and releasing without all the fun—those fish will hit and then run without you getting to play them. You only need a few basic, solid knots in your arsenal.

Maybe you're a beginning angler, and learning to tie knots can seem intimidating. Or you're one of those fly anglers who has fished with the long rod a decent amount, but you only know a knot or two—or you don't know how to tie the ones you do know, correctly.

The bewildering array of knots has resulted from variations on a few basic knots, in addition to the need for different knots to adjust different tackle setups. Tying knots properly is not all that difficult and can help

you land more fish. If you tie a knot poorly or if you tie a knot ill-suited to the situation, you will likely lose fish. And that defeats the entire purpose of fishing. Fishing involves enough variables that can cause you to lose fish without adding another to the mix. Properly tied, properly suited knots will help you cast better and land more fish. It's that simple. But learning and tying the knots is not all the knowledge you need about knots.

SOME BASIC KNOT TYING INFORMATION

Don't take knot tying for granted. Because poorly tied knots usually result in losing hooked fish, a bit of attention to the preparation phase of fishing can help you catch more fish in the fishing phase of fishing.

Buy the best tippet, leader, and fly line you can afford. Cutting corners on such important items of your tackle makes no sense at all. The better and fresher your tippet, leader, and line, the better knots you will tie and the fewer fish you will lose. Always check your line (and double-check your tippet and leader) before you go fishing. Look for frayed spots. These are weak links that could break when you have that lunker trout or huge bass on, the one you have been stalking all summer. Look for nicks too, especially after you hook a fish. If you tie a knot with a nicked line, the breaking strength of the line decreases dramatically.

If your monofilament or tippet is nicked, frayed, discolored, or just plain old, then go ahead and replace the problem section. Abrasions and other "bad spots" can seriously weaken your line's integrity. It takes less time to tie on more tippet or another leader before you hit the water than it does to do the same while you are standing knee-deep in the river cursing at the big fish you just lost. If your tippet and leader have been on your fly line all winter, take the time to replace the tippet, at the very least. Fly lines generally last one hard summer, or two light- to medium-use summers. If your leader or tippet is still on the spool from the previous fishing season, trash it. Heat and light (both sunlight and fluorescent light) can weaken your line.

If you keep losing fish because the knot unravels or the line breaks at the knot, you are doing something wrong. Unraveling can mean you tied the knot incorrectly, or did not cinch it tightly. Breaking at the knot can mean that the line was frayed or nicked—this happens frequently when you snip off the tag end of a knot, so be careful. You can also cut the tag end of the tippet tied to the eye of the fly too closely, and that will cause it to break or unravel. Be careful, on the flip side, not to leave the tag end too long or it may cause the trout to turn away.

Don't bite off the end of the tag end of line. This method does not cut the line cleanly, and your dentist will not be happy with the enamel you will invariably lose. You will end up doing it anyway, but we're saying not to do it. Do not overwrap your knots. If the directions say five or six turns, wrapping the knot eight times weakens the integrity of the knot.

Take time to tie your knots. If you have time to retie a knot when your tippet has slipped or broken because your knot was hurriedly (and incorrectly) tied, you have time to tie it right the first time. One way to avoid hurrying is to practice the knot at home, before you get on the water.

You can usually feel any nicks on the line when you run your hands up and down the line while tying a knot. Doing so quickly between your forefinger and thumb causes friction, and the heat from this helps straighten your tippet. You should also occasionally take the line with each hand and pull evenly and firmly. Don't jerk the line, just put steady pressure on it. The line and the knots should hold up.

We debarb all our flies before we tie them on.

When you "seat" your knots (make the final tug to secure the knot), don't jerk the line—use steady and even pressure. Don't wimp out, either. Knots will easily unravel if not seated properly. Be careful not to trim the knot too closely. You do want to trim the knot close and neat, but not so close that the tag end of the line can slip through or you accidentally clip the standing line.

An old angler's trick is to wet your knot. Most anglers have heard that spitting on the line before you tighten the knot helps. Guess what? It does. This old wives' tale works by lubricating the knot, which ensures that the knot slides correctly. Wetting the knot also lessens the amount of friction heat caused by tightening the knot. An old wives' tale you should not follow? Do not burn the ends of the line. You will still see anglers swear by this practice. Lighting the end of the mono only weakens the line.

Arbor Knot

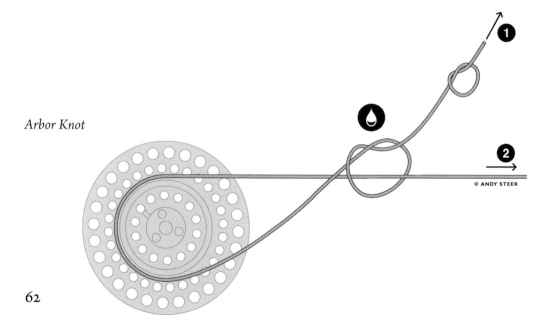

© ANDY STEER

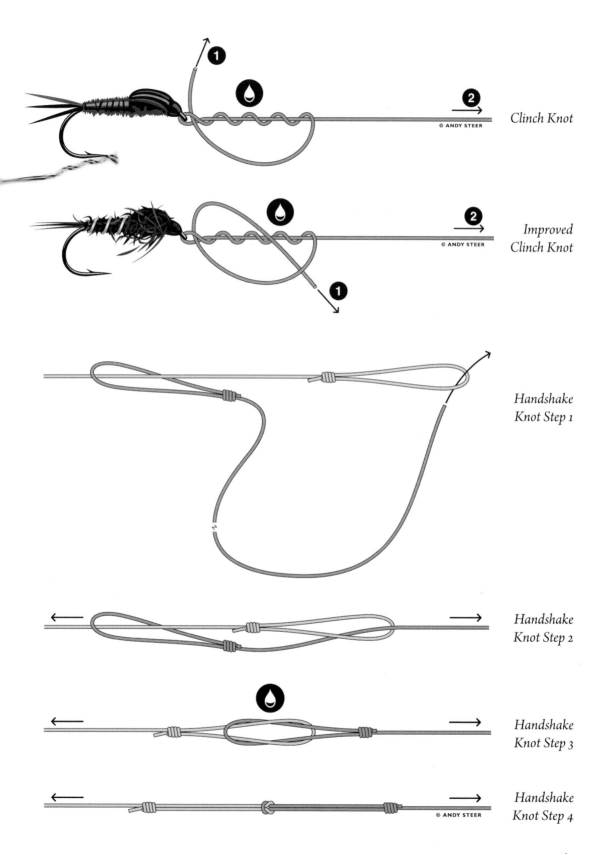

Clinch Knot

Improved
Clinch Knot

Handshake
Knot Step 1

Handshake
Knot Step 2

Handshake
Knot Step 3

Handshake
Knot Step 4

© ANDY STEER

63

Surgeon Loop
Step 1

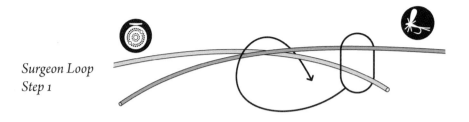

Surgeon Loop
Step 2

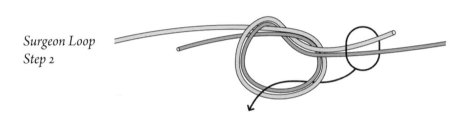

Surgeon Loop
Step 3

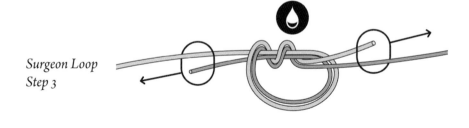

Surgeon Loop
Step 4

© ANDY STEER

64

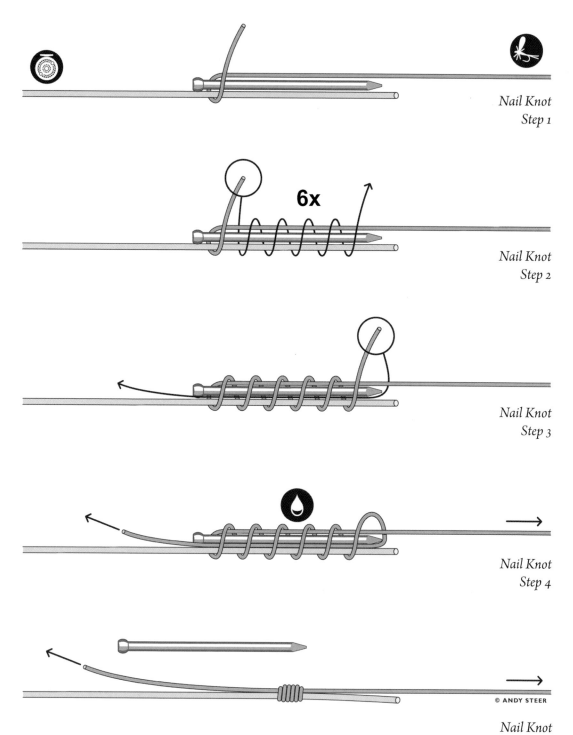

Nail Knot
Step 1

6x

Nail Knot
Step 2

Nail Knot
Step 3

Nail Knot
Step 4

© ANDY STEER

Nail Knot
Step 5

65

BUGS & INSECTS

We have to confess that while we are fairly knowledgeable about insects and hatches—especially Western stream insects—we are nowhere near as informed as many other scientifically minded colleagues. It's not that we don't appreciate their depth and breadth of knowledge. We do. We read their books and articles and learn a lot each time we do. But we just don't get as anal-retentive or as in-depth about bugs as they do. We even like the absence of hatches, in which case we employ aggressive prospecting methods.

We've seen days on end where the closest thing to a hatch was on the rusty AMC Gremlin with a flat sitting in the riverside parking lot. But we've seen other days on the water when the sun was darkened by clouds of insects. We've perfectly matched the hatch and had take after take. We've perfectly matched the hatch and had refusal after refusal. Weird thing. You can be perfectly imitating the insect, phase, color, and size while watching myriad trout feeding on the surface and yet you still won't get a take despite your best presentation. Frustrating, we know, but that's part of the fun and mystique of the sport.

If you are a beginning trout angler, you might have read or heard something about the aquatic insects that trout feast upon. Contrary to neophytes' general belief that trout eat Royal Wulffs and House and Lots, trout only find those flies similar to their favorite foods: mayflies, caddisflies, and stoneflies. And half the time, just as with lures, fancy-looking flies catch the eyes of more anglers than trout.

Grasshoppers make fat treats for trout.

You will find in books that these common aquatic insects have been given fancy scientific names. The study of insects is called entomology. Pretty high-fallutin' huh? Learning Latin names doesn't help you catch more trout. But learning the life stages of the insects the trout eat will help you catch more trout. It never hurts to learn all you can, but at least start with the basics. Flies usually don't look exactly like the insect you are trying to imitate. They are imitative, suggestive, and impressionistic. They look kind of like one of the insects trout eat. They look kind of like a stage of one of the insects trout eat. They provide the proper silhouette or shade or wing pattern or size or color of the insects trout eat. But they rarely look exactly like the insect.

The most abundant insects trout eat, the insects that you will be imitating with your selections of dry flies, wet flies, and nymphs, are mayflies, caddisflies, and stoneflies. You can find mayflies and caddisflies in almost any trout stream, and stoneflies in many of them. The life cycles of the insects vary in length and process, but in general, you will be trying to imitate the stages of the life cycles, whether winged adults or immature pupae.

Thumbnail Sketches

Caddisflies belong to the scientific order Trichoptera. Roughly tent-shaped, when at rest, adult caddisflies fly in a distinctive skittering pattern. Unlike mayflies, caddis have no nymph form. Their stages are the egg (which won't concern the fly fisher), larva, pupa, and adult.

In the immature phases, caddis larvae look like tiny grubs—wormy little things. These larvae build houses of twigs, rocks, and other debris and sediment in which they live, usually attaching themselves to rocks or other underwater structure. Trout find these cased caddis cocoons to be irresistible fare. This comes in handy when you are selecting an underwater fly to imitate them. The larvae mature into the pre-adult phase, the pupae. The pupa emerges from the case and swims (rises) quickly to the surface to hatch into an adult.

In the middle of a prolific hatch on West Fork Dolores

Mayflies are of the order Ephemeroptera. They are found everywhere, and are most easily distinguished by their upright wings. The larvae tend to live in soft bottoms, but can be found in rocky places as well. The mayfly has a short life cycle consisting of egg, nymph (larva), and adult. Generally though, silty areas are loaded with them. There are some 700 species. The nymphs, which are next to impossible to see, live out their time before becoming duns (the pre-adult phase), by burrowing, clinging, or crawling. These larvae usually have three tails. The dun sheds its skin (and is vulnerable to trout at that time) as it prepares to leave the water and finally ascend to the sky, as an adult.

The repeated dipping of an insect to the water is a sure sign of a mayfly actively laying eggs on the water surface. The adults die shortly after having lain their eggs.

A live stonefly

Stoneflies are members of the order Plecoptera. The stonefly is a clumsy, prehistoric-looking creature, perhaps more suited to a bad Japanese monster movie than to a scenic stream.

The adults are flat and long with great wings that, when not in use, lay down on their body. You may sometimes hear these called Salmonflies, but those are particular species of Plecoptera. The adults range in color from brown to black to golden to orange.

The life cycle of the stonefly—egg, nymph, and adult—is played out mostly on land. Stoneflies tend to like faster water, rocks, boulders, and overhanging trees. Keep your eyes open, and you'll probably notice the nymphal shucks deposited on tree limbs, rocks, and logs, where the adults have crawled out onto the shore. You will see the stonefly's peculiar flying pattern if you see an insect that's as big as a small bird and flying about as erratically as my grandmother drives, dipping and diving, sputtering and coughing and buzzing, then splatting onto the water. That's a stonefly.

Chironomid is the informal name for Chironomidae, a large family of flies predominantly known to fly fishers for their presence and importance on lakes. Chironomids are also found on tailwaters and rivers, and are sometimes called sand flies or lake flies. They superficially resemble mosquitoes, but to an entomologist it's easy to tell the difference. They don't bite, but apart from that they can be easily confused.

When we think of Chironomids, we think of imitating them with tiny patterns, in hooks sized from 18 down to 26, or even smaller. We also think of all the various colors they come in, how selective the trout are about taking them, and how hard the flies made to imitate them are to thread tippet through! Concentrate on the pupal and larval stages, to entice trout. If you ever pump the stomach of a feeding trout plumped up on these insects, you might find wads of a thousand or more pupae. If you find larvae in the stomach remains, you might see some that are surprisingly large, from a half-inch to an inch long.

Midges (Diptera) are tiny insects—what you have grown up calling gnats or no-see-ums. The term midge is loosely applied to any tiny flying insects, even incorrectly, small mayflies. You'll know midges by the fact that trout love the naturals and have a distaste for your small midgelike offerings.

OTHER THINGS TROUT EAT

Trout will eat a wide variety of species: Tricos, crustaceans such as snails, both mysis and freshwater shrimp, dobsonflies, craneflies, caterpillars, leeches, dragonflies, worms, annelids, damselflies, terrestrials such as grasshoppers, beetles, ants, crickets, baitfish, and even other trout—just to name a few.

This brown trout fell for a terrestrial pattern, a grasshopper.

One of the most important ways to learn about the insects trout eat is not from this chapter or from this book, but out on the stream or lake. Next time you go trout fishing, take the time to sit a spell along the river, looking at the trees for insects buzzing about. Pick up rocks from the streambed; turn them over and see what wigglies are crawling about underneath. You will see the cases of the caddisfly attached to the stone. Or maybe their tiny larva scurrying about on the slime adhered to the rock. Sometimes you can see both. If it is a rocky river, you can look at the dry side of big streamside boulders for crawling stoneflies, or their dry shucks they left behind. You can also see them on streamside willows.

Beginning anglers will often see trout rising in the river, but not stop and take the time to see what the fish are rising to. That's where a seine net comes in handy. Holding the net against the current, shuffle your feet just upstream of it, then carefully lift the net up out of the water, take it to the bank, and sit down and learn. You'll be amazed by the variety of insects the net traps, insects you never would see otherwise. (Don't shuffle your feet in this way to stir up the bait and entice fish—it's illegal in most places, and is also very unethical. Just try it this one time to see what we mean. And be careful never to shuffle over redds, because it will destroy them.)

Another trick to try when the trout are rising is to capture one of the insects that is flying about in the air. These insects might be dipping up and down, and you might remember (from articles and books that you have read) that these might just be mayflies. Use your cap to snag one and study it. This way, you can better gauge the size and coloring of the insect in order to better imitate it. Seeing these insects firsthand can help you understand how to better match the hatch in the future, to understand the life cycles of the insects, and also how the trout tend to see the insects. And in the end—whether you learn all the Latin nomenclature or not—you'll catch more trout.

THE ADVANTAGE OF DRY FLIES

It's been said that 95 percent of successful fly fishing lies in the fly. Or that the largest percentage does anyway. In fact, with all the gear and gadgetry that goes along with the sport, the fly is the only thing the trout should ever see. So in that way, to a trout, flies are actually 100 percent of fly fishing. Until one has at least a cursory knowledge of how flies relate to bugs, catching trout will always remain a mystical and elusive endeavor.

In other words, know thy flies!

It's the fly that's made the sport of fly fishing, not the other way around. You see, fly fishing is almost the opposite of bait fishing. So here's the main difference between flies and bait or lures. When you're bait fishing, the weight of the bait is what pulls line off of the reel in the casting motion. The heavier the lure or bait, the farther the cast. Well, most flies don't weight much more than a bundle of nose hairs or the lint from your belly button. So tying a fly to the end of your Zebco isn't going to produce a very lengthy cast. However, if you were to pull some line out first, and then flick the rod just right, you might get some sort of result, though probably still not much.

Early fly-fishing pioneers realized this, and realized that the weight of the line itself would be the only way to get their fly out there. It was a simple lesson in physics, and hence, fly fishing was born.

Most researchers believe that the first literary reference to "flies" and fishing with said "flies" occurred in *Ælian's Natural History,* printed ca. 200 AD, in which a Macedonian fly was described. So, like many things, the Macedonians may stake claim to yet another invention—fishing with flies. Then, in 1486, a piece titled The Treatyse on Fysshynge with an Angle (perhaps where the term "angler" originates?) was published in *The Boke of St. Albans,* by a nun named Dame Juliana Berners. Then, in 1652 John Denny published *The Secrets of Angling,* in which we find the first known illustration of an artificial fly. Immediately after, in 1653, the original mention of the term "Artificial flyes" comes from Izaak Walton in *The Compleat Angler:*

Cutthroats can be suckers for big, bushy dry flies.

"Oh my good master, this morning walk has been spent to my great pleasure and wonder: but I pray, when shall I have your direction how to make Artificial flyes, like to those that the Trout loves best?"

By the 1800s, the term "artificial fly" was being routinely used in angling literature, much like in this representative quote from Thomas Best's *A Concise Treatise on the Art of Angling* (1807), to refer to all types of flies used by fly fishers:

"The art of artificial fly-fishing certainly has the preeminence over the other various methods that are used to take fishes in the art of angling."

So lots and lots of other stuff was published since then, till now, and today, here you are reading this book and now you're learning about flies yourself. You've just become the most recent addition to An Extremely Brief History of Flies. Congratulations!

TYPES OF FLIES

Dry Flies

Dry flies imitate insects (typically winged ones) floating on the surface of the water. The water's surface tension (explained in another book not written by us), coupled with the arrangement of feathers, hairs (not nose hairs), thread, and other lightweight materials (not belly button lint), both natural and manmade, work in conjunction to keep dry flies floating and relatively dry. Most anglers "dress" their dry flies with a thin coating of floatant to repel water, which keeps them floating longer. But over time, say 20 to 30 minutes on average, most flies will become saturated to the point where they will no longer ride the waves anyway, floatant or no floatant. So we often choose not to use floatant. In short, you will need to continually change dry flies. This is one reason why learning the clinch knot (See pg. 63) will save you tons of time on the river.

The most amazing aspect of using dry flies is this: fishing with drys allows the angler to actually "see" the action. People can see trout seeing bugs. And as trout see bugs trapped in the water's film, they recognize them as a food source and rise from below to feast on them.

Often, this feeding behavior can be witnessed long before the first cast is made. Pay close attention to the water in front of you. If you see bulges, splashes, or rings, trout are feeding. During a hatch, or when there are lots of insects present, an angler can cast a few feet in front of a feeding trout and dupe them repeatedly.

Presentation

With dry flies, presentation is paramount. The fly should land as softly and naturally as possible. With time, you'll be able to cast with precision and delicacy. Practice in the yard with a fly you've snapped the shank off of. You'll get better with every cast. But since some flies are more productive than others, here is a list of what we believe to be the most effective and useful dry flies out there.

Stimulator

Many versions of the Stimulator exist, in large part because trout seem to be entranced by the shape of it. A variety of colors simulate bugs in various rivers in every region. Some have rubber legs, some don't. Some are royal (black and red), some gold, some orange. Some are big, some small. Whatever the arrangement, a Stimulator is considered an "attractor" fly because it isn't intended to imitate any particular bug, as most flies do. Instead, Stimulators possess characteristics of many insect species and seem to strike at a trout's curiosity more than anything else.

This is Williams's favorite dry because it floats high, it's easy to see on the water, it's great for a dry-dropper rig, and it can imitate everything from a moth to a spider to a caddis to a stonefly. Anglers love "Stimmies" during stonefly hatches as well. Just ask the trout.

Stimulator

Humpy

Humpy

Humpies come in an array of colors, but the most common and deadly are yellow, red, and chartreuse. Humpies, like Stimulators, are attractor patterns and are a go-to fly at midday, when the sun is directly overhead. They float super-tall and get their name from the distinguishing hump of bleached elk hair used for making the body. Their only downside seems to be that they start to sink rather quickly. Sizes 14 to 18 are the most likely to dupe wild trout from the depths, and they're perfect for fishing for cutthroats since most cutts tend to be nonselective surface feeders.

Once I was fishing in Cimarron Canyon, New Mexico. Williams couldn't make it so I decided I'd make him jealous by mopping up and rubbing it in. (Williams does it all the time, thanks to his iPhone. While I'm in Texas working, he emails fish pics in "reel time" from Colorado. Isn't that rotten?) It was mid-October, and not a single fish rose to a single fly all weekend. I was befuddled. On my way home I decided to pull over one last time and try a chartreuse Humpy. It was high noon. The sun had broken out and was searing straight down into the creek. Didn't matter at all, though. That fly saved the trip. A dejected and surly Mac changed his tune and came home with pics of 11 nice browns instead of the grimace I'd worn for two days.

Parachute Adams

Trout adore the Parachute Adams because it almost uncannily mimics an emerging mayfly, plus it can be fished as an attractor pattern as well. The simplicity of this fly adds to its mystique. Quite possibly it's the most important dry fly in an angler's box. Oftentimes, when all else fails, skittish browns and rainbows will rise to a well-placed, well-presented Parachute Adams because they appear so lifelike—seemingly half in and half out of the water. Have multiple sizes and variations of these flies ready at all times in your box.

Elk-hair Caddis

Trichoptera is the scientific name for a caddisfly. But the dry fly that imitates the caddis is far from technical. It's so simple-looking, it seems it shouldn't even work. But caddis are some of the most recognizable aquatic insects in the water, for humans and trout. They represent a substantial part of a trout's diet throughout its life cycle. The Elk-hair Caddis comes in a variety of hues, from black to tan to olive to ginger. There are tons of variations, all of which have their place. And because caddisflies are so varied in color in nature, the patterns you choose to take will require some method of research before fishing a new stream. Have several sizes and shades, but always keep the tans and olives especially handy.

Royal Wulff

A black and red licorice stick with wings? A cherry Jolly Rancher with a fur coat and skirt on? Trout aren't sure what they're supposed to be either, they just know they want to eat them. When Lee Wulff created this fly, he really hit on something big. The Royal Wulff is a wonderful fly to attract trout, and also when fishing a dry-dropper rig. Store some in #14–16, plus a couple of big, puffy #12s for the dry-dropper days.

More must-have flies are the:

- Royal Trude
- Blue Wing Olive
- Lime Trude
- H&L Variant
- Irresistible Adams
- Midge (black gnat and mosquito imitations)
- Light Cahill or Light Hendrickson
- Royal Wulff

Royal Wulff

WET FLIES

Wets resemble a wide array of underwater insects and baitfish beneath the water's surface. Wet flies imitate drowned terrestrials, drowned winged insects, aquatic insects, or larvae swimming to the surface to hatch; basically wet flies imitate insects in motion. They may appear as though they are attempting to surface, or else drowning, so perfect presentation and technique are unnecessary while fishing wet flies. However, most neophytes don't care to use wet flies because they can't actually see them in the water. Big mistake. Wet flies are just as fun, once mastered, and are actually more productive than drys most of the time.

There are two distinct varieties of wet flies: nymphs and streamers. Both are efficient fish-catching lures. And here are the differences between them.

Nymphs

A nymph is a type of wet fly that resembles an aquatic insect in various stages of life, such as pupal or larval. You don't really need to know that to be successful with them, because we have listed below some surefire nymphs that work most anytime, anywhere. Many are weighted with beads, or lead or copper wire. Since 90 percent of a trout's diet is sub-surface, learning to fish nymphs will often mean the difference between being skunked on a river and putting on a clinic.

We're nymph maniacs. That is to say, we like fishing with nymphs. And we like to fish nymphs one of two ways: tied directly to the end of the tip-pet and fished in a manner called "dapping" aka "nymphing," aka "short lining," aka "high-sticking" (see Nymphing and fishing multiple flies on pages 161 and 213); or setting up a dry-dropper rig (page 217), and fishing a nymph below a big, bushy dry fly. This is a particularly effective way to fish for trout because you present a double threat, one fly on top and one below, so you can hit trout in several feeding modes.

To begin what's called nymphing (or variations on how to nymph such as high-sticking or dapping or short-lining), flick a weighted nymph into fast-moving water where drys would typically sink, and just let it swoop through. Cast upstream and swing them through pools and pockets. Also, try dragging them across the current with a herky-jerky or twitchy retrieve simulating a swimming insect. Fish them unweighted on shal-low riffles in a dead-drift manner, which means no line strips. These flies will land trout nearly any time of day, in nearly any type of water, nearly anywhere on the planet. When you get better at fly fishing, you'll want to look into fishing with nymphs in the European method (the Czechs and Poles and French are particularly good at their styles of nymphing, which require great touch and feel.)

Must-Have Nymphs

Gold-Ribbed Hare's Ear. This fly looks like something you'd pull out of a dirty vacuum cleaner bag. But trust us, it doesn't suck. Hare's Ears will produce trout at any time of day or in any weather, and in any type of water. They can be used where caddis, stoneflies, or mayflies are suspected. In lakes or slow-moving water, fish near the bottom, using a sink-tip line, a long (9-foot) leader with a piece of split-shot a foot above the fly.

Copper John. Fly fisher and fly-tying innovator John Barr perfected this pattern over several years of experimenting with various mate-rials. With a sink rate roughly equivalent to that of a brick, this fly drops through the water quickly to get to deep-dwelling trout. This is Mac's favorite all-around fly, especially the red ones. Put him on

Beadhead Gold-ribbed Hare's Ear

Copper John Red and Copper

any water at nearly any time and he will find a trout with it. He loves fishing this fly about 18 inches behind a #14 Royal Wulff or a #12 rubber-legged Stimulator.

Pheasant Tail. This is one heckuva good fly. Fish the unweighted version just barely below the surface. On deep, still waters, fish a beaded version with a twitchy retrieve around weed beds, drop-offs, and cover. For streams, fish in soft, quiet pools, backwaters, slow currents, eddies, and so on. Cast upstream and let them ride down the bank, through pools and tailouts, and also try pulling them across the current.

Zug Bug. This fly seems to produce best when fished close to the bottom and worked slowly in ponds and lakes. It's probably considered more of a streamer than a nymph, but we have it listed here because you probably won't fish many streamers, and you need to fish this fly.

Brassie. A Brassie is a very simple fly: a hook, copper wire, peacock herl, and some brown or black thread to bind it all together. Brassies work, too, probably because peacock herl has iridescence about it that trout cannot resist. And the red wire may resemble a bloodworm as well, which will simulate a chironomid in certain stages of life. Plus Brassies have a certain flash about them that mesmerizes fish. Use Brassies with either brass or pearl beadheads, especially during caddis activity. They also fish well on stillwaters, down deep.

Universal Nymph. According to the developers of the Universal Nymph, "it's a beadhead, no, a Hare's Ear . . . how about a flashback pheasant-tail . . . could be sort-of-a Prince Nymph, maybe a Copper-John-alike or a biot-bug; whatever it is, it's versatile!" The reason they say this is because they literally took all the best qualities of the most popular nymphs and blended them into this one fly.

Damselfly Nymph. Most often this fly is tied in an olive-green color. We prefer the ones with brass beads for heads. These are crucial flies for alpine ponds and lakes where adult dragonflies and/or damselflies are obviously present. Fish them perpendicular to the bank and hold on tightly! Rainbows and browns will smash them.

Kaufmann's Rubber-Legged Stone. Stonefly patterns are very popular in the West. This fly is best fished on river edges and in fast, rocky currents, especially during stonefly hatches. Cast across the current and dead-drift them through riffles and seams. This is mainly a springtime fly, for late April and May, when clumsy stoneflies emerge from their slumber and litter the water.

Scud. Fish a scud mostly in lakes and ponds with vegetation and weed beds, either on the bottom, or at weed level. At depths past 5 feet, a long leader works wonders. Spring creeks can also be full of vegetation, so cast a Scud upstream and float it through currents and seams. Impart a slight twitch with an occasional light strip of the line and you'll find pay dirt, no doubt. You'll also fish scuds in tailwaters, but usually only a mile or so below the lake, or closer.

Prince Nymph. The Prince is considered an "attractor" pattern, which means that, like its dry-fly counterparts, it does not look like any particular insect, but rather is intended to create a sense of intrigue for fish. Cast beadhead versions of the Prince with a 7- to 9-foot leader as a part of a dry-dropper rig in all types of water and structure. A split-shot about a foot above the fly should get it down to about 5 feet, or even to the bottom, when fishing stillwaters. Use a one and two "beat" stripping rhythm.

Chironomid. Chironomids are the number one item in the diet of trout in productive stillwaters; from morning to afternoon approximately 25 to 40 percent of a trout's caloric intake are chironomids at some stage of their life cycle. This changes during the later hours, when they turn to feeding upon other insects near the surface.

For the vast majority of fly fishers, chironomids can be tough to fish because they swim vertically to the surface and will require you to have the patience of a glacier. If you're going to fish a lake or pond, bring a few of the following most popular chironomid patterns: Chromie, Ice Cream Cone, Bronzie, Red Brassie, Pearl Pupa, Thompson's TDC, Gold-ribbed Hare's Ear, and Zug Bug. Fish them just like you might jig for crappie—start at the bottom, and bring them up slowly all the way to the surface, twitching one or two times as you pause.

STREAMERS

So now we've come to streamers. Streamers don't necessarily imitate insects. They do something different. To predatory fish, they simply appear as a smaller baitfish. They are typically used on large rivers where the largest of fish are targeted. We recommend that newbie anglers to try the streamers below.

Woolly Bugger

This big, (often) black, burly fly suggests many foods for a trout, and has been responsible for more trophy trout than any other fly, and is something every angler needs to have in their fly box. We suggest using them in the deepest, darkest pools on a river on bright days, or trailing them behind you as you troll a pond or lake in a kayak.

Woolly Buggers can come in an array of colors, but black is the most common.

Zonker

Mac caught some huge carp one day with a Zonker on Lake Meredith in the Texas Panhandle. He chunked it out in front of this whale, hoping for more of a spook factor than anything else. Next thing he knows, that carp bolted to it and sucked it in and it was like the Thrilla in Manilla, except without all the jive talking. It was the first time we'd really thought of carp as gamefish, and we realized right then that the Zonker was for real.

Other well-known streamers: Mickey Finn, Black-nosed Dace, and the Muddler Minnow.

DRY-FLY ESSENTIALS

It's difficult to tie either of us down about our favorite flies, and since our favorite flies are all dry flies, any top-ten list we composed would be drys only. We put together this checklist of dry flies that fly fishers will want to include in their vests when heading to the trout streams any time of year.

One aspect we like about this list is that with these ten flies we are covered for just about any fishing situation where trout are looking at the surface. Most anglers know that the Adams will imitate just about any mayfly hatch, but the versatility of flies like the Asher, the House and Lot, and the Turck's Tarantula Asher are underrated.

Parachute Adams: This little gray-bodied fly doesn't look like much. It certainly doesn't have the pizzazz of the Royal Wulff or the high profile of the Stimulator. But if you want to imitate just about any mayfly hatch and have the ideal prospecting fly, you'll need Parachute Adams in sizes #10 to #20 in your box.

Royal Wulff: Looks like candy to you and the trout. This amazing pattern does not imitate any insect but still works like few other drys. Sits up high, works during all kinds of hatches and is a nice choice for the top fly in a dropper rig.

Elk-hair Caddis: Some like the Goddard version, others the Henryville, but the Elk-hair pattern is tried and tested. The Elk-hair Caddis works on all kinds of water, fished during a hatch or just casting blindly.

Asher: No one, but no one, fishes an Asher anymore. This is a simple fly, just palmered hackle. But few flies imitate terrestrials, water bugs, caddis, and mayflies and can be fished wet like this old standby. And it's easy to tie. It's a great fly for when nothing else is working.

Quill Gordon: Traditional producer. This eastern-style fly imitates many different mayflies. Not a bad prospecting pattern for slower waters.

Parachute Blue-winged Olive: Too many anglers underestimate the BWO hatch. Both the insects and the patterns are too small and difficult to see. But a parachute BWO can produce when all other patterns fail.

House and Lot: Big and ugly. The perfect attractor fly for medium to fast water. Looks like a spider, a water bug, a moth, a butterfly, a bee, and a grasshopper. You can see the fly, and so can the trout.

Patriot: This is a Charles Meck fly that looks like it was designed by a nationalistic circus clown. Red, white, and blue. But you'll salute the little fella when you see how many fish he'll catch for you.

Stimulator: One of the great Western flies. Rides high, draws strikes, stands up to use. Imitates various stoneflies and caddis. Few fish can resist it.

Turck's Tarantula: Is it a dry fly? A terrestrial? (Who cares?) This versatile fly is one of the most efficient searching patterns I fish. This big, buggy, rubber-legged fly imitates stoneflies when fished dry, and imitates baitfish, crawfish, and other swimming uglies when fished below the surface. It works consistently on any kind of water, but especially pocketwater, riffles, and runs.

Honorable mention: Stimulator with rubber legs.

Rubber-legged Stimulator

You have successfully purchased or purloined a rod and reel and your other gear. You're strung up, have your waders on, and you are facing the water. So now what?

It can be pretty daunting to look out at the water, see no trout, and then look at your open fly box. You see a weird array of all these flies someone gave you or that you bought, perhaps on our advice.

Remember to take time to observe. If there are insects in the air or on the water, then capture one. Is it an upright-wing insect, like a mayfly? Or a tent-winged insect, like a caddisfly? Do you have a fly tied that approximates the size and color and shape of that captured insect?

Here's the kicker—even though this fly might be part of a hatch, in the air and on the water, the trout may not want to eat it. So here's what we suggest:

Tie on an attractor fly with a dropper nymph below it. For instance, start with a Stimulator, and below that, 14 inches of tippet with a size 16 Hare's Ear Beadhead Nymph, or a similar combination, such as a size 14 Royal Wulff with a size 18 Prince Nymph beadhead below it, perhaps 16 inches. You are just prospecting, after all.

As you walk the bank, perhaps wade in the water, you will see more. Just watch and learn. Look for rising trout, riseforms, and insects both on the water and in the air. If the trout are not consistently taking the dry or dropper, then it's time to change flies. Don't keep on the same fly combination for too long. One hour is too long. But 15 minutes is not long enough.

If and when you decide to change your flies, mix it up. Match a fly you've seen on the water. Or, match a fly to the time of year. For example, in June, in the Western states, this means stonefly hatches will be the favored trout food. Move away from a larger attractor to a smaller one. Take off the dropper and tie on a smaller attractor dry. If you have been fishing a Royal Wulff, go with something different like an Elk-hair Caddis, or a sleeker fly, or a much smaller fly. Mix things up a little, and make mental notes for yourself as you go.

If the trout are going after your fly, but denying it at the last second (nosing it, spitting it out, getting close but turning away), several things may be going on:

1. Your tippet could be too big. Drop down one size or even two. You will hardly ever use a 4X tippet for a dropper rig, or even for the end of your leader. Go with 5X and smaller, trust us.
2. You could have tag ends of your tippet sticking out.
3. Your fly could be too big. Downsize by one or two, such as from a size 12 down to a size 14 or even a 16. Keep in mind, when matching the hatch, that earlier in summer, natural insects are larger. As the summer goes on, especially into the dog days of August, the natural insects will get smaller.
4. You might be close on your fly choice but not close enough. If you are using a bushy fly, consider changing to a slimmer version, say from an Elk-hair Caddis to a Henryville or Goddard Caddis pattern.
5. The hatch stage might be in emerger or spinner phase. Take off your dry fly and tie on an emerger or pupa, or drowned adult or shuck or spinner. The point is to experiment, and take mental notes of your experimentation so you can use those resources in the future.
6. It might not be the fly. It could be (and often with beginners, probably is) your presentation. You may be slapping the water, giving away your position, casting a shadow, creating drag, casting over fish, pulling your rod tip up so that it drags the fly, and so on.

One tenet we have about dry flies is that you must be able to see your fly, or be able to see where the trout is taking your fly. So if you have trouble seeing that fly, you can do a couple of things: Learn to judge, gauge, and sometimes just guess where the end of your tippet is. And tie on a fly that you can actually see. That doesn't necessarily mean a bigger fly. Nowadays, some small flies even have a fluorescent aspect to them, so you can pick out your fly in even the roughest water.

Fly Tips

1. Don't saturate your fly with floatant. It won't float well.
2. Dry your fly off from time to time. It will float better. One effective method for doing this is to false cast, but remember that several things can happen when doing this—you can spook the water, you can get hung up in a tree, or you could hook your fishing buddy. Alternatively, just retrieve the fly and dry it on a shirt or bandanna.
3. Keep your hooks sharpened.

4. Always make sure your hooks are not rusted.

5. If you store the flies you've used on a vest drying patch, you'll risk losing them since they can easily come off when you're walking through brush, or in your vehicle. Instead, dry them out when you're finished fishing, and upon returning to your vehicle, organize them right back in the storage boxes they belong in.

6. Don't give up on beat-up flies. You'll have some flies that work well, and as a result of abrasion, will have the wings unfurled or the body tattered, or hackle that has spun out of control. That fly can still catch fish. Those fuzzy flies that sink a bit can imitate different stages of insects: a dying adult, an emerging adult, a crippled insect, or a drowned insect. Try tying these worn flies as a dropper-emerger under a brand new, high-floating dry. You'll be surprised how well this will work.

7. We keep separate fly boxes in our collections, assembled for different purposes. We have a box for attractor dry flies, a caddis box, a stonefly box, a mayfly box, one for nymphs, a tailwater small-fly box, and a streamer box. When traveling light, we assemble a new box that includes selections from any or all of these existing boxes.

MATCHING THE HATCH

The insects are in the air and on the water. Trout are rising all around you. You've thrown the kitchen sink at the silly fish and they won't take a thing, not even a fly that looks exactly like the duns flittering about. What's going on?

One of the most common mistakes when reading a hatch is the tendency to disregard what you don't actually see. What you are seeing are the adults of the hatch, but more times than not, trout will feed more readily on the other stages of the insect cycle. The adults are big meaty choices but are also often the most difficult for the trout to capture. So any trout angler would find it beneficial to study and understand the stages of caddisflies, mayflies, and stoneflies.

The most important advice to learning how to match the hatch and catch the trout is simple: Observe. Start by picking up a rock. Turn it over. If you have done your homework, you can tell if those are mayfly nymphs or cased caddis.

Williams searches for the perfect fly to "match the hatch."

Pull out a dip net or seine net, hold it in an edge of fast and slow water, and take a couple of readings. If you know your nymphs from studying, you can tell what insects and what stages are active. Make sure to bend over and look very closely to see what insects you can spot on the water. Spinners are almost invisible at times.

Walk the bank and shake the bushes. Take a seat on high ground and watch the water. Don't fish for five minutes, or ten if you're patient. Begin by watching the insects alighting on the surface on just one section of water. Can you see trout feeding on the surface taking the insects? Are the insects landing in riffles or on flat water?

If you can see trout feeding, you can often see the whites of their mouths opening to take food. If you see trout and their tails pointed upward, they are probably feeding on nymphs on the riverbed. So look carefully, and you can probably figure out which fish you want to go after.

Most importantly, watch the rises. Watching the rises is an art form of study all in itself. Are the trout slashing? They could be chasing adult mayflies. Sipping? Then they are probably gently feeding on spinners, insects that become lifeless after reproducing. Porpoising? The trout could be taking crippled mayflies or mayfly nymphs. If the fish are jumping clear out of the water, they're probably chasing caddis emergers, which release from the bottom and rise quickly to the surface to emerge as adults. And, sometimes, anglers believe the trout are feeding on the top, which to anglers means dry flies, when in fact, they are taking insects in the surface film or just under the surface.

If trout are rising during a hatch, sight-cast to them; don't just cast blindly. Time the rises. Each trout, because of his holding station, will have a certain cadence. Try counting out loud (although in a low tone, so as not to spook the fish, or disturb other fishers) an individual trout's cadence, so that you can plan when to plop out your imitation. Cast above the rise ring. When trout go to the surface to feed, they move up several inches to several feet, then drift back down to their lies.

If you do all this, and the fish are still refusing your offerings, here are few tips:

TIPS

1. Try a smaller version of the fly.

2. Try a more subtle pattern of the fly (a lighter-dressed fly such as a No-Hackle).

3. Go to lighter tippet.

4. Change the color of next pattern.

5. Try a cluster pattern (Cluster Midge or Griffith's Gnat).

6. Go to a different phase of the insect like a pupa, larva, emerger.
   (A dropper rig is a good way to quickly find out what they are feeding on.)

7. Try new patterns like cripples, emergers, and stillborns. For instance, it helps to know if the caddis hatching are cased caddis, peeking caddis, spinning caddis, or egg-laying caddis.

The well-prepared angler will have different patterns, stages, shades, and sizes for the hatches that occur during the time period. Make sure you have various patterns in subtle shade differences and in different sizes. Many diehards bring their fly-tying equipment streamside, and some bring color markers for white flies to color them to match the hatch.

And if all else fails, and matching the hatch isn't working (and sometimes it won't), or there are just too many other choices that they like better than yours, toss out a big old Royal Wulff or a House and Lot. You'll be surprised at how often a change of pace like this will work.

TYING FLIES

We've been on rivers, back at camp, fresh out of the flies that are working, and having to tie up a dozen by the light of the campfire on a portable vise. We can tie basic flies that will usually catch fish.

Doc Thompson is a good friend of ours. He is a fly-fishing guide in the Taos, New Mexico area. He was the 2006 Orvis Endorsed Guide of the Year and, more importantly, the 2005 Orvis Fly Tier of the Year. Doc doesn't believe that the patterns he ties are all that amazing, even though patterns he designed are featured right on the pages of your Orvis catalog: Doc's Disco Hopper, Doc's Cork, and the list goes on and on.

Doc always disparages his own skill at fly tying, but he's one of the top fly tiers in the country.

We tell you all this because he can tie circles around us. We'd much rather buy his flies than tie our own, because—well, some folks play pro basketball and some folks watch pro basketball. Doc plays "pro hoops." We watch. We can't do what he does on the vise. We can tie serviceable nymphs, especially beadhead nymphs. But if it's a fancy fly, we're out of luck.

Doc has a practiced hand, a consistent rhythm, a feel around the vise and tying table. Heck, we have trouble even seeing the tiny aspects of the flies he ties up. Doc has to be proud of the flies he created. Neither of us will ever "create" a pattern that other anglers will purchase and catch fish with. Won't happen, partly because of our skill levels and low ceiling. Partly because fly tying is just not for everyone. Instead of sitting at a table creating new flies, we find ourselves poring over maps or reading guidebooks, or writing guidebooks. Neither of us has the patience or inclination. You might. Tying flies is an integral part of fly fishing, but you can learn fly fishing without fly tying. But you're not going to learn fly tying from us. We're being honest. Too many other experts have books out there that will do a much better job. You need to have to a big fly-fishing library anyway.

We recommend learning how to tie some basic flies. We can tie basic flies that will usually catch fish, but ours fail under close inspection. Too much hackle, not enough turns, poor clipping. But you'll benefit from taking a fly-tying class at your local fly shop or community college. You might love it. You might actually be good at it. Our friends who are good fly tiers usually find an added depth to the sport as they while away the winter hours (and we circle our favorite flies to order, in the pile of fly-fishing catalogs) and make fun of us for not spending hour after hour, turn after turn, looking at our own microscopic creations of feathers and fur.

Our friends who are fly tiers will tell you that you can save money, that the artistic endeavor increases your understanding and enjoyment of the sport. They are right. But so are we. To tie or not to tie: That is your question.

FLY BUYING ADVICE

Where to buy flies? Everywhere. We have both tied flies in the past, but nowadays only tie up beadhead nymphs in bulk. We like to build a fly box that has a few of each of the flies we always count on: five or six size 12 Royal Wulffs, four or five size 14 Royal Wulffs, three or four size 16 Royal Wulffs, five or six size 14 Parachute Adams, and so on. Then, when we get to a location, we visit local fly shops and see what patterns they tend to use. You walk the line on buying eye candy vs. what really works, but the act of purchasing 10 to 15 flies at a fly shop means that you give something back for all the advice you're getting from the guides; and you find some exotic or unusual patterns you've never seen before.

Inevitably, if you get on the river and have a successful pattern, one that is working when no others are, then you will get that one super-duper fly stuck high in a tree and it's your last of its kind. That's why we run a constant inventory on our fly boxes and try to keep backups on hand. Believe us, if we are on the river or lake, and there's just one pattern working, the other guy is going to have some awfully powerful leverage in trade negotiations.

You can, of course, learn to tie your own flies. Especially if you are a millionaire, because fly tying, until you quit, can be an exercise in budget futility. We know a few anglers who know these other anglers who swear they save money by tying their own flies. Okay.

So where to buy your flies? Try 'em all. Order a few dozen from one of those back-of-the magazine discount places. Order a few dozen high-end flies from a catalog company such as Orvis or L.L. Bean. Find some online fly shop stores and pick some unusual patterns you don't see in all the usual places. And like we've said, visit your local fly shop and talk to the guys behind the counter; walk out with a couple of plastic cups of flies. Just don't buy any flies at any big discount store that ends in "Mart." Not unless you want the flies to virtually disintegrate on your first drift.

We love tying beadheads because they're easy, and we lose a lot!

TIME TO CAST

ASSEMBLING YOUR ROD

Putting your rod together for the first time is a simple childish pleasure that satisfies the id in all of us. But it needs to be done with delicacy and fortitude simultaneously.

Once you get the pieces of your rod out and they're ready to go, we suggest you start with the tip end and go down to the butt. Where the rod pieces connect is called the ferrule. Most ferrules are extremely finely tuned to each individual rod, which means the tip section of your rod may not fit the rest of your buddy's rod that's the exact same make and model. So it's important that you connect the joints properly every time. A broken or split ferrule typically means the whole rod is ruined.

So, take the tip end, and find the next section of rod. Slowly fit the two sections together, with your guides being offset about an eighth of a turn. You want to simultaneously twist and slide the two pieces together until there is resistance. Press them firmly into one another, without ramrodding them. You're not drilling for oil.

Once you have those two sections together, sight down the guides and make sure they're lined up precisely. If they're even a tiny bit out of whack, simply twist the pieces till they align. Repeat this process until you have all the sections of your rod connected and aligned. You can test your work by giving each joint a slight tug. If they're secure, you're ready to attach your reel.

ROD DISASSEMBLY TIPS

When disassembling the sections, use the same twisting motion as you pull the sections apart. Some guys actually do this process behind their backs. They look as though they're hiding some technique from you, or they're about to do some magic. Never mind that. We don't understand why you'd want to do anything behind your back. Just do it at chest level and you'll do fine.

Also, if your rod has metal ferrules, we strongly suggest you drop some saliva on the male end before assembling; otherwise, you may have to use a lighter for a brief moment to heat the sections until they will come apart. Williams and I had to do that procedure with his Hexagraph once.

Attaching the Reel

There are a few types of reel connections these days. One of the simplest styles—usually found on lightweight rods—is called cork and rings. This consists of two rings that look like wedding bands around the cork handle. All you do with this style is place your reel seat on the flat part of the cork grip, making sure your reel knob is on the appropriate side. If you're right-handed, the reel knob is on the left, and vice-versa.

Next, slide the rings over the ends of the seat to secure the reel to the rod. Then just slip those wedding bands over the feet on the reel. Snugging them up too tightly will damage the cork. Leaving them too lose will result in the reel falling off. It's up to you to figure out how snug the rings need to be.

Uplocking reel seats are another style. They are found on almost every rod heavier than a 3-weight, and are super easy. You just place your reel foot into the groove on the grip, sliding the front reel foot into the hood of the seat. Next, you twist the threaded back end of the seat until it "up-locks" the reel onto the grip.

Again, if you're right-handed make sure that the reel knob is on the left. Unlike bait-slinging reels, where the reel knob is often on the right for right-handers, the fly reel hangs below the rod when in the hand, and the knob is on the left.

Line-to-Reel Connection

Putting your line on your reel for the first time is a tricky endeavor, and we recommend letting the overly exuberant dudes at your local fly shop do it for you. They'll be very adept at this and won't mind doing it at all. If you were stringing a new guitar you wouldn't do a good job of putting the strings on. The same is true with fly line. However, if you insist on doing it yourself, here goes. Hope you haven't lost your mojo.

First, you'll need to know how to tie two knots—the arbor knot for securing the backing to the arbor spindle of the reel, and the nail knot for attaching the fly line to the backing. For both of these, refer to Chapter 2 (pages 62 and 63). The arbor is easy. The nail will take practice, patience, and dexterity to master.

The trickiest part of putting line onto your reel yourself is knowing how much backing to put on the reel. You need enough so that the coils of fly line are as large as they can be. But if you put too much backing on, you'll run out of room and your fly line won't fit on the reel. And when that happens, you'll have to pull all the fly line back off, cut the difficult-to-master nail knot you just tied, then remove an arbitrary amount of backing, hoping you pull enough off so this doesn't happen again, then redo the whole process of tying the nail knot and reeling in the line.

If there are any tricks to knowing exactly how much backing to put on a reel, we don't know of them. Most fly lines will have a recommended footage amount of backing to use printed on the box, but it's only an ap-proximation, and how the hell do they know what reel you have? More than anything it will take practice, and a few times of messing up before you get it just where you want it. Good luck.

A great way for a beginner to connect lines is loop-to-loop. Whether you are connecting your fly line to your leader, or leader to tippet, loop-to-loop is the quickest and easiest method.

You want to aspire to cast like Mel Krieger or Lefty Kreh, but just like a golf swing, just aspiring to swing like Ben Hogan or Greg Norman is not easy, and the process is not going to happen overnight. Your cast will probably be crappy at first (and that's why we'll instruct you to keep things short and easy at first) and your learning curve will be steep, and you may never swing like Greg or cast like Lefty.

Mac has stopped his backcast, the rod is loaded, and he is beginning his forward cast. Remember—don't drop your arm!

Elbow pool

One common problem is that you'll do well with your casting early but then get greedy, want to be a pro, and you'll start casting longer and longer until you overpower or underpower your stroke, have line flying around your ears and eyes dangerously, get frustrated because there's just too much to remember and too little success. So you give up the sport. We don't want that.

We don't want you to learn the standard cast first. We want you to learn a more basic, useful cast that will allow you to experience more success and less futility.

The one-handed cast is so simple you won't want to advance to the standard cast. Grasp the rod with your casting hand—grab the cork handle as though you were shaking hands with someone. This is your rod hand. Your grip needs to be firm but not suffocatingly tight, and needs to allow your index finger or any combination of fingers of your rod hand to cover the line against the rod.

You'll want to extend about 1 to 3 feet of fly line out from the tip of the rod. You will have 7 to 9 feet of leader attached to the fly line. We recommend 7 feet as opposed to 9, by the way. The less line the better for a beginner. Note: If you have a 7-foot rod, 7 feet of the line will be on the rod so what we want is for you to only have 1 to 3 feet of fly line past the tip, to go with 7 feet of leader.

We'll be using the one-hand casting trick. No need to worry on your first few outings with 10 to 2 o'clocks or strip hands or arcs or tight loops or any of that. We want you to start with a one-handed, in-control method, using short lining and dapping. As you get better, you will learn how to use your line hand or off hand, resulting in the eventual standard fly-fishing cast. But success breeds learning, we believe.

We begin with your fly rod, reel, and line. You tie on a 7-foot tippet to your fly line and pull out 2 feet more fly line. That gives you 9 feet of leader and line to play with. You pull out this 9-foot combination of line and leader and grab the rod butt as if you were shaking hands, making sure your finger covers the line so it can't release. You'll be fishing one-handed, without stripping line or shooting line. The idea is to be in control, with a basic, no-frills, abbreviated cast meant to help you learn how to drift, read water, and possibly catch fish with minimal problems.

Do not tie on a fly just yet.

Stand on the bank. Face upstream or most of the way upstream. This means your shoulders should face mostly upstream but still toward the river. We like a slightly open stance where your right foot aims to the river and your left foot aims up the bank line. If you're right-handed, place your left foot slightly upstream of your right foot. Let your rod arm bend slightly, even to the point of your arm being bent at the elbow at a 90-degree angle.

Extend your rod arm and slowly move the arm to your right, downstream. The end of the tippet should be touching the water. Keep moving your rod tip (watch the rod tip, not your arm or wrist) to your right, downstream. Stop.

Your shoulders should be mostly facing upstream while your right arm (your rod arm) is extended not quite fully downstream. Let your rod hand wrist turn slightly over from left to right as though you were opening a pickle jar.

Imagine yourself throwing a baseball. While holding the rod. Not too much wrist, okay? You push through the throw, letting your hand stay extended but not dropping below your waist. The first one sucked, right? Let's try it again.

The idea is to minimize your backcast and go ahead and position your rod as though you had used a backcast stroke. So line up again, let your rod tip lie parallel or angled slightly up, extend your arm downstream, and stop. Now throw the ball. Not too hard, but still use a short, springy forward motion and then stop. You can now experiment with a slow toss or a quick burst and find what works for you. Some folks will find that a tiny wrist flick at the end of the forward cast works for them.

If you were wading in the water, you'd make your forward cast, let the fly drift down below you, extend your arm, letting the water move the fly downstream, and then in one easy motion, throw the ball (make a forward cast) to where you wanted it to land. Don't let your arm drop below your waist.

If the baseball throwing analogy isn't working, think of it this way—consider the rod a hammer. From the downstream start position, you are swinging a hammer to hit a nail that is somewhere in front of you waist to face high. Not knee high or river high. That means you're dropping your rod tip too low and you won't cast well that way. If you were to swing a hammer at an imaginary wall in front of you to hit an imaginary nail, the wall and opposing matter would stop you. Bring your rod forward with some force, not too much and not too little, and let the imaginary wall bring your rod to a stop somewhere in front of you. Try this a few times.

You should be able to get in the downstream cast start position and cast forward. Tie on a fly. You're ready. Make sure to de-barb the fly because you are not that ready. You will be using two drift methods your first few days out—high sticking and dapping.

FALSE CAST

A false cast is a "regular" fly-fishing cast that is not intended to land the fly upon the water. You'll use false casts to change direction, to shorten or lengthen the line, or to dry off your fly. Don't false cast too much or you'll get hung up in trees or line fish.

*Mac is stripping and mending to match the
current and keep his drift drag-free.*

Say you've just cast. Let the current take the fly downstream. When
the line is taut, with your arm extended, use a tight, short forward motion to propel the line and fly upstream. No need to false cast today.
This is a modified roll cast. We like a flatter forward stroke, especially for
beginners, a cast that does not emphasize much movement over your
shoulder. You can cast over your shoulder on your forward stroke, but it's
safer and easier to cast as if you are throwing, slightly to the right of your
shoulder but not so low as to be sidearm.

Keep your backcasts to a minimum; use the water as your "backcast"
as much as possible.

In other words, you cast upstream, holding the rod tip up so the least
length of line is on the water. It's okay if the leader/tippet is on the water
and a little bit of line, maybe a lot or even all the line if you are casting
across stream. As the fly comes to you, floating downstream, slowly lift
up your arm, raising the tip of the rod so you can easily and quickly raise
the tip to set the hook and control line.

Above, high-sticking, with the arm in position for a quick backcast and below, in position to easily backcast and forward cast.

Keys to this Easy Cast

1. Keep your rod-hand on the line all the time.
2. Let the current be your "backcast."
3. Keep a short, tight forward stroke.
4. Raise the tip of the rod as fly floats downstream, as if you are a puppet master.
5. Let the fly go all the way downstream and make your line tight.
6. Repeat.

Face at least partly upstream, and remember to watch for obstacles behind you.

As you get better, you don't have to always let the current tighten the line. You can and should sometimes use a short, tight backcast followed by your forward stroke. Don't drop your arm when you go forward or you won't hit the mark and your arm will get tired. As you get better at it, you can let out a little more line. Don't get overconfident and let out too much line. You are not ready for that.

Look behind you. You shouldn't have to cast perpendicular to the river because you should be facing upstream or at least partly upstream. If there's a limb or brush or a person or a bear behind you, don't start the backcast. Remember that the line and tippet goes out 9 feet and you have a 7- to 9-foot rod.

Don't try to power the cast. Simply stroke forward when you feel some tension.

Don't have the fly upstream of you. It should be downstream or slightly off to one side.

When you backcast with this grip and setup, you aren't going to make the fly go any farther by powering the stroke. You know how it feels already when the fly goes downstream: You feel some tension and you simply stroke forward. Now you will do the same thing, but in the air.

Do not have the fly in front of you or upstream of you. It needs to be slightly downstream or off to your side.

If you have loose line or a belly in the line, you run the risk of hooking your ear, or worse. Keep your line fairly tight downstream of you and slightly off to your side.

Think minimum motion. The backcast is short, and by that we mean that you don't have to make a big deal about it. With force, you move your hand and arm back a foot and open your wrist a tiny bit, then snap forward while moving your arm back that same foot.

It's like hitting a nail with a hammer. If you take a huge swing, you won't hit the nail. If you take too small a swing, you won't drive it through. You know how you let the hammer rock slightly in your hand on the upswing? That's what we want you to do with this short stroke. It's not a wrist thing. You move your entire forearm and wrist, not just your wrist.

Keep your casting hand slightly over the rod, not on the side or under it. This keeps you from breaking your wrist too much on the backswing—in other words, your wrists don't need to be floppy.

You want to feel the tug on your backcast. It won't be much because you don't have much line out. When you feel the tug, you rock your hand slightly and push forward, then stop quickly. This lays the line out straight right where you want it.

You have the mechanics of the short hammer cast down. Next, try a cross-chest short hammer cast. Sound hard? Nope, it's easy. Instead of taking the rod tip back to your casting side, you will angle your body differently.

Instead of holding your left foot more upstream, your right foot should be more upstream. You will face totally upstream or slightly closed, which means your chest should now face more of the bank than the river. You will repeat all the same mechanics as the hammer/baseball cast, except you'll be doing the cast over your left shoulder, or out away from the shoulder in a ¾ manner.

Let's say you have a machete in your rod hand. You are walking through tall grass. You have been asked to cut off the tops of the grass, say, the top few inches. The grass is about 4 feet tall.

The start and position of a backhanded or cross-body cast

The second part of a backhanded cross-body cast

As you walk, you take the machete up over your left shoulder, bring it to a stop, and in he same motion, bring the machete back across to cut the grass. You wouldn't want to bring the machete too far across your body or you might cut yourself. So you should go back, bring it forward, and stop somewhere out in front of you and somewhere in the middle of your chest, as if a line shot out perpendicular to your chest.

We call this a cross-body cast. When done properly, the line tends to land with a curve that has the belly on its left side—the end of a parenthesis.

The cross-body cast works best when you are wading on the right side of a stream and wish to cast close to the right bank, when you have an obstacle behind you and to your right.

There are many other uses for the cross-body cast, sometimes called the backhand cast. We like to use it as we wade upstream because it's easy on the arm and very accurate. You get a full range of targets in front of you and to your sides. We use the cross-body cast in an upward motion over the shoulder, then a slight downward motion, stopping while the arm and wrist are still above the waist.

Things to remember about the cross-body cast:

Keep the rod tip away from you. You don't want to have the rod tip arc over your shoulder, close to your face.

It's a fairly flat cast, ¾ is best.

Use it mostly when you are casting on the right side of upstream. That way you keep your backcast out of trees and brush and you also get your fly and line positioned to float and mend better.

You won't have an arc or belly in your line if you use the cross-body cast, but you are likely to when you are on the right side moving upstream.

You can use the curve to your advantage when you want to place the fly around a rock, so in those cases, use the regular cast.

When you have gotten fairly confident with the hammer and machete casts, try letting out some more line. Don't get too excited and try an extra 5 feet on the first try, but try 6 inches of line. One way is to let the 6 inches of line fall between your line-control finger and the reel. When you cast forward, after the rod has passed your shoulder, lift up your index finger and the line will fly through the guides. In this way, you don't have to backcast as much line. You can eventually take out even more line, say 12 to 18 inches, let it hang between your index control finger and the reel, and shoot out the line on your forward cast. At some point, you'll end up with too much line to cast and control with this one-handed technique, and it will be time to learn the standard cast.

THE STANDARD CAST

Our book is designed for beginners and those with a little more experience. We don't think you can learn to how to make the standard cast properly from any book. You need to go to a guide or a fly-fishing school, or take lessons from your fly shop. You need to watch videos of experts casting. You wouldn't learn the standard golf swing from a book. If you try to learn a golf swing on your own, you develop really bad habits. Don't get us wrong; you'll want to read up on standard casts once you have gotten lessons.

Here are some of our tips for when you are out on the water "learning" and practicing this standard cast.

What do you guys mean by stripping line? Instead of controlling the fish by reeling in line on the reel, you'll do so by retrieving the fly line with your fingers. As you strip or pull line with your line hand, guide the line through your outstretched index finger of your rod hand.

Keep things short and tight. Your mistakes will come when you try to do too much, cast too far, or use too much line.

Don't drop your arm too far behind you. Dropping it does not give you more power, only less.

Don't aim. That's the bad habit from spincasting that you want to drop. What we mean by "aim" is don't aim at the water. If you aim, aim at an imaginary target at or near eye level. The fly will drop from that point and hit the mark.

Don't drop your arm too far in front of you. You will lose power and accuracy.

Let the strip hand really work for you. You'll figure out that if you keep line tension with that hand, your rod will load better and you'll cast better and farther. We really pull the line with our strip hand, so try it.

There are times when you can sidearm your backcast and forward cast and cut through the wind or create a curve cast.

When you cast forward, let the line shoot. That means you must not have the tight grip on the line that you did when you loaded the rod.

Williams lays a fly right up against the bank.

*Classic upstream
casting position*

*Below. No obstacles behind him,
Williams works up the left side,
casting to choice spots from the
middle run to the far bank.*

When you are fishing with someone who is a better caster than you, stop and watch. Emulate his or her motions. Ask for advice.

You'll notice that good casters make everything seem so smooth, just like pro golfers and their swings. Their trick is not smoothness. Their trick is knowing when to stop the backcast and when to start it—acceleration and deceleration. It's a timing thing.

With proper timing come distance and accuracy.

Buy the right rod for your casting ability.

If you don't practice, you won't get better.

False casting lets you redirect your fly and line and it allows you to let out more line. Just don't overdo it.

Your "River Runs Through It" cast won't always work. On your lawn or in the driveway of your local fly shop, you will be able to practice the old 10 o'clock/2 o'clock cast, loading the rod, maintaining your plane, keeping a rhythm. But on the river, trees get in your way. Rivers bend and turn. Limbs hang over perfect lies.

The rod does all the work once it's loaded.

The fly line is lying horizontally, but look at Mark's arm and hand—he keeps it fairly perpendicular.

Wade gently and cast as you wade.

Learning the perfect cast can be a lot like learning the perfect golf swing. In theory, you can always make it better, more efficient, transfer the load of the club better, and so on. But on the course, as on the water, it's all about scoring.

What are the swings/casts that will help you in less than ideal conditions? As when learning the perfect golf swing, the process can become bogged down by physics, science, and too much analysis. Sometimes, it's better to just get out and try it.

There's no doubt that you'll need to know the roll cast, the reach cast, the double haul, the curve cast, and the bow-and-arrow cast, but there are other overlooked but useful casts that don't require hours of practice and don't look all that pretty, but keep you catching trout.

These are blue-collar casts, not trick casts, casts you will use on streams and lakes over and over when you find yourself in unusual situations.

These casts include the

- *cross-body cast*
- *S-cast cast*
- *sidearm cast*
- *steeple cast*

We'll walk you though each of these casts later on. In this installment, we'll dissect the steeple cast.

The steeple cast is useful in most places where a roll cast comes in handy, but has some additional applications. I've also found that many beginners and intermediates never quite get the hang of the roll cast, and find the steeple cast easier. The steeple cast can be used when you have trees or other obstacles behind you. The cast is named for the fact that the backcast travels in a straight-up plane to the heavens, like a church steeple.

When you strip in line with your line hand (also called off hand), re-member to clasp lightly back down with your rod hand or fingers. That gives you more control if you need to set the hook. As you get more expe-rienced, you can move your line hand away from the index finger of your rod hand. The steeple cast has a couple of advantages over the roll cast. One, the line is not on the water, so the line won't drag, spook the fish, or be affected by the current. And if you have extra weight on the line (split-shot or two flies) it's much easier to lift the line off the water to cast.

And with the steeple cast, you can change direction in midair and you can be more accurate with your target than with the roll cast.

Sequence 1 of a steeple cast

Sequence 2 of a steeple cast

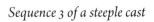

Sequence 3 of a steeple cast

114

Step by Step

1. Begin with your rod in the standard casting position.

2. Start your backstroke like a sidearm cast and then swing your arm into a vertical position. The idea here is that instead of casting 10 to 2, your rod tip should travel more of a 9 to 12 path. When the rod tip reaches the 12 o'clock position, stop the rod abruptly to load the rod and allow the line to lay out overhead.

3. Since this isn't a perpendicular cast and you start the cast out in a sidearm plane, keep your reel face facing forward and your arm angle mirroring the angle of the line until it reaches its apex. In other words, this isn't a cast where the line has a clear back-and-forth path, so you will need to let your forearm imitate the path of the line or the line will get tangled with your rod tip.

4. Keep the backcast (which is really an "upcast") over your casting shoulder, and once you get the hang of it, bring your arm a little over your head. Keep the line high and tight, like a taut clothesline fastened to a point directly over your head. If you drop your arm behind you, all hell will break loose. Don't do that.

5. Punch hard through the forward cast and stop your cast at the 9 or 10 o'clock position. If the line is getting tangled on the upstroke, your extended arm is not following the angle of the backcast/upstroke line. Another way to keep the line from tangling is to use more of an outward and upward sweeping motion on the backstroke, like waving a wand or conducting an orchestra.

Bow-and-Arrow Cast

One day, you might be tight against willows or cottonwoods on the bank. For those hard-to-reach places, into pocketwater, under limbs, and spots where you have no backcast room, go to the bow-and-arrow cast to drop your fly on top of fish. This is a cast you must first practice without a fly on your line. Take out 2 to 4 feet of fly line. Grab the tag end of the tippet between your forefinger and thumb. Leave no slack. With your rod hand, hold the fly line tight against the rod.

Point the rod tip toward the spot where you want the fly to land, extending your rod arm, holding the end of the tippet tight. Pull the tag end tighter until the rod tip bows. You should look somewhat like you are shooting an arrow.

Get ready to release. With the rod tip held at a slight angle, and importantly, without moving the rod when you let go, release the tag end of the tippet. The end should drop softly wherever you were aiming.

Mac with a bow-and-arrow cast because he has no other way to place the fly.

Another bow-and-arrow cast. Mark is using his left hand and the loop is solid and about to uncoil.

Tie on a fly. Repeat the steps but insert this instruction: Grab the fly at the bend of the hook between your forefinger and thumb. Be careful, folks. There's not much more painful or embarrassing an experience than impaling a thumb or finger just by trying to cast.

Again, if you have a decent amount of tension and the rod is bent back and you don't move the rod, wherever you point it, that's where it's going to land.

You can also curve the bend of the rod to your left or right so you can get the fly under obstacles. You'll put your fly into tighter spots where no other anglers have fished, you'll catch more fish, and it's a cool-looking cast to boot.

Begin fishing by simply flicking the fly out into the water with your hand first. Hold the rod in your casting hand, and the fly in the other, and with a swooping motion, let go the fly and flick it out there. Strip off some line, and begin casting.

Keep the wind in mind. The last thing you want is a fly in the eye or ear. Fish on the proper side of the stream when possible so that if there is a wind or breeze present, it's not blowing your cast into you, but away from you. Proper means the side where you won't get hooked because of wind.

Don't pop your fly on your backcast. This ain't Spanish bullwhipping class. It's a delicate, almost effortless motion. Go easy; slow down. If you're popping, you're not waiting long enough on the backcast. Wait to feel the rod load before coming forward on the forward cast.

Trap the loose line under the index finger of your rod hand.

Yvonne demonstrates proper grip, good posture, and attentive listening while learning the standard cast.

Lifting the line . . .

. . . and making another backcast

After you learn the one-handed cast, do this next: Cast one-handed but control the line with your left hand and the fingers of your rod hand. Casting less line is far cooler than casting too much line.

When in doubt—and your cast feels like a train wreck—stop, slow down your stroke, and visualize your loop going right where you want it. Then start your cast again.

SEQUENCE OF THE STANDARD CAST

IT'S ALL ABOUT
THE TROUT

SPECIES OF TROUT

Even though fly fishing has grown by leaps and bounds and now includes
chasing largemouth bass, saltwater fish like permit, speckled trout, redfish, and inland gamefish like peacock bass and tigerfish, most American
fly fishers are in hot pursuit of one fish: trout. That's where we focused
this book. But trout come in many forms and fashions (some hair-split-
ters like to call them species). So it's important to be able to identify and
distinguish the various species of trout you might catch, just as it's important for hunters to know what species and gender of birds are flying
overhead before they shoot.

Since many trout species feed and behave differently, anglers can actually learn these behaviors and key in on specific species of trout during
certain times in certain waters. Some of us actually target specific species
of trout by selecting certain flies, or by fishing with nymphs in a certain
area, or drys in another. Once you've fished for a while and have seen

Beautiful rainbow

these behaviors over and over, firsthand, you'll learn how to key in and target specific trout species as well.

We'd like to introduce you to the usual suspects. Here they are, in the order in which they appear. (Not actual size.)

Rainbow Trout

Scientific Name: Oncorhynchus mykiss

Other Names: There are quite a few subspecies of rainbows, which in turn means there are many other names for them, like redband, redstripe, bow, Kamloops, and others.

Native to the American Pacific coast, including Alaska, bows are now widely found in most states, including the eastern drainages of the Rockies, Appalachian drainages, and the Great Lakes states. They inhabit every continent but Antarctica, hence rainbows are by far the most dispersed and most popular of all the trout for fly fishers. They reside in coldwater streams, rivers, and lakes, and can tolerate slightly warmer and less pristine waters than brook trout.

Rainbow trout are called "rainbows" because they boast the well-known reddish-pink band stretching down each side, about the midline, that many say resembles a rainbow. (We don't think so. We think they their pink stripe resembles a pink stripe. But who are we to rename them "pinkies"?) This stripe may range in vibrancy from faint pink to a radiant red. We have both caught rainbows where no sign of a red stripe exists at all (rather boring). And we've also landed others where you'd swear the fish was bleeding out its scales (rather amazing). Often, hatchery fish are far less colorful and pretty than wild rainbows.

Rainbows have the telltale streamlined salmonid body, though their shape and coloration vary widely depending upon their diet, age, gender, habitat, and degree of maturity. Their body shape will vary greatly, from slender to thick, from fat to skinny, from long-nosed to blunt-headed. A rainbow's back might range from bluish-green to a deep olive tone. The lower sides are normally silver, fading to a white belly. Small black spots or speckles are present over the back, above the lateral line, as well as on the upper fins and tail. These spots are smaller than cutthroat spots and also a different shape, not usually as round as the cutthroat's markings. In some locations, the black spots of adults may extend well below the lateral line and even cover the entire lower side.

Rainbow trout can be positively identified in a couple of ways. There are 8 to 12 rays in the anal fin. (Not that you should be picking up a trout and looking at his anus.) The mouth does not extend past the back of the eye. The rainbow also lacks the teeth at the base of the tongue that some other fish have. (Who needs teeth on their tongue anyway?)

Another rainbow

River or stream dwellers normally have more intensely colored stripes and the heaviest spotting—more so than their lake-dwelling counterparts, anyhow. And during the spawn they usually turn a darker color. Spawn typically sets in around late March and rolls on through midsummer, depending on runoff, temperatures, and geographic location. When water temperatures begin escalating in late winter and early spring, adult rainbows instinctively retreat to shallow gravelly riffles in streams, or to shallower waters in lakes and ponds. A female will prepare a redd or nest utilizing her tail, approximately 4 to 12 inches deep and 10 to 15 inches in diameter. In it, she will dribble 200 to 8,000 eggs, and a male will soon fertilize the entire batch, then cover them with gravel.

If you want to mop up on rainbows, try fishing in late spring, after the spawn and before runoff, as well as in the fall, when rivers are lower and summer fishing pressure has diminished. Rainbow trout are voracious feeders and strong swimmers willing to hit a wide variety of flies. We catch most of our rainbows in seams and in fast water. You will too. Seams are where faster-moving water meets slower water and they seem to be rubbing past one anther. This "rubbing" of waters is visible on the surface. Seams are nice places for a trout to hang because they suspend in the slack water, and when they see food passing in the faster-moving food lane, they'll dart out to grab it, then move back into the slack.

Rainbows also seem willing to swim in faster channels than brown trout of equal size. This is probably because browns tend to dominate pools and chase other species upstream. When a rainbow is hooked, its first instinct seems to be to tail-walk on the surface while shaking its head back and forth to try and throw the fly. It's our opinion that they don't realize they have a hook in their mouths. They only know it's not something they have ever felt a bug do before, so they want to spit it out and let it fly away. Some rainbows, for instance in the San Juan River in New Mexico, do a short tail-walk (or none at all) but do love to run and get you into your reel. Kamloops rainbows sometimes love to dive and run.

The fight you might expect from a rainbow is less than that of an Apache trout in the White Mountains of Arizona, but more than that of the koi in the neighbor's pond. (You really shouldn't be fishing in your neighbor's pond or fishing for koi, by the way.) Rainbows will jump and jive and give you a run for your money, but they tire easily, and may die if you don't net them quickly. That's bad. Try at all costs not to harm the trout you catch. See our tips on catch-and-release fishing to learn what not to do once you finally hook a trout.

A beautiful example of a brown trout

Brown Trout

Scientific Name: Salmo trutta
Other Names: German brown, squaretail, Loch Leven trout.

Browns are "true" trout, first introduced to America from their supposed native land of Western Europe in the late 19th Century. We are convinced no one truly knows from which part of the globe brown trout truly hail, because in our research we've read that browns are native to Germany, Greece, Russia, Afghanistan, Iceland, and many other places.

Browns are generally tougher to catch than rainbows and brookies— but only a little tougher, depending on conditions. They're often a little bigger than rainbows in the same water, but only a little.

Browns will often bite beadhead nymphs most of the day in most waters. They will also take well-placed drys in calmer slack water and on the edges most of the day in most waters.

Brown trout will rarely do the aerial acrobatic dance that rainbows will, coming out of the water to shake the fly free, as do largemouth bass.

Instead, a brown's instinct is to go deep, then run upstream or down, and zoom all around until either it is exhausted, or you are. This quite often works in their favor.

Younger browns are often silvery yellow. Slightly older browns will age into a brassy or buttery yellow overall color, especially in streams, with dark spots intermixed with reddish-orange spots along their flanks, each spot surrounded by a light halo. Old browns are just that . . . old and brown. At all ages, they have squared tails and light-colored fin tips, which help distinguish browns from other trout. What's cool is that depending on the river, the geology, the minerals, the season, and all kinds of other things, brown trout can vary in color and vibrancy tremendously. Some brown trout have lots of red in their coloring. Others have more yellow, especially in their bellies. Brown trout are now found from coast to coast in America, with populations in all but a few very Gulf states. Most live in streams and rivers, with some lake-dwelling populations. They tolerate higher water temperatures than rainbows and other trout species. This is important to know because brown trout will be among the most downstream species, so if you're wanting to target-fish brown trout, you'll know to fish the lower ends of streams. (Typically, brookies tend to dominate the upper headwaters, then rainbows and cutts intermingle between them and the browns below.)

Browns are territorial and usually dominate pools or holes, so other trout will have to move up- or downstream from them to survive. They also cannot interbreed with any other species of "true" trout. Only brook trout (char) can successfully breed with browns, to create offspring called tiger trout.

Browns, especially older ones, tend to feed mainly beneath the surface, so nymphing with beadheads and subsurface flies tends to dredge out the rogues that refuse to bite on dry flies. However, during active hatches and on calm, clear days, it's possible to catch brown trout on drys such as Parachute Adams, caddis, and stonefly patterns and terrestrials just as easily.

Brook Trout

Scientific Name: Salvelinus fontinalis
Other Names: In many places brook trout are known as speckled trout, brookies, or squaretails.

Brook trout

Brook trout are not really "trout" at all. Brookies are actually char, so really they should be called brook char, which they are in parts of Canada. So just call them brookies, like us, and play it safe.

These smallish fish are native to the northeasternmost states and Canada, including the Appalachians. Today populations thrive in almost all Western states, where they live in only the clearest, cleanest coldwater streams and lakes. Because of this, brook trout serve as dependable indicators of the quality of the watersheds they inhabit. Strong wild brook trout populations demonstrate that a stream's ecosystem is healthy. If water quality is good, you'll know it—brookies will be present.

Brookies are often many anglers' favorite freshwater fish, where beauty is concerned. The large mouth extends past the eye. Color variations include olive, bluish-gray, or almost black above the lateral line, with silvery or whitish bellies and vermiculate (wormlike) markings along their backs. Brooks sport crimson spots surrounded by bluish halos along their sides. Perhaps the most distinctive characteristic of brook trout are the white tips along their lower fins, with the remainder of the fin fading to a reddish-orange hue. The tail fin is squared off, or rarely slightly forked, hence the nickname squaretail.

During spawn, male brook trout will become neon orange red along their sides. Brook trout are vicious feeders and will take dry-fly patterns at nearly any time of day. They are possibly the easiest trout to catch. We suggest you find a stream known to hold large numbers of brookies to learn your tactics. Kids and adults alike love to learn to fish for trout on high-elevation headwaters because the wading is easy, and brookies will take even poorly presented flies. Their meat is delicate and flavorful as well. One bad thing about brookies is that they repopulate so easily that they crowd out less aggressive native species like cutthroats.

Cutthroat Trout

Scientific Name: Oncorhynchus clarki (or *clarkii*) in honor of William Clark, co-leader of the Lewis and Clark Expedition of 1804–1806.

Other Names: Cutthroats are often generalized as "cutts," almost always preceded by their subspecies name, i.e., Rio Grande cutt. There are no fewer than 14 recognized subspecies of cutthroat in North American geologic history—and that includes two extinct, unnamed species.

Common Subspecies: Rio Grande, Bonneville, Yellowstone, Snake River fine-spotted, Colorado River, greenback, Lahontan, westslope, coastal, Whitehorse basin, yellowfin, Paiute, and Humboldt.

A beautiful cutthroat

Another fine example of a cutthroat trout, showing its amazing coloration

Most cutthroat species are found in the headwaters of cold, gravel-bottomed streams and rivers and some mountain lakes. They are indigenous to the Western United States and again, are not actually trout, but members of the Pacific salmon family. Yes, the cutthroat is just another of the many fish colloquially known as trout. Most populations dwell in freshwater streams throughout their lives and may reach weights of 20 pounds or more, but most will only push 2 pounds. In the old days, cutthroats reached large sizes and prodigious numbers but were either fished out by settlers or pushed out by environmental degradation.

Cutthroats can and often will breed with rainbow trout in the same streams and lakes, creating offspring referred to as cuttbows. Species of cutts vary widely in size, coloration, and habitats. Though their coloration can range from golden to gray to green on the back (depending on subspecies and habitat) all populations feature distinctive red, pink, or orange marks on the underside of the lower jaw. This is usually the easiest identifying mark of the species for the casual observer. As adults, different populations and subspecies of cutthroat can range from 6 inches to 3 feet in length, making size an impossible means of identification.

Apache trout

Apache Trout

Scientific Name: Oncorhynchus apache

Apache trout are a beautiful golden or yellowish color with medium-size dark spots or flecks, evenly spaced along the sides and tail. Their fins are tipped with a white or orange color, and the tops of the Apache's head and back are often a light olive color, and they have the appearance of having a black stripe through each eye. A telltale cutthroat slash mark appears below the lower jaw, varying in color from bright orange to yellow to gold.

Indigenous to Arizona, it is one of only two species of trout native to that state, the other being the Gila trout. Residing in clear, cool streams in the White Mountains that flow through coniferous forests and marshes, this species has since been introduced into several lakes in the area. Some of our favorites are Hurricane, Sunrise, and Hawley Lakes.

The Apache trout's original homeland can be traced back to the upper Salt River watershed. Historically it was found solely in the headwaters of the White, Black, and Little Colorado Rivers above 5,900 feet elevation in east-central Arizona. However, now you can find them in isolated streams outside the White Mountains region, like the Pinaleno Mountains, Mount Graham, and the North Rim of the Grand Canyon. We have found Apache fishing to be almost like an extreme sport. They are often easy to dupe with drys, and typically put up a vicious fight! The Apache is officially designated as Arizona's state fish, and a special permit is required to fish for the Apache in most places. Check your proclamation for details.

Gila trout. Photo by Melanie Dabovich, USFWS

Gila Trout

Scientific Name: Oncorhynchus gilae gilae (Is there an echo in here?)

Found exclusively in south-central New Mexico, this nearly extinct species populates only a handful of small, clear streams. The Gila trout is closely related to the Apache trout. They, too, may possess the two spots on either side of the pupil in the eye. Gila trout, on the other hand, are characterized by numerous small dark speckles on the upper half of the body. Otherwise, Gila trout might look very similar to an Apache—olive, golden, or buttery yellow in color.

Salmon

Scientific Name: Salmon are anadromous, which means they travel upriver from the sea (or sometimes from large lakes, such as the Great Lakes, where Pacific salmon were introduced in the 1960s) to spawn. Atlantic salmon are *Salmo salar* (in the genus *Salmo,* like brown trout), and were the first salmon to be classified.

Salmon are special. They are born, live, and die in very unique ways. During the course of their lives they live in both salt- and freshwater habitats. Young salmon are born in freshwater streams. They swim and play for about one to three years. They also feed heavily on a variety of foods, building strength to take the journey out to sea.

They may spend as many as three to five years maturing at sea, then make the miraculous return trek back to the exact same stream in which they were born in order to spawn. Some studies have proved that they return to the exact spot where they were hatched because they know it's a safe place for their young to grow up.

Amazingly, salmon journeys can be hundreds, even thousands of miles from stream to sea. Sadly but beautifully, after Pacific salmon spawn, they just die. One minute they're knockin' fins, next thing you know, they're pushin' up daisies. Atlantic salmon can withstand the rigors of migration to survive and spawn more than once.

And just so you know, salmon do not eat during their migrations to and from the sea, so you catching them (especially Atlantic salmon) is challenging. Instead of eating, their focus is on the spawn. A female can lay almost 1,000 eggs for every pound she weighs. Before a female salmon exhausts her supply of eggs, she will have made several "redds," or nests, that can be 10 feet long and 4 feet wide.

There are five species of Pacific salmon: king (aka Chinook), coho (aka silver); chum (aka dog); sockeye, and pink (aka humpback). All Pacific salmon belong to the genus *Oncorhynchus*. There are many subspecies of salmon, one of which is a special treat for fly fishers: Kokanee salmon—sockeyes that do not migrate out to sea because they are landlocked, or trapped inside a lake. These fish taste amazing with their delicate pink meat and flaky texture. We suggest tossing flies to these guys! Colorado's Blue Mesa Reservoir is a well-known Kokanee fishery.

Fly fishing for sea-run salmon requires heavy tackle and specialized rigging. Beginners will need to go with an experienced friend, or hire a guide. They will help you learn how to rig your line and cast certain ways that will pay off dividends. What's called "chuck-and-duck" is probably the most common and easiest way for salmon fly rodding.

Lake Trout

Scientific Name: Salvelinus namaycush

Other Names: Mackinaw, lake char (or charr), laker, touladi, togue, and grey trout. In Lake Superior, anglers frequently call them siscowet, paperbellies, or leans.

Lake trout are freshwater char (of the same genus—*Salvelnus*—as brook trout) living mainly in deep, coldwater lakes in northern North America and Canada. They can grow to huge sizes, the world record lake trout being a whopping 65 pounds. They willnot leap from the water for you to photograph them, but rather, they're deep divers and put on lengthy underwater tug-of-wars. Most caught on fly rods are taken with sinking lines and patterns that imitate baitfish. Siscowets or "fat trout" are seldom caught on flies because they live at extreme depths.

Lake trout. Photo by Naoto Aoki

In summer, lake trout rise to depths of 50 to 100 feet, but in spring anglers can catch even heavy monsters in water of 20 feet or less. They prefer water from 40 to 52 degrees F, while siscowets lurk at depths of 300 to 600 feet, where it's just plain cold. (Fly rodders need not worry about them, though. You won't catch one with a fly rod. If you do, you probably didn't need this book.)

In most waters, lake trout feed heavily upon small baitfish like ciscoes, sculpins, and smelt. But in other lakes they feed almost exclusively on plankton, insects, and crustaceans and won't reach the size of those fish-eating giants. Lakers are the oak trees of the trout world, slow-growing but long-lived, sometimes reaching an age of 40 years. In the far north, it may take 15 years for a Mackinaw to reach 2 pounds. So although most of you will not be looking to catch a lake trout with a fly rod until you are experienced in casting, fighting trout, and releasing, we wanted to introduce you to lakers, because eventually we'd like for you to go try.

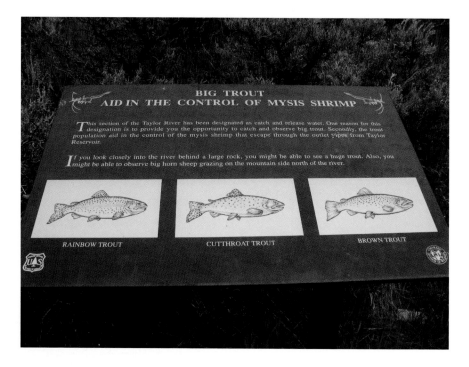

How do you spot trout? Good question. The obvious ways are that you can see them rise, jump out of the water, swim with their dorsal fins sticking out, or hold in extremely clear water. But those are the easy ways to spot trout.

Polarized glasses are essential. Not your father's sunglasses but some good polarized sunglasses made for the outdoors. When you try on a pair of good polarized sunglasses and look at a lake or stream, you'll immediately know what we're talking about. You can see under the water. You can see the lower half of that boulder that rises out of the middle of the river.

So you can see now. Next, stealth. Part of why rookies don't see trout is that they are not sneaky enough. They walk right up to the bank and peer out. The fish have hidden. Even with a submarine, you wouldn't see them. So hide behind a tree, a rock, or other cover, don't cast a shadow, and watch your footfalls.

Next, you have to know where they should be. They'll hide behind rocks, under overhanging limbs, and at current edges. Look for shadows, movements, know how they move and feed and swim, and of course, rise. Watch more than just what's right in front of you.

It's all about the trout.

FOAM MEANS TROUT

Why? You'll see foam lines on rivers. Sometimes they travel on top of runs, sometimes they empty into a whirling eddy. Foam lines are clues to where to fish. Foam carries debris and insects; they are cafeteria lines that convey insects to the trout. Trout will shadow these foam lines knowing that these are the routes for insects.

Staying far back means that as this angler's cast falls, only the last foot or two of the leader, and the fly, will hit the water. That's stealthy.

In lakes, you hide and watch for cruisers. In flat spots on the river, you watch upstream for rises while you are fishing. Watch insects on the water. You'd be surprised how many times you'll see a quick take that you would have never noticed if you hadn't seen the stonefly buzz around, land, and then float downstream.

Initially, seeing trout is not easy. But with practice and stealth you can gradually improve your fish-spotting skills. Let's say you're at a riffle-run-pool configuration. Creep up to a good watching spot. Hide behind a tree or a big rock, or just squat. We sometimes like to get on a hill above everything just to sit and observe. Some trout we spot easily. They break the surface. They cruise an area. They rise, then settle back to their holding spots.

You'll see a shadow that looks like a trout. The tail of the trout-shaped object weaves back and forth. The trout shape doesn't hold in exactly the same spot and may move from side to side, forward and back. The trout shape may even disappear, only to reappear. Sometimes, you are watching algae or a plant or a stick or a limb. But after awhile, you'll get to where you'll see more and more trout.

If you stomp right up to the bank, you won't see trout. If you let your shadow fall across a pool, you won't see trout. If you wade where the trout are holding instead of casting from other places (like the bank) you won't see trout. If you cast your line across trout (trying to reach another trout) you won't see those trout any longer—they'll vanish.

Sometimes, if you don't see any trout or any rises, you should look deeper. Watch for tails upright as the fish feed head down. See if you can spot any white mouths agape as they feed, or quick flashes as they turn. One time, when we were much younger, trout were rising in front of us and we denied it. That can't be trout right there. "Right there" was in the bounciest, roughest water in the entire river, a washing machine chute between two canyon walls. The flash of their noses, the crimson slashes; we saw the trout but as beginners we'd grown accustomed to looking for trout only where we'd had success before. We didn't look past those limited environments to see that trout hold in all the water, just at different times, for different reasons.

Right
This rainbow trout is cruising in search of something to eat.

Below
Find the trout. At first glance, this trout looks like a dark rock.

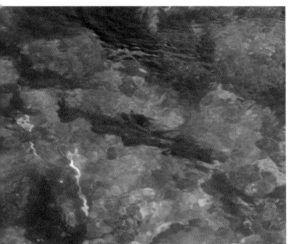

Fish breaking the surface

Over the years, we've come to like this truism: if you thought it was a trout you saw, it was. If you thought that was a flash, it likely was. You'll get fooled from time to time. That wavy tail is really vegetation. That dark back is just a submerged limb. But most of the time, if you watch closely, know where to look, know what to look for, it's a trout.

So where are the trout? They are hiding, that's for sure. If you see them, they might die because you could be a predator: an osprey, eagle, river otter, or determined angler. So they hide. They have to choose where to hide. They can't hide where they'll have to fight the current so tremendously that they burn up more calories than they could take in from food.

Trout can be anywhere, but they're not. They are swimming and holding where they can get food (mostly insects) easily, and not have to fight the current so much that they can't take in more calories than they burn up, and avoid predators. More often than not, trout will shelter themselves in deeper water, behind or to the side of rocks, in a V-shaped crevice in the stream bottom, under an overhanging tree, or basically anywhere where it makes things more difficult for you to catch them. Most trout will not move more than a few inches or at most a foot to feed.

When certain insect hatches are in full force, trout will sacrifice some of their safety so they can gorge. That's why you'll see rising trout in water that, just moments before, appeared to have no life at all. Trout are lazy. Trout are efficient. Trout are not going to expend more energy chasing food than the calories it will return. Trout will not hide and feed. If they are hiding from you or any other predator, they won't be eating anything until they quit hiding and begin feeding.

Trout have personalities, sometimes. What one is eating, another is refusing. Where one cruises a pool, the other lounges under a rock outcrop. Brook trout slash at your offerings with reckless abandon, while brown trout sometimes get spooked by passing clouds. Rainbow trout love to feed in fast water and perform acrobatics; browns seem to love slower water and slower rises. And yet, all this can be turned on its head. Trout are not all that bright, though sometimes they seem that way. But they are good at one thing: surviving. And oh yeah, avoiding your fly.

Think seams and edges.

Trout are camouflaged. They are good hiders. They don't like your shadow or footfalls. So just because you don't see them doesn't mean they are not there.

Typical Trout Lies

1. Under ledges

2. Under cutbanks

3. Around rocks and boulders

4. At the edges of chutes and runs

5. In pocketwater

Trout are well camouflaged and often hard to spot.
A dorsal fin protruding above the surface can help.

6. In soft water protected by a ledge, limb, or similar obstruction

7. Near drop-offs

8. In riffles

9. At edges where fast, rushing water meets slower water

10. In pools

11. On flats.

Note that flats are tricky, and best fished with long leaders, a modicum of skill, and during a hatch.

Riseforms

Watching for rises is the simplest way to spot trout. Beyond that, rises don't tell you much, or at least not enough. You see a rise, but unless you see the trout, you won't see where the trout originally started from. When you see a rise, take a seat or hide behind something and watch for the next rise. You'll be surprised how regularly timed these often are.

There have been entire books written about rises. You know what we readers can decipher after all these words? Not much. Sure, there are some consistencies with rises—the slashing style is almost always a trout chasing caddis, but sometimes it means they are going after grasshoppers. The tail-up/nose-down feeding style is usually trout feeding on pupae, but sometimes it's not. Porpoising usually indicates trout taking emergers. So rises tell you where they are and perhaps what they're eating, but honestly, you don't get much more than that to use to get them to take your offering. The two things we like best about rises are that you know there are fish, and that they are eating something. Those are good things.

Jackpot!

We watched these trout feed while we hid behind a tree 10 feet away.

You can see how a trout's camouflage hides it. Look for fins, movement, and shadows.

SOME GENERAL RECURRING RISEFORM TYPES:

1. *The sip:* The trout rises slowly, and only its mouth seems to break the surface. The ring is small and subtle.

2. *Fin-and-tail rise, or porpoise:* This is a confident rise, where the trout shows its head, then the dorsal fin, and finally the diving tail.

3. *Submarine:* The submarine doesn't happen often, but we saw it recently on a small creek in northern Colorado. Like a sub, the trout's entire body breaks the surface, and the fish takes an insect and submerges. Reminds us of Captain Nemo's *Nautilus* in *The League of Extraordinary Gentlemen.* Cool.

4. *Streaking fin:* This is out-of-water, dashing craziness. You'll know it when you see it. It's startling, disconcerting, frenzied, and fun as all get out.

5. *Sudden splash:* This rise will shock you in its suddenness and concentrated fury.

6. *Tail up, nose down:* This is not so much a rise as it is witnessed feeding. You'll often see more than one trout in the same location when this is going on.

7. *White mouth open, down deep:* The trout are obviously feeding on nymphs or pupae, but you'll often be able to entice them to rise to the surface with the right presentation and fly.

8. *Bulge:* You see a bulge on the surface and the ring, but you don't see the trout. This occurs often during a spinner fall, but the sip can also occur then.

The ring of a rise is always a good sign.

Close observation can help you discern the meanings of different riseforms.

WHAT SKILLS DO I NEED?

Try to learn or advance one new skill each time out. Don't make the skill a huge one, like double-hauling or casting all your line, but simpler stuff, more like learning how to fish a nymph more effectively, how to tie a dropper rig, or how to cast with a curve.

The trout are looking to where the food is coming from. So when you cast, don't cast where you see the trout, but above the trout. This way, your fly floats to the trout so the trout can see it, evaluate it, and then move to the fly.

POSITIONING, STEALTH, AND PRESENTATION

Positioning

First rule of Cast Club: Don't cast to the farthest spot on the river. Second rule of Cast Club: Think before you cast. Third rule of Cast Club: Look for seams and edges. Join the club.

Mac approaches

Mac lost it, so he immediately casts to his left a foot or two.

*Mac kneels and casts
close to bank nearest him.*

The idea is to reach the closest good trout lie first and then fan out to the other good trout spots without lining or spooking trout. First, size things up. Where are the top trout lies in this section? How can I reach most of them, beginning with the closest lie?

Let's say you come to this awesome pool. The water shoots out between two large, mostly submerged boulders. Some might call this a chute. In the middle of the pool is a boulder as big as a mammoth, and it sticks up out of the water about 2 feet. On either side of the boulder, you see a run that, 20 feet down, turns into dead water and then tumbles over smaller rocks and becomes riffles. You will want to hit the edges. Begin at the bottom of the pool, which means the riffles. So where do you position yourself? You're going to be on one side of the pool or the other. Common sense, right? So you're on this side, the left side of the river—this means the water is flowing downstream, and as you walk upstream, you'll be fishing on the left side. Simple enough.

Stand (or sit or kneel to remain hidden) and observe. See any trout? Remember to put on your polarized glasses. Do you see any trout holding near that boulder in the middle? Do you see any rises near the chute, on either side? Behind the big boulder? As you observe, imagine yourself casting to a certain spot. How will the fly float? Imagine your fly line. Is it landing over crosscurrents so you'll have to mend quickly? Can you make a backcast from your position without catching a tree or bush? How will you turn your body to your landing zone? Are bugs on the water or in the air? Watch foam or insects as they float downstream so you can get an idea of how your fly will travel. Do any branches or plants pose problems for your drift?

You're ready. You want to cast as close to you as reasonably possible.

Here's what we would do at this pool.

Strip out the amount of fly line you want on this first cast. Let part of it belly up between the reel and the first guide on the rod. Hold the rod flatly (almost level) and parallel to the bank as you face three-quarters upstream. One hand holds the rod. Your index finger keeps tension on the fly line. The fly hangs over the water or just above the bank.

The idea here is to use only a forward cast, a type of roll cast, in one quick motion to put the fly just a few feet up and in front of us. Our goal is to let the fly drop close to the bank, where we suspect a trout is holding in the cut under the overhang.

Mac hooks up with another.

Mac gets both hands on his line and rod to control the trout.

Mac has control and is playing the trout.

In one quick forward motion, we make the forward stroke. Lift your index finger so the slack line shoots out through the guides. We stop sharply but smoothly and let the fly drop to the surface. A trout pounces on the fly but we miss the fish. Great. But we know they are there and they like our fly.

So we plan to quarter the next round of casts. We will cast to the right of our first cast by about 6 to 9 inches. This is a case-by-case basis, by the way, with nothing set in stone. The idea is to cover water by fanning out our casts. The second cast lands and begins to drift quickly. We lift our rod so that less fly line is on the water, and we turn to follow the fly as it drifts. These two things are elemental and key:

1. Lift your rod tip as the fly floats.
2. Follow your fly by turning your body and pointing the rod in the general direction of the fly on the water.

We make the third cast (a foot to the right of the second), then the fourth and fifth as we fan our casts. We use very little backcast (but it's okay to backcast; just keep things simple.) Nothing. But we did see two flashes of silver under the water on one drift. We know those are trout. You might not have noticed, but in time you will. If we don't get a hit soon, we'll retie a longer dropper, or change out nymphs. For now, it's time to cast to that sweet little slick that's tucked between the chute and the rock and the run. There's got to be one right there.

Bam. There is. Fish on. We maneuver the trout by getting its head up quickly and then forcing him through water we already fished. It's a 12-inch rainbow. With a flick of the forceps, the fly is out and the trout is swimming back to its hiding place. Next cast.

We work our way upstream identifying the landing zone, the drift line, obstacles—even where water twists and turns or will cause a belly. If and when we catch one along the drift, then what?

We work in sections. You don't have to cast all the way across the pool to catch that one annoying rising fish. You don't cover all the water in one cast and drift. We cast in quarters and in that way we'll cover all the good water over time. When we finally reach the chute and have more or less covered the pool and all the good trout lies, we move upstream to the next good spot. Don't go back and refish this pool right now. Let it settle.

Mac has moved the trout away from the unfished water so as not to disturb it.

Mac moves the rod back, keeping the tip up, leaning forward with his net.

Mac releases the trout.

Don't fish downstream except in extreme circumstances. Why not? For starters, you're standing upstream of the trout, which are generally facing upstream. Two, your footfalls and shadows might be reaching the fish downstream of you. Three, it's more difficult to hook up with the strike and you might end up pulling the fly away from the trout.

Remember this: We fish upstream or slightly across-stream, but still upstream. Exceptions to fishing upstream include when you are swinging caddis pupae or other nymphs so they rise at the end of the drift (this is called the Leisenring Lift). You might also have to fish downstream when you can't put the fly in front of a fish any other way.

Stealth

Stealth when fly fishing means several things. Shadows on the water. Footfalls. Debris from bushes as you walk through them. Wading when you shouldn't be. Casting your line over fish. Too much shadow casting. Putting in at the wrong place. Fishing to the wrong spot first. Bad drag. Lifting the line on the backcast and slapping the water. Too forceful a forward stroke, making the line slap the water. Knocking pebbles or rocks into the water.

You get the idea. Don't reveal that you are a threat to the fish.

We've been known to crawl on our bellies or shuffle on our knees to lower our profile so the fish won't spot us. We use natural cover to hide behind (trees, bushes, rocks, slow deer). If you can't hide behind something or go prone, don't just walk up to the edge of the river. Stand as far back as you can but still observe. By the way, the trout can't hear you talk, as long as you are not talking underwater. Trout can tell if you are splashily wading, knocking rocks around, clanking into things, that sort of thing.

Presentation

When fly fishers speak of presentation, they are primarily concerned with how one lands a dry fly upon the water and keeps it looking real and natural. But achieving this takes a series of actions before it can happen. Presentation is the most crucial skill in fly fishing; practice all other aspects of the sport properly, and you'll still miss fish if presentation isn't perfect.

Several components go into perfect presentations: setting up, fly positioning, and mending, to keep the fly looking realistic throughout the entire drift.

Mac is set up for the next cast (and yes, he caught a few more trout as he crawled up this pool).

Mac approaches a cutbank with stealthy, quiet footfalls.

Mac leaning out and around a huge boulder used as a shield.

Setting Up: Setup can be from either an upstream position or down-stream position from the fish you're trying to catch. Setting up can refer to where you are in relation to the trout lie, your body positioning, as well as where the fly hits the water in relation to the fish.

Almost always, your position setup will be from a downstream position casting upstream, or from the bank casting across and upstream. (There are times when you can move upstream and let a fly drift downstream in what's called a dead drift. Let's discuss only upstream fishing for now.) What you're hoping for in "setting up" your position is a series of checks to which all answers are Yes:

You've spotted a lie and hope to cast to it, but does it appear rewarding enough?

Are there any overhanging limbs or surface obstacles that will impede your cast?

Is it safe to cast, play a fish, and catch a fish from where you are?

Can you get a fly to the strike zone and keep it there long enough?

If you do catch a fish here, is it feasible to believe you will net it safely without harming yourself or the trout? If you can go through this checklist in your mind, and "Yes" is the resounding answer to all of them, it's time for you to cast.

Fly Positioning: Dropping the fly upon the water does not always have to be done perfectly. Too hard, too far back, too far to the left—it's all going to be okay. However, when it's done in an imitative manner, as a bug would naturally land on the water, it yields the most desirable results. And dry flies should be cast and "set up" in front of the trout, or at least above the lie you're hoping to catch a trout in.

Stoneflies and fat terrestrials almost slap upon the water, while teeny-tiny midges might land as delicately as a dandelion seed upon the grass. When casting the fly you've chosen, don't forget how that fly should land and present it in that manner.

Earlier, we said that when the fly hits the water it doesn't have to be perfect. This is true, because many times a trout is caught several feet beyond where the fly alights on the water. Perhaps the landing is what awakens the trout to its presence, but it's mostly a perfect drift that triggers a trout to strike. Keep this in mind. So what if your fly splats upon the water too hard? Just let it ride all the way through the lie. We have dozens of memories each of when we unsuspectingly caught trout behind us downstream as we were casting forward. It's the drift that counts most, not just how it lands.

Mending: Mending line means simply manipulating, in various ways, the fly line already on the water after the cast and during the drift, usually to prevent the fly from dragging unnaturally. For example, if you're trying to drift your fly through a spot across the stream from you, but the current in the center of the flow is faster than the current where the fly is, the faster current can grab your fly line and "drag" the fly downstream at an unnatural speed. You can solve this problem and get at least a few feet of more natural drift by using the rod tip to gently lift the line off the water and toss (mend) a loop of slack slightly upstream, to prevent your fly from dragging. As your fly-fishing skills improve, mending line in any direction necessary to achieve a natural drift will become second nature, and you'll find yourself doing it automatically when you see the fly dragging, or otherwise not behaving the way you want it to.

You gotta keep that fly looking real. If you were to drop a bug on the surface of a moving river, it might create rings at first. That's normal. But it wouldn't have a wake behind it as though it were waterskiing. Only an object being dragged across the water leaves a wake, and trout know bugs don't do that. This is called drag, and it's your foe.

If you can see or feel drag anywhere near your fly, it probably won't catch a trout. Most trout fear drag and bolt at the first sign of it. In order to keep drag from spooking trout, there are several things you can do to combat it.

Mending is the method employed after the line is on the water so that you can better achieve a drag-free float. You flip the line with your rod tip. Cast upstream. You'll notice that you just cast across a faster-moving run that is now bellying your line and will soon pull your fly (which you dropped perfectly onto the great-looking slick spot). Lift your rod tip and flick the line in front of you upstream. You may have to keep mending, because that pesky fast current keeps bellying your line, but that's okay—it's part of fly fishing. Now practice.

Fish casting upstream, and let the fly drift naturally down toward you. As this drift is occurring, you'll notice your line pass between or beside your legs if you don't raise your rod tip to take up the slack, or strip in the line at the same rate as the river flow.

Mending can be a tough skill to learn, but you will do it naturally and automatically the more you fish. If you're in the stream and casting directly upstream, just strip in line at the same rate it's coming to you.

And don't try to cast all the way to the headwaters! Stick with 25- to 30-foot casts at most in the early days.

If you're on the bank and casting across water, mending is a different ballgame. Here, you'll notice that stripping in line won't suffice. Instead, raise your rod tip up and move the tip upstream in a semicircular motion, then either just lay the line back down on the water, or try to "flick" the line in that semicircular motion upstream. The point of all this is to try to get the longest drag-free drift you can. Practice picking up the downstream line and placing it back upstream. This is what fly presentation is all about, and once you've got this part down, you're on to achieving Jedi status with a fly rod!

READING THE WATER

Knowing where to put the fly is the single most important skill in trout fishing.

An angler who can read water but can't cast well will outfish a skilled caster who cannot read water, every time. What's interesting is that for smallmouth bass (and to a lesser degree, largemouth bass) so much of what works for knowing about trout, also works for bass.

On this stretch of river alone, you get a nice bend, a side pool, an eddy, and some riffles.

Reading the water can be tricky on some trout streams, but there are some general principles that apply to trout just about anywhere you fish.

To learn how to read water, an angler must consider the habitat from the trout's perspective. A trout has three major concerns in finding a place to hold: cover to protect him from ospreys, eagles, otters, kingfishers, and other predators, including humans. The trout must locate a lie that doesn't require it to expend any more energy than it'll take in. The trout needs food, so his lie must provide him with opportunities to feed frequently.

Cover

Trout don't need much structure for cover. Trout will use rocks, fallen trees, limbs, undercut banks, weed beds, roots, and even shade for cover. Depressions in the streambed make for good cover because the trout's back markings and the depth of the water make it difficult to spot.

Energy

Trout will rarely hold in fast water for very long. During hatches, trout will move out into the riffles to feed, but will typically return to less demanding holding spots when the hatch is over. If a trout were to hold in the faster water for too long, it would quickly burn up more energy than it could consume in insects or other food. Trout will hold in the slower water, near the faster water that carries food.

Food

Food is the main thing on a trout's little mind. They look for food all day long, usually insects, and search out the places where those insects live and collect. Ever see those stretches of foam on the surface of a river? Those are floating cafeterias full of trapped insects, both dead and alive, and hungry trout eagerly line up alongside them for lunch.

Let's dispel one myth right off the bat: Trout do not always face upstream. They certainly face upstream a great deal of the time—but not always. They face where the food is coming from—into the current. If a trout holds in an eddy, it is entirely likely that since the water swirls around, his eyes might be trained downstream instead. Angular cutbanks where trout might hide can make trout face across stream.

*Pocketwater on a
local stream*

Trout will hold around rocks, but since the biggest fish get the best lies (the lies with the most cover, the least resistance, and the most food) other fish will hold in several places around the rock, and not always upstream.

Water running downstream takes circuitous routes, and as such, trout will face in whatever direction the water happens to be bringing them food. A simple and effective method to read water is to think "edges" or "seams." These occur where the faster water meets the slower water, places where the water is broken by a rock, a limb, or a different current. Look for edges where there is any change in the water, such as where a chute of water dumps through a channel, leaving the fast water churning in the middle. The edges of the fast water are where the trout will be holding.

High-stick nymphing can be very effective.

In a pool, the smaller trout will hold at the edges of the head of the pool, while the larger trout will hold at the edges of the tail of the pool. The current through the pool will bring the fish a continuous supply of food while they sit on the sidelines, rising or cutting out into the food line only when they spot a piece of pie or a cut of meat that pleases them.

So look for edges and seams. Cast your fly in the seam between the quick current and the slower current and you'll be surprised by how many more hookups you'll get.

NYMPHING

Have you ever watched a fly fisherman angling from atop a boulder, holding his rod high, moving it from side to side like a maestro's baton, then slinging his presentation back upstream only to conduct it downstream again? You must have wondered, what in the world he was doing. We can answer your question: That angler was catching more trout than you were.

We are dry-fly kinds of guys. We like fishing pocketwater pools the size of a washtub with big attractor dry flies and watching a trout shoot from the depths to wreak carnage on the offering. But catching trout is more important than maintaining our dry-fly-purist ethic, so we too occasionally hop atop a boulder and conduct a water symphony. It's called high-stick nymphing, and if you fish swift streams with multiple currents, plunge pools, or long deep runs where the fish stay deep, it's something you need to learn.

High-stick nymphing (aka short-line nymphing) gives you greater control of the fly, reduced drag, more sensitivity to strikes, quicker hooksetting, the ability to move the fly through the trout's strike zone, and close proximity to the action.

You're standing on big boulders on a medium-size stream casting dry flies to the glassy pools of the pocketwater. Occasionally, you induce a trout to shoot up from the depths to take your offering. But to catch more trout in this swift water of multiple currents, you need to get flies down deep to where the trout are holding.

The techniques of high-stick nymphing are simple but deadly. You need to sneak up on the trout, hold your rod high, and maintain total line control throughout the drift. We have taken complete fly-fishing beginners on a river several times and taught them high-stick nymphing, and each caught trout in solid numbers all day long. Some veterans say this is an art, and when you watch a true artist who knows how to read underwater, it is. But even we "paint-by-numbers" anglers can paint a pretty picture with this technique.

Trout in swift streams hold under foamy, deep, or broken water, and cannot easily spot an angler even at close range. The fact that they can barely see makes dry-fly fishing on this kind of water iffy at best. The key to success is to reach the fish where they are holding and to present the fly in a natural manner. To do this, the fly needs to be moving at the same speed as the current where the trout lie, with as little drag as possible.

Most of the time, this means effecting a dead-drift presentation (moving the fly at the same rate as the current), but during caddis hatches, it can mean you'll need to use a downstream-and-across-and-up presentation (known as the Leisenring Lift). In high-stick nymphing, you will need to control excess slack by moving the rod to the side as your fly floats downstream. Place the line under your index finger of your rod hand quickly and strip in line immediately.

With the extra weight of a nymph, think about flattening out your arc (aka opening up) so you don't swing the fly by your ear.

We liken high-stick nymphing to "walking the dog" with a yo-yo. You keep the end of the string high enough so that the yo-yo walks along the ground. The same holds true for high-sticking, but you vary the height of your hand depending on the terrain. Keep the line somewhat taut and the rod held at a 45-degree angle as you guide the nymph from an upstream cast through a downstream drift, constantly adjusting the tension, depth, and speed to match the current.

For our high-sticking, we use weighted flies on 4X to 6X leader on a floating line. Some anglers swear that the lighter the line, the less resistance from the current and the more efficient the drift. We do believe fly fishers should always get by with the thinnest diameter leader they can, but in foamy pocketwater, we often like the thicker tippet to help absorb the punishment it takes from hard strikes and bumping rocks and carrying the extra weight (with split-shot and heavier flies).

We like beadhead flies because they get down deep when they hit the water on our upstream cast. Many anglers like weighted flies, tied with metal wrapped under the body to add more weight to the fly. Another technique is to fish with two flies (for example a nymph and an emerger) with weights on your leader.

Two things here: One, it's not as much a cast as it is a sling, fling, lob, or flip with weighted flies. Two, the trout tend to take the fly just after your upstream fling, so you need depth and line control. When you are controlling your rod tip, mending line, and keeping the fly where you want it, you often look like a symphony conductor moving the baton up and down, back and forth. Beginners will sometimes miss strikes because they aren't controlling the line from start to finish. So what should you do? Fish with your rod-hand forefinger held tautly on the line to ensure good line control.

More advanced anglers should make sure to strip in loose line with your line hand as it moves through the air on your upstream cast. Move the rod from side to side to control excess slack. In shallower water, you can watch the trout take your nymph—it's almost like dry-fly fishing underwater.

During your forward cast, eyeball the amount of line you need to mend. Then, in what will become second nature, pull in slack with your left hand and abruptly stop your forward cast, driving the fly into the water and removing most of the slack, allowing you to control the drift.

When performed properly (and this technique is not at all difficult to pick up) high-stick nymphing will make you a better angler with a fly. Sometimes referred to as short-line or tight-line nymphing, high-stick nymphing is an effective method of catching more fish by conducting your own trout symphony.

That said, not all nymphing anglers like to high-stick. They might use a South Platte method, a technique related to Czech nymphing. And Czech and short-line nymphing are either the same thing or close cousins, depending. Czech nymphing is a style of short-line nymphing where there are no strike indicators, the leader construction is created so two or three heavily weighted flies can get down deep, ideally to the bottom. Longer rods work better with this technique. Ditto fast water. The flies themselves hold the weight, not the leader. It's a learned technique that requires a great feel. These short-line methods use less leader, say 15 to 20 feet, with the angler keeping the line fairly tight and bumping along the bottom so to stay in contact with the fly at all times. It's not easy, so forget about it till you get a lot better.

Dead-drifting nymphs is an easier (we didn't say easy, just easier) technique that is also deadly effective. This is like dry-fly fishing but with a nymph. Cast your fly above (upstream of) where you think a trout is holding. As it slides under the water, carefully gather the slack with your line hand and rod tip, lifting to maintain contact with your nymph. The takes are usually subtle, so you have to get a feel for this technique. Don't get crazy with a lot of line; keep it short, say 10 to 20 feet of line and leader. You can dead-drift with an indicator and watch the indicator. Dead-drift and high stick/short-line nymphing are cousins too, by the way, but there's a bit more slack with dead-drifting.

DRAG

Your fly is affected by drag when it doesn't act like the insect it's imitating. Drag can mean that the fly encounters resistance, leaves a wake, or otherwise behaves unnaturally. Drag happens when the fly comes upon cross-currents, or when the line pulls the leader-tippet-fly combination. You don't want drag unless you are trying intentionally to skitter a fly on a beaver pond or are imitating a caddis adult.

Keep line off the water and you won't have to mend so often to avoid drag.

Strike Indicators

Strike indicators come in many shapes, sizes, colors, and materials, but the idea behind an indicator is that while your fly is underwater, you need something attached to the line above the surface that will "indicate" when a trout is messing with your fly. Indicators range from foam stick-ons to fluorescent yarn to little bobber things with toothpicks. There is even a new style indicator that is like a rubber bubble the size of a grape.

Some purists mistakenly assert that using an indicator is cheating, or somehow diminishes the purity of nymphing. Hogwash. Using an indicator improves your strike success by 25 percent or better. Studies show this. Why handicap yourself? It's legal and ethical and functional. If you plan to nymph without a dry-fly dropper, you'd be crazy not to use an indicator. As a side note, if you practice Czech or short-line nymphing, you don't use or need an indicator—but that's the exception.

WET-FLY PRESENTATION

Presenting wet flies like nymphs and streamers is not nearly the problem dry fly presentation is. But it does require some thought. Here, presentation is less about how the fly lands upon the water, and more about how it flows through it.

Keep in mind that bugs must appear realistic, and must appear to be doing realistic things. Since bugs don't actually swim, they must travel through the water naturally, as though the water is carrying them. This means no bugs will be traveling upstream, or zipping across fast water. So don't drag your flies upstream and expect trout to be that dumb. Keep your wet flies in the strike zone all the way through pools and riffles, till the very end, letting them drift at a natural rate, with maybe a jitter or a jolt here and there to impart some sense of liveliness to them. Presentation with wets is not too difficult to figure out. Set up, present the fly, let it drift, and recast. Natural drifts are key to fishing with wets.

HOW TO HOOK A FISH (OR HOW NOT TO HOOK A FISH)

Keep control of your line. What does this mean? This means avoid having big bellies in your line, which means you must mend from the moment the fly lands, to the pickup. If you have a belly in the your line, when you lift your rod tip, you have so much slack and so much resistance from the current that the fish will have time to spit out or shake off the fly.

Another facet of line control is keeping the line near the reel touchable. You need to be able to put drag on the line with your finger or fingers. This is why, for the first time out, we recommend keeping the same length of fly line out and keeping your index finger on the line with the same hand that holds the rod. When you introduce two hands into the process (and this is a process) you complicate things. Complication leads to failure, and that's why so many get into the sport only to leave.

An iridescent rainbow trout

Because Jorgen had so little line on the water, he didn't have to move his rod tip up very much to hook this fish.

Fish on!

Rookies often yank the rod back as if setting the hook on a bass. That won't work with trout in many cases. Instead, you quickly lift the rod tip up. You do this with your wrist and forearm, not just your wrist. Fly fishing is not a "wristy" sport, and if you overuse your wrist at the expense of your arm, you'll make mistakes in casting and catching, plus you'll tire out your arm. When we say "lift the rod tip up," what we mean is this:

Your arm is slightly extended, mending line as the fly floats downstream. If you're moving along in your mending skills, you can use your off hand to strip in line as the fly floats down, too. Fish hits. You continue holding line with your off hand while lifting the rod straight up. You do this quickly, with some force but not too hard. There's a balance to lifting the rod quickly, forcefully. No arc. Straight up. This motion sets the hook. If you let go with your off hand, you will have too much slack till the lifting takes up the slack. If you are using the one-hand-only technique, you lift the rod straight up as if you were conducting a symphony, remembering to keep your finger or fingers on the line, pressing it against the rod.

Note: Eventually, you'll set the hook with a less straight-up-and-down motion, but if you start off thinking you can arc the hook-set, you'll not get what we're trying to do.

So you see a trout jump and take your fly. What do you do? Hopefully, you have line control. Many beginners aren't watching the fly, so they don't see the fish take the fly. But sometimes you don't see the fish take the fly because the fly isn't visible. How do you know that a fish has taken it? If you are watching your fly and it disappears, you should have enough line control to gently lift your rod to remove slack. You'll then feel the tug and can more fully embrace the hookup. If you aren't watching the fly and are instead watching the mending of the line, you're going to miss fish. On setting the hook, learn to strike quickly, immediately. If you start missing fish, and you have ruled out (for the most part) the pattern and presentation, then strike more slowly next time. This is especially true when the trout are rising slowly instead of slashing.

Sometimes, you'll find that you'll be too slow or too quick on the hook-set. Sometimes it's you. Sometimes it's the way the fish are taking the fly. Last summer, we were casting to eager greenback cutthroat trout on Lawn Lake in Rocky Mountain National Park. We could see the 14-inch beauties rise slowly from the dark depths to submarine up to our dry flies sitting on the surface. We'd watch them open their white mouths and suck in the flies. We kept setting the hook but the fish would get off.

Why? Because these were slow-taking trout. We were used to fast-taking trout in rivers. After a few missed fish, we talked and realized that we needed to wait a count or two before we lifted the rod tip. The greenbacks came up, slowly opened their mouths, took the fly, and slowly submerged. Then we would set the hook, and we caught lots of trout.

Another trick you can try is to keep as much line off the water as possible. Don't have so little line out and hold your rod so high that it pulls the fly as it floats, but if you find a balance, you can have the fly on the water with very little tippet on the water. If you keep line off the water, you'll be surprised how little you'll have to raise your rod tip, perhaps only a few inches. This method will help you catch more fish.

PLAYING AND LANDING YOUR FISH

So you have hooked up with the fish. Now what?

This aspect of fly fishing is where many anglers fail, and because of that failure, get frustrated with the sport. You'll hear from veteran long rodders to keep the rod tip high and bow to the jumping fish and all that jazz. Kinda.

Biggest mistakes? Rushing. Not knowing what to do with the line, with your hands. Lowering the rod and holding it parallel to the water. You won't find absolutes here, but you can typically do these things and be successful.

Don't point your rod tip down. Don't level your rod. Don't point the rod at the fish unless it's bent. The tippet will break. Why? Because your rod is a shock absorber, and if all the weight and pressure are on the tippet, it can't handle a fighting fish. Let your rod do the work.

REEL RETRIEVES

Do I ever retrieve using the reel? You bet. When you finally tie into a strong, feisty fish, that creature will run and dive and pull out all your slack forcing the fight to the reel. But for a beginner, think of the reel as just a lineholder until you figure all the other things out.

(You'll find this out the hard way, but one day you'll catch and play a nice-size fish. The tippet and leader—let's say 5X—does a fine job of not breaking while the fish is in the water. You'll stupidly lift the fish out of the water, and that puts all the weight on the leader. Pop, the tippet is broken, the fish gone.)

So you have a fish on the line.

You probably have loose line. Don't try to reel it up all at once. There will be too much going on. Worry about keeping the tip high, your rod butt firm and in control. The fish will pull out the loose line. As you get more confident in your abilities, you'll naturally keep the line tighter when the fish hits and you'll figure out how to raise the tip and strip line with your off hand to take up slack, all at the same time.

The fish doesn't want you to bring it to hand or net. Some will tail-walk and show amazing acrobatics. Some will immediately dive to cover or to the bottom of the lake or river. Others will zig and zag, running away from you so that your slack line zips away and the reel comes into play.

Finesse goes a long way when playing a fish.

Playing a trout with rod tip held high

Some Things to Keep in Mind When Playing a Fish

1. Rod tip up. Can't put it any simpler than that.

2. Rod angle doesn't have to be straight up and down but you don't want to get it close to level.

3. If it's a small fish, you can simply strip in line until the fish is near you, but make sure to get the fish's head above water so you can control it more easily.

4. Once you have a semblance of control, you want to position yourself to maximize your chances of bringing the fish to net. Look for obstacles that could cause problems. If the fish runs downstream, do you have a clear path?

5. Look out for obstacles. Cattails or willows or tall grass can get wrapped up in the loose line that dangles below the rod or reel.

6. Even if you have been stripping in and have a good bit of loose line, as long as you have control of drag at the point of the reel or above the reel with your off hand, you're in good shape. Don't panic. Not yet.

7. If the fish is big or strong enough, it may run far enough and fast enough that you will have to let it take line from the reel. This is why you need to set your drag on your reel to a moderate level: not a loosey-goosey drag but not a tow-a-car drag either.

8. If a fish runs and you decide to horse it, chances are you'll break off that fish. Don't horse the fish. It's okay to let them run. Over time, you'll learn when to use your rod and when to use more finesse. Use light pressure at first.

We try at first to get the fish's head out of water. If you do that, you control the fish and shorten the battle. If you can't do that, you've either got a nice fish on or you've foul-hooked the fish.

Use your off hand to let the line run with resistance (aka drag). You can press the line gently against the rod grip, putting slight pressure on the line to act as drag. When you feel slack, strip in with that off hand and then put your index finger of your rod hand on the line to pinch it against the rod—or reel with your off hand quickly so as to put the fish on the reel.

Later, after many moons, you will learn to set the hook toward something. One of the best ways is to turn the fish into the current. In this way, the fish is working against both the current and your rod and line. How do you do that? Turn your body toward the current, the rod tip (if it were extended and not bent) pointing upstream.

Later in the process, you'll instinctively notice if there are problem areas where the fish could run, such as a fast seam, a big rock, or over-hanging limbs. You'll position yourself beforehand, and have an escape strategy. It'll take time but it'll happen.

You can be more assertive with playing your fish than you think. Sure, you don't want to just reel it in without caution, but think about the times you have stuck your fly on a tree or under a rock and how much force it took to break it off.

Get the fish's head out of the water. You get control this way.

There's a fine line between playing out a fish and exhausting a fish. You want to learn to control the fish as quickly as possible and get the fish to hand, and released.

Pump the rod to help subdue it quicker.

Change your rod angles and positions to help control the fish more quickly. When you raise your rod tip to its highest position and then slowly lower it, you can then reel in or strip in line. When the fish is near, some beginners make the mistake of reeling or stripping in too much line and putting all the weight on the tippet and leader; or getting the fish so close to the rod tip that you cannot fully control the fish and you won't be able to bring the fish to hand or net.

Occasionally, you'll have to lay the rod level to fight a fish. But your rod will be bent and you'll be trying to move a fish in an advantageous direction.

When you get a fish that takes out the slack in your line and starts pulling on the reel, you can palm the line to make your own drag, or palm the reel itself or let the fish drag against the reel's resistance, which is why you need to not set it to its heaviest drag setting.

Always be aware of hook safety. Debarb all your hooks by crushing the barb against the shank with pliers. You do not want to have to remove a barbed hook. You must usually push it through your unbroken skin and cut it off with pliers. Debarbed hooks make it easier to release fish, too.

CATCH-AND-RELEASE BASICS

What is catch-and-release? Why practice catch-and-release fishing? A better question might be, why not? The philosophy of catch-and-release is pretty basic: You catch the fish, you release the fish. Some look at catch-and-release fishing as a moral issue. They believe that eating the fish you catch is just plain wrong. We think that attitude is elitist, shortsighted, and a subject better left for the fishing forum. If you really believe in the moral high ground, don't fish. Catch-and-release fishing does several positive things other than make stuffed shirts happy. The practice leads to bigger fish. If you put a fish back instead of keeping it, it gets bigger. Bigger fish produce better progeny. And fish that survive in the wild produce fish that will have those same survival characteristics.

There's nothing wrong with keeping a fish or two for the frying pan, but if you keep too many—if too many people keep too many, and if too many people keep too many big ones—the quality of the fishery declines eventually. And with the world's fisheries getting more and more pressure from the growth of sport fishing, it makes sense for us to keep their future health in mind. We once talked to a couple of anglers from Texas and this is how the conversation went: "We've fished Red River since the 1960s. We used to fill coolers full of big trout, many over 20 inches long. But now, we still go there, and we just don't see the size or numbers of trout we used to catch."

Cradling a trout before release

We nodded and walked away. Really? You kept the best of the river's trout, the progenitors that passed on their genetic and hereditary advantages and you did it year after year, and then you wonder whatever happened to the population?

To us, it makes sense to just leave the fish so you can catch them again (and they'll be bigger.) Release so you can keep the trout populations healthy, so their sons and daughters will be there for your sons and daughters. Fish are a replenishable resource.

If you do practice catch-and-release (and chances are you'll have to at some point, since so many rivers and lakes rightfully now have regulations requiring it) you need to do it correctly because if you don't, it can harm the fish. Catching and handling fish can build up their lactic acid, increase their body's pH level, and tire them out. If you tire out a fish and release it improperly into the water, that fish can get caught in the current and swept away. It also becomes more vulnerable to predators, and because of these and other factors, it might not survive after you went to all that trouble to release it.

Gentle release of a trout

Releasing a trout into the current

Some anglers like to preserve their catch with a taxidermy mount for their living room wall. But we think the best-looking ones are either photos or taxidermy mounts created from photographs of the fish, not the real deal—and that creature is still swimming the water for some other trophy hunter. And catch-and-release is not a concept only for trout, but for all species. So practice catch-and-release fishing if you want to see healthy fisheries in the future, producing fertile, strong fish populations for generations of anglers to come.

Smart Catch-and-Release Practices

1. Minimize contact. The more you touch the trout, the more you put the fish at risk.

2. Don't squeeze the fish too hard because you can damage its internal organs.

3. Trout have a protective slime coating protects them from disease, so the more you handle the trout or the more time it's in your net, the more slime comes off.

4. Keep the trout in the water as much as possible. Release the trout as quickly as possible.

5. Use pliers or forceps or a hook remover instead of your fingers.

6. You know this already, but debarb your hooks, and this catch-and-release practice goes a lot more smoothly for you and for the fish.

Cradle the trout and they'll move away when they're ready.

7. Wet your hands before you handle the fish.

8. Don't lip a trout because it will damage the fish and if you release it, it will starve. We don't recommend lipping bass either, unless you intend to keep that fish. Don't touch the fish's gills.

9. If the hook is too deep to retrieve safely, cut the line close to the hook. The hook will dissolve over time.

10. If you don't have to remove the trout from the water, don't. If you have to do it for a photo, have the photographer get ready for you while the fish is in the water.

11. Use two hands for all but the smallest trout.

12. Don't just let them go. Control them with a gentle touch. You may have to turn them upstream to let water flow through their gills, but do so in slack water or sometimes, you will let them go and the current will just carry them downstream.

13. If you have revived a fish properly, it will swim off under its own power.

14. If you thought you revived a fish but it swims off only to turn over and lose control, go fetch the fish and revive it again.

HOOK REMOVAL

The "loop method" is for hook removal for you! The loop method of hook removal is an effective, safe method for barbed hooks. Create a loop about 4 to 6 inches long using your strongest tippet. Pass the loop over the eye of the hook and pull it gently up to the top of the hook bend. Here's the creepy fun part—push down on the eye of the hook so that the hook eye touches the skin. With a sudden, strong burst of a tug on the line loop you made, pull up and away from the hook eye. Yeah, we know, gross right? But very effective, and usually it doesn't hurt.

The water on the Florida is cold (so says Yvonne's expression).
We're using the buddy system until she gains confidence.

SAFER WADING: TIPS ON HOW TO WADE

Sounds simple enough, doesn't it? Wading. Walking in the stream, walking in the shallows of a lake, walking in the surf. How difficult can it be? Tips for wading? You bet.

We have fished with beginners and veteran anglers alike and have seen all kinds of risky, even stupid, behavior watching them wade. We have seen a close friend cross a stream which at best is only 15 feet wide (not enough to be dangerous, right?) and he got caught up in a wicked current and swept downstream 20 yards. He was okay, wet and embarrassed, but it could have turned ugly, especially if he had hit his head on a rock. He paid for it later with our chatter around the campfire to be sure, but a little foresight and strategy and my friend would have crossed the stream without incident. Quick story.

Williams: Years ago, when my nephew Bryan was about 12 or 13 years old, we mistakenly taught this anti-establishment young man how to wade and fish by himself. He's a great kid but one who has always figured that rules meant breaking them must be more fun.

Bryan went off on his own on a small creek, with very few places over his knees. In a few moments, I heard his faint cries for help. He had crossed at the deepest place and gotten swept off his feet and tangled in a web of limbs along the shore, sort of a beaver dam in the making. When I got to him, he was trapped and barely able to lift his head above water. In this same stream, just a few weeks before, a 50-year-old man had a similar mishap and drowned. Don't be flippant about wading safely.

You'd be surprised how many anglers develop strategies for casting and catching but never consider how wading can both make their excursions safer and help them catch more fish. Our first rule of wading rivers and streams? Don't wade if you don't have to wade. So many anglers feel some sort of urge to get in the water because they need to get their waders wet, or they've seen too many fly-fishing advertisements with the angler shadow casting in the middle of the Firehole River. All too often, anglers wade in the very areas they ought to be fishing, walking right through productive lies.

Every year, in both big and small rivers, in 1-acre lakes and lakes best measured in square miles, anglers drown. Wading is inherently dangerous. Even if you are a world-class swimmer, currents and impediments can work against you, so all anglers need to learn how to wade more safely.

We have a longtime fishing buddy, Kenny Medling, who is an aggressive wader, always wanting to toss one cast into that toughest-to-reach spot to catch that elusive big fish. He gets himself drenched and in tight spots all the time. But he is built like a Mack truck, has no ankles, and is as strong as a water buffalo. Nevertheless, he uses caution. Wading is safe if you're smart about it.

Top Wading Tips

Use a wading staff. We recommend a solid staff instead of the collapsible kind. We don't use wading staffs but we should. We rationalize not carrying staffs by convincing ourselves that we are still young, strong, and know how to wade. Do as we say, not as we do.

Wear proper footwear. Wear nonslip rubber soles on rivers, cleats on rocky streams, wading boots in the surf. And you need to make sure that your footwear has good ankle support to avoid getting sprained ankles.

Wear waders. Being soaking wet is one of the worst feelings. Don't buy into the myth that if you wear waders and you fall in you will turn upside

Michael Fiore leaves a larger wake than the more experienced Williams. As you learn to wade, you'll discover how to do so more efficiently.

down when your waders fill up. Water in your waders weighs the same as the water all around you. It's not heavier. But it helps to wear a wading belt with your waders to keep your waders from billowing out like a parachute—the currents will carry you and move you in ways you don't want to move. So wear a belt.

Keep one foot on the ground when you wade. In tempestuous water, we like to move one foot forward, the other forward, come to a stop, plant both feet, reevaluate the direction we are moving, then move again.

Don't make rapid or aggressive moves when wading.

Read the water just as you would read it to gauge where the fish are. Using your polarized glasses, project a course to wade that maximizes your ease and safety while also putting you in position to make the casts you want to make. Find a safe route.

Shuffle your feet. Sounds simple enough, but it keeps you from making rapid or aggressive moves and ending up in the drink. If you move slowly, it also doesn't spook the fish.

On big water, both lakes and streams, wear a floatation device. We know it sounds cumbersome, but manufacturers make U-shaped flat floats that lie flat and unnoticed until you pull a string and voilà—instant float. When you wade in the surf, you ought to wear a lifejacket or inflatable device in case you step off where you didn't mean to step off.

Don't fish without a buddy. This is the best advice we can give you. When you fish with a buddy, and are crossing big water, interlock arms for increased safety.

Wade a stream diagonally, moving downstream. Take the angle, take it slowly. You will be surprised when you get in fast-moving water that is more than 2 feet deep because it can lift your feet off the ground and sweep you over in a flash. Look for slower water and solid footing.

Point your forward foot toward the current. Keep your rear foot planted firmly.

Do not cross on big submerged boulders. They are likely slippery, and any rapid or accelerated movement leads to problems.

If you fall, especially in a big river, pull your knees up, face your feet downstream and lean back, using your hands as best you can to navigate and get to the bank. Try not to panic. You don't want your head underwater banging into rocks. If you stay calm, you can reach water where you can stand up or swim to the bank.

Again, do not panic. Assess the situation and have forethought about what you should do. Then do it.

If you do not carry a wading staff, keep your rod in your upstream hand and if you slip or start to fall, jab the rod handle in the water to immediately stabilize yourself. The current tends to push you upright.

If you fall in and get soaked, dry out your clothes to avoid hypothermia. And "pruny" feet will get blisters quicker than dry feet.

Don't wade on the redds of spawning fish.

Keep your balance. Don't cross your legs. Don't lean over too much.

The bottom line: The less you wade, the less you spook the fish, and the less you put yourself in harm's way.

7

STRATEGIES, TACTICS & TECHNIQUES

TERRESTRIALS

It's summertime, and as the glorious spring hatches fade into memory, it's time to remember this: Trout like ants. Trout like big juicy grasshoppers. Trout like easy meals.

There are those veteran anglers who have divined knowledge of the trout's affinity for the ant by luck or by keen observation, and know that trout will take an ant pattern when all other patterns fail. Common sense tells us, then, that if the trout likes ants so much, why not skip the other patterns and start the day's fishing with an ant? In the absence of a hatch, we often use a hard-shelled ant as a dropper under a more conventional dry fly. And it works.

Terrestrial insects are important foods for the trout, much more consistent year-round in their availability than some aquatic insects like

Foam Ant

Cinnamon Ant

stoneflies or *Hexagenia* mayflies or crane-flies. This holds true on most streams, big or small.

Ants, grasshoppers, beetles, inchworms, and crickets—to name a few terrestrials—are fat and juicy meals for trout. For years, Harry Murray has been touting the virtues of fishing the Mr. Rapidan Ant on small mountain streams. Rainstorms wash ants into streams in great numbers, and after a shower, trout will often eat ants and nothing else. On the Guadalupe River in Texas, the trout key in so intently on ants that an estimated 20,000 of them died a few years ago when they feasted on deadly fire ants, which poisoned the trout when digested. A lot of days have been saved by fishing a Chernobyl Ant pattern or a Clear Coat Ant. Some anglers like floating patterns for ants, while others prefer theirs to sink.

Hoppers, Beetles, and Inchworms

Most anglers are familiar with fishing grasshopper patterns occasionally. They limit this practice mostly to meadow streams. What a shame. Hopper patterns are big and fat, easy for the angler to see, and make excellent searching flies.

Hopper patterns come in all shapes and sizes and colors, as do grasshoppers, so we tend to carry numerous patterns in a box devoted solely to terrestrials. Try hoppers anytime it's windy—these leggy insects are often blown into the water, even in canyon streams.

Try floating a fat beetle when rising fish gobbling up all the Tricos on the water, except for your size 24 pattern. You would also be surprised at how many times a trout gulps down the beetle pattern that looks just too plump to pass up.

Beetles work well on all kinds of water, but don't be without several colors, patterns, and sizes on slow-moving, clear streams and especially on spring creeks, where they are deadly. Modern patterns are often tied of foam with a bright orange spot on the back, making it easier to follow the fly.

Try an inchworm fly (there is such a pattern, called "the Inchworm," although you can always use the classic fly, the Asher) where you have overhanging limbs and brush. Trout will often lie in wait for the worms to drop. When you fish hoppers and beetles and crickets, try to cast them so they splat when they hit the water, just as the naturals do when they land. One way to do that is to continue your forward cast past your normal stopping point.

Make sure to carry terrestrial imitations in many sizes, even as small as size 14. Most anglers think of terrestrials as big insects, and they often are, but there are many times when it is necessary to downsize your fly to get an interested fish to take. We use Stimulators from size 6 to 10 as substitute hopper patterns but it does seem the more authentic patterns typically work better on meadow streams, especially in August.

So make sure to fill your box with a variety of terrestrial patterns. Try using these fat flies more often. Ants are your new secret weapon. Or tie on an Inchworm when faced with overhanging limbs.

And the old standby hopper pattern can be used more frequently, especially when prospecting and fishing blind. But we will say that we have caught few fish on cricket imitations, and have seen very few crickets on the water. But we do carry two different cricket patterns just in case. You never know, right?

TIPS ON GETTING YOUR FLY OUT OF TROUBLE

When you get your fly stuck, you can usually get it unstuck, though sometimes you can't do it quickly or easily. Here are a few tricks we use. But if these don't work, you have to consider whether or not it's worth it to cross that deep pool, shimmy up the tree, or break your rod. Sometimes, it's smarter just to let that $2 fly go. Really, don't break your rod just to retrieve a fly. Here are some sticky situations and how to get out of them.

Across the pool: The best way is really cool. Strip out some line, an extra foot or two. Then roll cast. Yeah, the fly is embedded in a log or under a rock, but if you perform a forceful roll cast, it usually works.

Caught in rocks under the water: Strip in line and move the rod forward, tip down. Play conductor. Move the rod around. Reach out as far as you can on the other side of the sticking point. Reach and wiggle. Slowly move the rod tip underwater and back out. Don't panic, and don't do anything with force or you'll bust off. Walk upstream, downstream, across stream. Usually, just changing position will get you out of this mess. This also works if you are on a lake in a personal watercraft of some sort.

In a tree: If your rod tip can reach the limb, this one is easy. Reel in all your line and move your rod tip toward the fly. Reel in line until the rod tip touches the fly. Push forward with the tip, and the fly should pop off. If that doesn't work or you can't reach the fly with your rod tip, sometimes you can bend the smaller tree limbs forward until you can retrieve the fly.

Caught under a submerged log: Change position, use the reach and wiggle technique, use the "in-a-tree-push-the-tip-against-the-fly" technique. If all else fails, you have to consider whether it's worth going to the log and reaching in the water to dislodge it with your fingers.

Bird's nest: Sit down. You're not going to get rid of this mess standing up. The best way is to cut the fly or flies off your tippet, but because the fish are rising and you're all excited, you won't do that. Look for tight sections of line that are trapping other loops. Pull these trapped loops free. Actually look at the tangled lines and see if you can solve the puzzle. If you get it untangled, make sure there are no wind knots or bent tippet. Oftentimes it's just to cut your losses and retie your rig.

In a trout's mouth, but the trout is wrapped up in something: Mac had this happen on Upper Beaver Creek one summer. The fat brook trout he'd hooked wrapped itself up in a submerged bush. Mac had to take off his shirt and chest pack and submerge most of his body underwater to grasp the fish with one hand and untangle the mess with the other. Trout have tiny toothlike ridges in their mouths that will easily fray your line. Tippet gets caught in their mouths or in their gills or around their tails. Take your time, loosen any tightness, and work carefully.

Wind knot: This is an overhand knot put in the leader by poor casting or tricky wind. Wind knots reduce the breaking strength of your leader by a lot. Cut above the wind knot and retie tippet and your fly.

Getting your fly out of trouble sometimes takes a team effort.

What if it is so stuck that the fly won't come loose at all? You better be very careful here, because this is where you can break your rod. Rather than pulling with all your might, level the rod tip to where all the pressure is on your leader tippet and pull back slowly. The line will snap. The other, safer method is to simply clip your line closest to the snag.

Spring creek fishing

SPRING CREEKS

If you are a newer fly angler and you choose to fish a famous river, say the Henry's Fork or the San Juan or the Green or Spring Creek, you're setting yourself up for failure if you don't hire a guide. And if you fish a famous water that is a spring creek or tailwater and you don't hire a guide, it's all luck—usually bad luck. There will be finicky trout in difficult conditions, often requiring tiny flies, very fine tippet, and long leaders, knowledge of hatches and phases, all requiring long, accurate casts and perfect presentations. All these things conspire against rookies—and even against veterans, too.

Spring creeks are fairly uncommon, since their water sources come from underground aquifers instead of from snowmelt and rainfall. Sure, there are underground springs all over. But a spring substantial enough to create a trophy trout fishery is rare.

However, they do exist, the Henry's Fork of the Snake River (Idaho) and DePuy (Montana) being two of the more famous in the U.S. Fishing a spring creek is a different ball of wax, and quite a challenge. You'll need to learn a particular spring's idiosyncrasies in order to have success.

First, know this. Spring creek fishing can be difficult and frustrating. Here's why spring creeks are different, and some tips on how to combat the adversities.

Water temps don't fluctuate as they do in others streams, but instead remain relatively stable. So you won't see the same series of hatches you would on a mountain stream as it warms up. Stream flow is more constant and unchanging, since the aquifer "pushes" the same amount of water year-round, unlike snowmelt and rainwater, which is erratic and pulled by gravity. Therefore, the various species of insects that exist in a spring creek are limited because of the consistency of the temperature. That doesn't mean that large numbers of insects won't be there. They certainly will be. Just don't expect many different types of insects.

Mineral and alkali content is typically elevated. This translates to large numbers of insects (but relatively few species) trout enjoy feasting upon. Spring creeks lack the structure that creates broken, frothy whitewater. The surface is often glassy quiet, and unremarkable. This means that stealth and presentation, as well as patience and technique, are paramount.

Trout in spring creeks tend to congregate in small, packed areas rather than spread out and hide behind structure, since there often isn't much subsurface structure. Spring creek trout almost always feed during the early morning and evening. But often you can catch them in the daytime too, as long as you fish with diligence and careful observation.

Spring creek trout will often fall into a "rise cycle." They might rise every 3 seconds, 4 seconds, or 5 seconds, dipping back down between rises for safety. It becomes an almost predictable rhythm. Don't cover a lot of water on spring creeks. Instead, stay in one place and observe. Watch for feeding patterns. Cast to fish you see feeding, and time your drifts to just before they rise. This way they'll see the fly coming upon the rise. Stay put, and throw drys, nymphs, and terrestrials, all in the same water, repeatedly, until something gives.

Spring creek trout are often more about size than numbers. They get huge. Be prepared to keep them on the surface during the fight, not letting them go too deep or under driftwood.

TAILWATERS

Tailwaters, also called a tailraces, are trout streams formed by the outflows of dams that form reservoirs. Bottom-release dams often create extremely cold flows, since the water being let go is from the bottom of the lake, as opposed to the warmer, sun-heated water at the surface.

Pocketwater on a freestone stream in a canyon

Some of the country's best trophy tailwaters include the Taylor River near Almont, Colorado, and the San Juan below Navajo Reservoir, New Mexico. In both rivers, trout gorge themselves on tiny bugs—seldom on big ones—and become behemoths through consuming large numbers of insects, as opposed to large insects. This means fishing with tiny fly patterns, which many anglers find tedious and boring.

Tailwaters can be tough to fish because the best fishing tends to be closest to the dam, and trying to figure out the specific technique and insects to be successful can and often will take several trips.

For instance, one can spot a newbie a mile away at the San Juan or the Taylor, and not by his cast alone. At either place, if a guy is tossing big drys around, he's probably new. Very few anglers have success with big drys below those two dams, for several reasons. Since the stream flows out of the reservoir above, it doesn't have a lot of room to create habitat for insects until it's a half mile long or so. Also, so much food is continuously being released from the lake that trout often need not even look at anything else.

At the Taylor, you'll need to set up your rig with a tiny subsurface fly imitating the nearly microscopic mysis shrimp that bless the lake above in astronomical numbers. And you'll probably want to utilize a small bubble indicator and extremely light tippet. Trout in the Taylor grow to sickening sizes, eating little else than mysis shrimp, so it's hard to get them to turn and look at anything but an imitation of one.

At the San Juan, you can float dry flies (one experienced guy we know tosses #10 Royal Wulffs in the mornings and does well), but you're better off fishing microscopic midge patterns—around size 22—tied to a specific San Juan rig utilizing Amnesia and extremely fine tippet. The rainbows in this section rarely take anything else. And when a San Juan trout finally does take a fly, it does it so subtly that a novice probably will never know it. All the while he might be fishing the right fly and rig, and have trout hitting it all day, but just never knows it and thinks he's getting skunked.

Newbies might fail miserably on tailwaters. They show up unaware that there is a very targeted way to fish these unique streams. They think they'll fish like a freestone stream with the usual cast of flies and casts, but they just won't get takes that way. On many tailwaters there are strategies, techniques, and fly patterns that are specific to that water and that work consistently when nothing else does. Read up on any tailwater you'll be visiting before you get there to know exactly what flies work, how to set up a specific rig, and also how to fish the setup.

Big Rivers

Big, boisterous rivers often require a unique skill set and an almost hometown knowledge of the structure beneath the surface. If you think you can just cast a lot of line across a big river like the Conejos or the Arkansas, without first learning how to mend line, you'll likely not catch a thing.

The more line that's on the water and the more complex the currents on the surface, the more you need to mend. Mending is a skill that pulls out the bends in the line caused by microcurrents. Microcurrents, eddies, and seams can make different sections of your line drift at different rates of speed, eventually creating drag on the fly.

Mending is done in several ways. You can simply lift the rod and pull line off the water and literally lay it farther upstream, or do a "tossing" or "rolling" motion, pitching the line upstream to slow it down. Until you can mend line, you'll get drag on big rivers nearly all the time.

Big rivers will also threaten beginning waders and force them to cast from the bank, which limits them dramatically. If a river looks scary, it's probably too big for you, and you may not be ready for wading it yet. Play it safe and fish from the bank or in shallow water until you're more adept at being more than knee-deep.

Big rivers can be finicky. The larger the body of water, the more prone it is to acting like a lake. Search for seams, slack water, deep pools, and pockets. You'll hear that you should parcel out the river, attack only small sections of it, but that's easier to read about in a book than it is to do on the water. Sometimes the biggest waters are the toughest to fish, and they need to be given the respect and time they deserve.

Small Streams

Small streams can make even seasoned anglers look ridiculous if they don't attempt to learn to dap and short line. New anglers and those accustomed to larger rivers want to cast lots of line and catch trout from far away. In reality, most of the trout we catch are within 20 to 25 feet. Small

Sure footing is essential on the edges of frothy, fast-moving canyon water.

streams will require covering water, stealth, and a Herculean shoulder for hours of dapping. But once you get that shoulder in shape, you'll land more fish in small streams than you ever dreamed possible.

Small streams often need not be waded, but can be trekked along the banks. Fish upstream, moving at a brisk clip in search of only the most productive lies: pools, pockets, edges, overhangs, and seams. Match the hatch, or toss drys like Yellow Humpies, Irresistible Adams, H&L Variants, Lime Trudes, and Royal Wulffs, in sizes from 16 to 20 when no hatches are visible.

Doc Thompson's Tips for Fishing Small Streams

(Doc is a friend of ours. He has been a fly-fishing guide in northern New Mexico for 15 or 20 years.)

Small creeks often leave anglers holding their heads low, cursing the hike in and out, surrendering to the perception that these highly balanced gems are nightmares. Fortunately, dreams of solitude and native trout come true here. However, a small sacrifice must be paid for these dreams. Great physical and mental demands may be placed on a body, including scratched-up arms, scraped knees, unexpected branches in the face, and casting headaches in tight quarters. Experiences like these result from failure to prepare for such encounters. The following tactics have all been proved effective on small streams. Study them, learn them, and practice them.

Spooked fish are hard to catch. Scared trout run for their lives, giving up morsels of food drifting by while seeking shelter. Even the greatest anglers can't catch spooked trout. Approach the stream quietly, with soft feet. Sound echoes through clear water four or five times faster than through air. Heavy, loud footsteps send out an early alarm that an intruder is approaching.

Implement the "closer-lower" Method; the closer you approach the water, the lower to the ground you must be. Avoid sudden movements.

Find cover behind boulders, trees, and their shadows. Hiding your profile behind natural objects will help keep you out of sight of the trout. Keep your rod parallel to the ground, with the tip behind you. The last thing you want to do is sneak up on a rising trout only to spook it with your rod tip reaching 8 feet in front of you.

Show your rod only when your ready to cast, and keep its shadow off the water. The slightest unnatural object or shadow is enough to send trout fleeing.

Use the longest and lightest leader and tippet possible. Light tippets appear almost invisible to trout, as well as allowing for a cleaner drift. Fluorocarbon leaders and tippets refract less light than monofilament.

Delicate presentations and drag-free drifts are a must. Most insects hatch without so much as a dimple on the water, so your presentation must imitate the natural insects well. Free-floating insects are often trapped in the current and don't create much commotion.

Casts include roll casts, sidearm casts, bow-and-arrow casts, and fly dapping. A solid casting repertoire allows you to cast in virtually every situation. Be creative when casting in tight spots.

Prevent your shadow from looming over the water. Trout know what shadows are natural and what shadows just appear out of nowhere. A sudden shadow alerts trout.

Maintain a level-headed approach. Don't panic. As you approach a pool have a game plan laid out. If you pooch the pool, move onto to the next one with a new game plan.

Small streams and creeks require a high degree of delicacy, which is next to impossible to learn on a large river. Fishing small streams brings you in closer contact with Mother Nature. Unfortunately this closer contact means nervous trout, but then again, what a great challenge we are presented with—trying to fool Mother Nature and wild trout. Novice anglers and those less acquainted with small beautiful gems should take time to learn these tips and avoid moving like the proverbial bull in a china shop.

CAVEAT PISCATOR (ANGLER BEWARE): SPRING IS HERE. A LIST OF DOS AND DON'TS BY AMY BECKER WILLIAMS

(Amy is Mark's wife and a darned good fly angler. She is also the most organized of the three of us, and a great fishing buddy.)

Most anglers I know have a spring to-do list. I'm working on mine right now. If you're anything like me (or more like my husband), you've forgotten that you left that one reel in the shed back in October, and it still has the bird's nest you promised you'd get undone this past winter. So, get ready to start your own list by ticking off the essentials below gathered from experience and local fishing enthusiasts.

Step up your gym routine. Strength and stamina come in handy when trekking to the pristine waters where the most beautiful trout lie. Hiking several miles into a lake, and obviously back out, is not uncommon for me when I'm in search of trout and mountain solitude.

Get your must-haves. One indispensable item of gear I cannot live without for backcountry angling is my Korkers. those cool hybrid hiking/fishing shoes with interchangeable soles. If you've ever hiked on scree slopes, you know how valuable hiking soles that grip the ground can be. Sole choices include, rubber (natural and/or synthetic) and cleated. Sierra Trading Post often has good deals on them. Try www.sierra tradingpost.com, or www.korkers.com.

Save your feet. My great friend and fellow fishing buddy, Chad McPhail, is looking forward to building his spring gear collection with a pair of Orvis Easy-on Side-Zip Brogues. You don't want to wait to buy your boots till June because you sure don't want to waste time getting in the water since you've waited since autumn to fish.

Inspect your gear. Spring waters are still cold, so take the time to check your waders and neoprene socks for leaks. Most waders come with a one-time repair kit, or at least an extra swatch of fabric. If not, try Aqua Seal and Cotol 240 or the Simms Gore-Tex Wader Repair Kit If you end up needing new coverage, you can't go wrong with anything in the Simms line of gear.

Take inventory. Empty your vest or tackle box. Throw away old tippet and fly line; the older the line, the weaker it will be. Toss out old monofilament, replace expired attractant, and sharpen lures and flies. You'll still need a few replacement flies. (Surely a few were left behind on rocks and limbs.) McPhail is packing his fly box for spring with plenty of droppers (nymphs) including red Copper Johns and Hare's Ears. For dry flies, he says: "I never go without Stimulators (with rubber legs), Humpies, caddis imitations, and Parachute Adams."

Check your pack. Need a new vest or pack for spring? The boys and I recommend Fishpond packs. Choose from chest packs, waist packs, and backpacks so you can tuck away your lunch, water bottle, lures and flies, gewgaws, and gadgets.

Dust the cobwebs off your rods. Check the line guides for breakage and cracks. Even the slightest nick can break a line and ultimately release the big one before its time. Take some practice casts in the yard to make sure all mechanisms are running smoothly and to get your muscle memory back for fine casting. And girls, if your grip is small, you may like R.L. Winston's Joan Wulff Favorites, with smaller grips and lighter weights.

Early spring ice breakup

McPhail, and other fly fishers I know—myself included—go with the Dorber. McPhail loves to hit the water with Monic's MDT, Micro-Double Taper fly line.

Clean and oil your reels. Last season's dirt and debris can wreak havoc on performance. For a how-to, Google "fishing reel maintenance." If you're wanting to replace your reel and don't mind a used model, take a look at this Web site that highlights used reels through eBay: www.flyfishingsupplies.blogspot.com.

Go shopping. Okay, ladies, shop for fishing gear just like you were shopping for spring clothes. Looks and comfort count. You may not catch more fish, but you'll be more comfortable and look good trying. Patagonia and Simms both offer great breathable waders, cut just for women. Patagonia's Women's Watermaster Waders are constructed for easy pit stops. What a relief!

Your rod and reel have been sitting in the corner this winter. Before you go out for your first angling excursion only to "remember" that the reel has that big bird's nest you ended the season with last year, or the rod tip snapped off in the door, you might want to pull out the tackle for inspection, check your gear and make sure when you leave the house, you are as prepared as you can be.

If you plan to venture out and about this fishing season, you'll need to make sure you insure yourself against emergencies. If there's an accident, it's a long way on a Forest Service road to reach medical attention. And it's easy to find yourself in the middle of nowhere. At least it is for me.

Checklist:

1. Put together the most complete first-aid kit you can. Add a smaller version for your vest or fanny pack.
2. Look in your tackle box or fly vest. Sharpen all hooks.
3. Check for frays in all your lines and tippets.
4. If you plan to boat, check the boat for leaks. Check the motor. Do you have enough life jackets? Where's the paddle, just in case? Flares? Emergency snacks?
5. Many anglers travel by car, with the luxury of a cellular phone, a convenience much debated in the Fishing Forum. Cell phones in the car (not on the stream) are a good way to protect against all the outdoors nasties. You can also carry a CB radio (remember those?) or another kind of handheld radio.
6. And since you're going to be in your vehicle, check and double-check your tires, engine, transmission, and so on, and then check them again. Veterans carry toolboxes in their cars, right next to the tow rope and/or chain, high-beam lantern, and first aid kit. I carry a gallon of antifreeze because my Blazer once overheated in the middle of Arizona on an old logging road during the heat of summer.
7. Is your spare tire in good shape, is it aired up? Is it one of those wimpy doughnut spares? Get a real spare if you travel in the outdoors.
8. Have you changed your air filter? The dirt stirred up on these roads can clog yours up and lower your car's performance.

9. If you are not an accomplished outdoorsperson, and you will be deep in the outdoors, hiking to a distant lake or stream, make sure you bring someone who is accomplished. Pack a small survival kit, travel with a compass and the appropriate maps, and learn how to use them properly.

10. One critter that should cause concern is microscopic: *Giardia lamblia*, a waternborne parasite found in most untreated water sources in North America. Don't drink untreated water, even spring water, even if you are in the deep backcountry, even if the water is cold and crystal clear. Beaver fever is nothing you want to catch, so carry water in your fanny pack or a top-rate filter cup.

11. What about dangers you might encounter? How about hypothermia, altitude sickness, lightning, extreme sunburn, landslides, high water, falls, sharp rocks, slippery rocks, scree slopes, tree limbs, and other naturally sharp objects, which can poke eyeballs? Dress in layers at higher elevations, wear sunglasses to protect your eyes, wear shoes with grip soles and ankle support, and bring along raingear and warm clothes.

12. Pack sunblock, sunscreen, or suntan lotion, even if it's cloudy over head. You can buy the waterproof kind, but the best idea is to keep applying it throughout the day.

13. A two-dollar bandanna is one of the most useful items you can take fishing. Stuff it in a pocket and you'll be glad later on. Wear a cap this time out. Better yet, wear a hat so the brim protects your ears (or your balding pate) from sunburn.

14. Rain gear, anyone? You're going fishing, so the odds that it will downpour just increased significantly. And a cheap rain parka folds up as small as a bandanna and fits nicely in your vest or tackle box.

PACKING LIGHT/ESSENTIAL GEAR FOR FLY FISHING

Don't break your back carrying too many accoutrements on the river. Take only what you need. Go light. The trout only want your flies, not all the junk in your trunk! You gotta learn how to shed the nonessentials.

Taking a fully loaded vest and chest waders to fish a step-across stream for an afternoon is like taking a tractor-trailer rig full of stuff to a primitive campsite in Alaska. Sure, some of us could pack the bastard full to the top with gear, but why?

Filling up every pocket on the vest with gadgets and doodads is a great excuse to shop for the latest products. We ain't gonna tell the old ladies—we do it all the time. It's like helium for the ego. But trout are after one thing: flies! Almost everything else should be no more important, and gear should be essential for getting the fly to the trout, or for safety. No more. No less. Here are some important tips for lightening the load.

Ditch the Goofy Gadgetry

Leave the extra weight behind. It's surprising how much gear can be avoided simply by learning to tie successful knots. Fly-tying contraptions and line-to-leader connectors are two of them. They are both rather expensive, and connectors are far less effective than a good old-fashioned, well-tied nail knot. Learn to tie effective knots, and straighten leaders with your thumb and index finger.

Line basket. Who needs it? Unless you're fishing the salt or for stripers, really, you don't.

Entomology kit. Wha-huh? You may end up being a bug nerd, and that's fine, but . . .

Tape measure. Smallish trout need not be measured by anything other than your eye. One trick is to attach a special measuring tape to your net or rod.

Mosquito annoyer. We've seen dudes with these on. Stop it!

Creel. Come on, practice catch-and-release.

Hook sharpener. Iffy, but ditch the thing. Sharpen your hooks before you go out. If you tie your own flies, sharpen the hooks and crush down the barbs at the tying vise.

Water thermometer. Unless you're going to make Jell-O, who cares what the temp is? Downsizing from a trinket-laden vest to a smartly designed chest or waist pack forces one to carry only what is needed.

Purchase ultralightweight gear, such as waders, boots, and reels—every ounce makes a difference when you're scrambling over rocks and fighting through brambles, or shuffling through moving water. Less gear equals less weight, which translates to better coordination when wading the river, and less fatigue in the legs and arms.

Fewer tangles and messes with gear and gadgetry mean less headache and frustration. Less time playing with gadgets yields more time with the fly on the water. All of which leads to the payoff: more trout!

What is essential, then? What should an angler carry on those lighter days when the full-on arsenal is impractical? Here's a comprehensive checklist of trout-fishing rudiments. Nothing else is needed. Remember this list! Learn it. Live it. Love it.

1. ID, licenses, and permits
2. One small, loaded fly box
3. One extra leader
4. Two spools of tippet
5. Pair of nippers
6. Forceps
7. One strike indicator
8. Floatant
9. Split-shot
10. Lip balm
11. Small amount of flagging tape

Anything absent from this list might actually be necessary, such as sunscreen, a lunch, and polarized glasses. (Or, some people might actually deem a cigar, a lighter, and a 750ml bottle of Scotch as must-have items. Let's face it, "essential" is a relative term.) However, many "extras" are best used before hitting the river, or left in the vehicle, or don't actually need to be stowed away, i.e., polarized lenses. Sunglasses are critical, but are worn, not necessarily packed.

Follow these tips and see if your hours on the river don't become more comfortable and productive. Packing light allows anglers to reap results. Too many beginning anglers give up because they've not only caught few fish but because they're tired as all get out by day's end.

HIRING A FISHING GUIDE: WHEN TO HIRE ONE, AND WHAT TO EXPECT

Why hire a guide? If you already know everything there is to know about fishing, don't read this. But if you want to pick the brain of someone who takes fishing very seriously, someone who is on the water as many days in one year as you have been in your entire life, then hiring a guide makes a lot of sense.

You might very well be an accomplished angler. But can you double-haul? Tie a Bimini twist or nail knot without a hitch? Guides can teach you how to tie some of the local hot flies, read the water, improve your casting, handle a boat, and countless other useful skills.

A good fishing guide is invaluable, especially on unfamiliar water.

Say you want to hire one of these guides. You want an expert to take you on his (or her) home waters and put you onto more fish than you ever caught before. You want this expert to teach you how to unlock the mysteries of this body of water and perhaps, since you are paying hard-earned money, catch a fish big enough to impress your circle of friends back home.

But how do you hire a guide? Where do you start? Most tackle shops and fly shops either have guide services or book for them. Most states have guide associations, and you can get those phone numbers from the state wildlife departments to find the guides in the area you want to fish. Many guides also advertise in sporting magazines, newspapers and club newsletters, and more and more have their own websites.

Say you've found a guide. Now what? Let's look at a list of things to consider before plunking down your money.

A guided river float trip by pontoon boat

What are your expectations? Are you looking for a solid day on the water where the guide puts you in position to catch a lot of fish? Or are you in need of a beginner makeover, with the guide teaching you how to cast, tie knots, unravel bird's nests, and the like? Or do you just want to get out of the house, don't know the lay of the land, and need the expertise of a professional?

Let the guide know your skill level—your actual skill level, not the level you sometimes reach on your best day. The guide needs to know how well you cast, how frequently you fish, if you've dropped a line in this fishery before, or even if you can take a fish off the hook. If the guide is equipped with an accurate idea of your skills, he can put you on the right kind of water and maximize your opportunities. Your guide knows the local water, how the trout feed, if there is a behavioral drift and how to fish it, times of hatches, and so much more that would take you a lifetime to learn. Why not hire the benefit of their wisdom?

What are the duties and responsibilities of the guide? Most guides do not fish while guiding. If you are fishing from a boat, you'll be amazed at how the guide processes so many things at once. Your guide is asking you questions about what you do for a living, watching for upcoming hazards, thinking about the weather, about what the fish will be feeding on at this time of day, whether he remembered to pack the Grey Poupon for the sandwiches, and—if this hot spot holds no fish—where to fish next. Most guides provide tackle and flies. Most guides feed you lunch. Many provide transportation, tippets, and usually have rod-and-reel outfits set up and ready to use.

Don't be afraid make sure you get what you want up front. Ask for references, and to talk to your guide before you commit. Hiring a guide is relatively expensive. Make sure you know what the guide will provide, what happens in an emergency, and where you will be going. Ask the guide what kind of fish you'll catch and how big they average. But beware of any guide who promises you the best fishing haul of your life. Guarantees in fishing are for fools (except in Alaska, of course).

Money. Most guides give a price break to take out two persons at a time. Taking along a fishing buddy is a no-brainer, since it cuts the price in half. You had a good day on the water. You want to give the guide a little something. How much to tip? Consider this: Guides are running a business. The guide's fee may seem like lot of money just to take folks fishing. But guides don't work every day. They work only when someone wants to hire them. They have a specialized base of knowledge, especially about their own waters. Guides who own their own businesses pay for liability

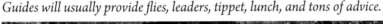

Guides will usually provide flies, leaders, tippet, lunch, and tons of advice.

and auto insurance, flies, lures and tippet, gear, rods, reels, lunches, and gasoline. It all adds up.

And those guides who work for someone else might only realize one-third of the money you plunk down. Did the guide act professionally? You can determine if they tried tactics and strategies to optimize your chances of catching fish. Did they give a darn? Twenty percent of the fee (always in cash) is a common tip for a job well done. Anything less says you think the day was less than you expected. Tip more if you can afford it, and you had a great trip. Guides can't make the fish jump onto your hook. Never judge the day's on how many fish you catch. It's the whole experience, and the guide's attitude that matters.

One last note: The best way to find a great guide is by word of mouth from other anglers whose opinion you trust. Top guides don't even need to advertise: They get plenty of business from word of mouth and returning clients.

STILLWATER FISHING

Lakes and ponds can be tough to fish until you learn the behaviors of trout in stillwaters, and the insects found in them. Most trout in stillwaters spend a lot of time cruising the edges, swimming parallel to the bank, often between the bank and where the water drops off into the dark depths. You'll want to learn to cast flies like size 16 to 18 red Copper Johns, Beadhead Princes, and damselfly nymph imitations, and to drop them in front of cruisers and strip them in using an irregular retrieve. Just remember that in lakes and ponds it's mainly about finding fish that are rising to emergers, finding trout on the edges, and duping trout with the proper imitation at the proper depth using the proper technique. Sounds easy, right? Fly fishing in stillwaters is related to fishing rivers of course, but there are many differences. Forget much about what we've told you about insects and food. There are two ways to fish a stillwater: from the shore or in a watercraft.

First things first. Where in a lake do you find fish?

The littoral zone varies from lake to lake, but basically it's the area from the shoreline to where the sunlight doesn't penetrate well. Where the sunlight doesn't penetrate, plants don't grow, which means no insects or

Facing above. A calm, reflective morning on Trappers Lake.
Facing below. Canoeing on the Blue Mesa Reservoir

aquatic life, which means no trout, because they swim where they can eat. On many lakes, this shallow area extends from the shore to about 25 feet deep.

The drop-off zone is where the green plant growth is maximized, where trout can hide, where trout avoid the heat of shallow water on hot summer days, and most important, where the edge of the shallow water drops off into deeper parts of the lake. So you want to concentrate on the shallows and the drop-off zones, not on the littoral zone. That means that casting way out in the middle of the lake is often a fruitless endeavor. There is also, in many lakes, a midlake or deepwater zone that gets enough sunlight to support chironomids and other insects. And in shallow high-country lakes, this shoreline water is warmer, too.

Where else to fish in a lake? Look for weed beds, springs, and stream channels.

Fish in lakes typically cruise. Unlike stream trout, they don't stay in one lie. They respond to the oxygen levels, the light coming through the water, the plant life, the temperature, and other conditions. Watch for cruisers and risers. Risers are just cruisers that decided to eat something close or on the surface.

What do they feed upon? Terrestrials, chironomids, mosquitos, damselflies, dragonflies, baitfish, leeches, scuds, caddisflies, water boatmen, backswimmers, snails, mayflies, eels, worms, and other slimy weird fish food. They have a soup bowl full of food.

Personal Watercraft

You've probably fished in a boat, so you're pretty familiar with that kind of fishing. But what about in a personal watercraft? What is a personal watercraft? This means a belly boat or float tube, a pontoon boat, or another kind of one-man or one-woman watercraft.

When you are in your personal watercraft, you'll want to troll, for sure. That's your number one plan of attack. You have to paddle or use oars or flippers, so there's work involved. You'll want to wear a personal floatation device (PFD). You'll want a longer rod more than you'd want on a stream. A personal watercraft can cost less than $200 (a float tube plus flippers) or as much as $1,000 bucks (a deluxe pontoon boat or even a pram.) If you really want to cover a stillwater, you have to get you're a personal watercraft of some sort.

A shallow lake calls for a boat or float tube.

Lake fishing is much more variable than river fishing. What kinds of variables? Water temperatures, waves, rain, clouds, shadows, ledges, drop-offs, inlets, outlets, submerged rocks and trees, grass, algae, water clarity, morning or evening vs. high noon, and a whole bunch more. Lake fishing is tricky, worthy of an entire book of its own.

Trolling is simple. Let your fly sink and begin paddling.

What's not easy is catching fish while trolling. There's more to it than meets the eye. Do you need a full-sinking line, a sink-tip line, or a floating line? At what speed do you troll? What will your path be? Do you troll from this point to that one? How will the wind affect your trolling?

Let's say you don't want to troll but you'd rather find a spot on the lake that looks promising. Lake fishing, because of wind and long casts and bigger fish, because you may be in a low-slung belly boat and need to pick up line easier, requires longer rods. A 9-footer is good. When you cast to a nice lie, perhaps to the side of a big rock, how will you retrieve it? Long, slow strips? Short, quick, intermediate twitches and retrieves? No movement at all, which is probably the most effective but most difficult technique? Why? Because it's tough to do nothing. Will you imitate a surface insect and tie on a dry fly? If you do, will you skitter and skate that sucker, or will you let it sit perfectly still and wait for a trout to take it? We can't answer any of these questions for you because you have to factor in all the variables we mentioned earlier, and no two days on the same lake will ever be the same.

Casting from shore is a key to understanding how to catch fish, even when you get out in your boat. Don't cast as far as you can and hope you get to the big ones. It doesn't work like that with trout lakes. Don't cast perpendicular to the shore. Don't cast blindly without at least taking time to watch for five or ten minutes, looking for any cruisers or risers.

An ideal lake for personal watercraft

This lake is ideal for trolling.

The trout are sure to be lined up at this inlet.

Casting blindly or what we call "prospecting" requires several elements. Don't stand right up on the bank. Step back a bit. Hide behind a rock if you can. Cast at angles and if possible, cast parallel to the shore. But don't just stand on the bank and cast straight out as far as you can.

Casting to cruising trout is both exciting and nerve-racking. Lead the trout. Use a long leader so that it can't spot you. Try to drop the fly a few inches on the other side of his intended path so you can twitch it to you if need be.

High-country stillwaters are often both beautiful and challenging.

Concentrate first on inlets and outlets, whether you're on shore or in a boat. What rod to use? A 9-foot, 5- or 6-weight is a good choice. But if the lake is windy or the fish very, very big, you might move up to a 7-weight. If you are on the shore and backcasting with trees, pull out your roll cast. Floating fly lines cover the shallow zone, which is the water between 2 and 20 feet in depth. The floating line is ideal for nymphs, pupae, emergers, and dry flies. A slow- or intermediate-sinking line is a solid choice for fishing the next deeper section of the lake, up to 20 feet deep, good for fishing the deeper parts of the shoal such water. A fast- or extra-fast-sinking line provides good coverage up to 40 feet deep and is effective for fishing dragonfly nymphs, leeches, and shrimp along the drop-offs.

When you hear the term "pocketwater," you may be tempted to think it's where you haul out your trusty Popeil's Pocket Fisherman, as seen on TV. It's not. So what is pocketwater?

Ever come to that point in the river where the water cascades into puffy white spots, places where the water swirls and eddies into tiny smooth pools, where rocks and boulders sit like sentinels all over the river and cause pockets of short glass all around them? That's pocketwater.

The water moves in all directions, foamy and white and quick. Traditional lies are often difficult to read, which means the trout can and will hide in any and all likely lies. What are likely lies? Anywhere there are edges, like seams and current breaks. Around any rock. Where the water color changes. Where the shallow water drops off a ledge into a deeper pool.

In pocketwater, the river moves furiously, broken by the rocks and streambed and trees. Pocketwater trout fight this constant maelstrom and grow athletic and broad-shouldered. They become opportunistic feeders and fierce fighters when hooked.

Think less casting, more control.

Mac is fishing pocketwater by dapping, highsticking, and keeping his line under control.

Pocketwater angling rarely requires long casts. In fact, you will want to keep your false casts to a minimum. The idea is to have a short and manageable amount of line and tippet outside the rod tip.

Casting is not as important as how you manage the line as it hits the water. Since you don't want much more than 6 to 9 feet of combined line and tippet out, your casts should be tight and short, sometimes more of a pick-up-and-place-down than a true cast. Many anglers just kind of flip the fly back upstream.

Pocketwater is an ideal time to practice your high-stick nymphing. And with dry flies, since you want to keep as much line off the water as possible (to cut drag), the technique is much like high-sticking.

Pocketwater Tips

1. You seldom get long drifts. Line control is essential. Mend often.

2. Keep as much line off the water as possible, and keep your line somewhat taut.

3. Keep your rod tip high so you don't have to move far to set the hook.

4. When your fly hits the water, be in position to set the hook. Pocketwater trout must hit their prey quickly since the water flows so fast. And pocketwater strikes are usually explosive. Be prepared.

5. The water is broken, which means you can't see the trout, and more important, the trout cannot see you. Use this to your advantage by getting close to the lies.

6. Fish all likely lies. Sounds simple, but you'd be surprised how often anglers wade right past good trout holding spots.

7. If you fish a subsurface fly, make sure to have enough weight to get the fly down quickly. A 50-yard stretch of pocketwater may offer 100 or 200 casting opportunities. Be persistent and work all of it. An inch or two one way or another can make a lot of difference.

8. Fish the foamy pools, the plunge pools. If you don't get strikes at first, especially with dry flies, sink the dry or add a weighted nymph. These are the lies of the big boys, so work them with different presentations.

9. Fish the glassy water with dry flies. Be delicate.

10. Use a heavier-gauge tippet than you would in other trout water; 4X is not too thick. Why? You won't have a lot of room or time to play a trout. Fool him, catch him, and land him. Don't mess around.

11. Pocketwater tends to hold caddis and stoneflies. Weighted caddis and stonefly nymphs are the most deadly imitations you can use.

The remains of a stonefly

FISHING MULTIPLE FLIES

Take this to the bank—the riverbank. If you are fishing with only one fly, you are missing out on catching all the fish you could catch. You are catching only those fish that, like you, love dry flies.

Think about it. If one is good, two is better. Trout feed on subsurface foods as much as 90 percent of the time, so the adage has it. This may or may not be the true-to-life percentage but the bottom line is that by the nature of living in water, most of the trout's food is underwater.

Mayflies and caddis and stoneflies and baitfish and crayfish and mysis shrimp live underwater. Subsurface flies meet the feeding expectations and the behavior patterns of trout and their food. When trout feed on insects on top of the water, they rarely do so to the exclusion of subsurface goodies. Trout think subsurface first, surface second.

By adding a second fly, the angler gains greater coverage. Even if the trout are keying on insects on top of the water, two dry flies or a dry fly with a subsurface dropper covers more water, and more lies.

I don't see as well as Mac does, and it's getting worse every year. When trout are feeding on small adult mayflies, I just can't see my size 20 or 22 Adams on the water very well. My trick is to tie as my first fly an attractor fly, one that I can see well. Then I add 16 inches or so of tippet to the eye of the attractor fly. Next, I tie on the size 20 Adams. This way I can follow the attractor and know to look out 16 inches to locate the smaller fly. It's deadly, by the way, and I often get hookups on the larger fly even in the middle of a hatch of small mayflies.

What the heck are multiple flies? If you fish with more than one fly, you are fishing multiple flies. These can be two or more nymphs, two or more wet flies, a large streamer and a tailing nymph, a dropper rig with a dry fly followed by a nymph, or two dry flies.

When you fish a dry fly with a subsurface fly below it, you are appealing to the interest feeding trout focus on and below the surface. You are imitating two different stages of insect life. Another benefit to using a dry fly above a nymph (or even a strike indicator with multiple flies) is that it aids you in detecting strikes.

Some critics call the dry fly, when used in this dropper rig, nothing more than a strike indicator, anathema to dry-fly purists. But I can't tell you how many times I have caught trout on the dry. The trailing fly and tippet between don't seem to turn off the fish. In the absence of a hatch, a dry fly and dropper nymph (or two nymphs with a strike indicator) is the ideal prospecting technique to locate trout.

To set up a dry fly/nymph dropper rig, tie on a dry fly, preferably a size 12 or 14, something that floats well such as a Royal Wulff, Trude, Elk-hair Caddis, or Parachute Adams.

Depending on the depth of the water, cut a piece of tippet from 12 to 18 inches long. Using a cinch knot (sometimes called a clinch knot), the same knot you used to attach the dry to the leader, tie the tippet to either the bend of the dry fly or the eye. Don't worry. Even on a barbless hook, the tippet will not slide off. Promise.

You should have a dry fly attached to your leader with a piece of tippet 12 to 18 inches dangling off it. The nymph you select should reflect the types of insects this water holds (rocky water has stoneflies and caddis; still, sandy pools hold mayflies or craneflies, and so on).

If you are prospecting, use a generic nymph like a Hare's Ear, Prince Nymph, or Pheasant Tail. We use beadhead nymphs most of the time, but you can use BB shot to weight the nymph by attaching them to the tippet between the dry and the nymph. Because BB shot tends to fray or wear the tippet, we choose beadheads. You can cast this rig upstream as you would a single dry fly, remembering that the nymph has added weight.

One trick is to cast upstream, let the flies float free until they pass you, then let them work downstream and across, sometimes submerging the dry. But don't stop here. This is important to making this work. Although you will catch quite a few fish on the downstream curve, and we've watched this a thousand times, a trout will typically follow the flies, sometimes shooting several feet from its lie, and when you lift the rod tip and lay it back down, sometimes a couple of times, the trout will hit. The dry acts like a drowning insect trying to escape, and the nymph acts like a pupa or larva or immature adult rising to the surface.

In fact, there is a common belief, which we adhere to, that multiple flies draw attention to each other, and even simulate insect behavior. In clear Colorado (and Arizona, Utah, Montana, and more) streams, we've fished two nymphs, running them through a deep pool. We've watched as trout turned initially to the dry, passing over it, then slashed at the trailing nymph.

On the San Juan River, we use a streamer, like a Bunny Leech, followed by a smaller nymph on the dropper, swung across current. (Mark's brother-in-law Kenny is deadly with this setup.) Trout often attack the streamer, swatting at it, then dive after the following fly, usually a small midge or egg pattern. We believe the trout see a smaller insect escaping from a larger predator, and are drawn to the action.

Think about fishing two dry flies as well—the larger fly closer to the rod tip, a smaller one underneath it. Be sure to check the attached tippet often. The monofilament is bound to get tangled around the flies every now and again. Check for frays, wear, and knots.

Try fishing two soft-hackle wets during the next hatch and rise. The soft-hackle wet flies can be deadly with their undulating movement. While most anglers get frustrated tossing patterns that match the adult insects flying about, you should cast multiple wets, one in brown and one in gray, or two different sizes or stages of development, and you will catch more trout.

The wets (which are traditional winged wets, soft-hackle wets, and wingless wets, sometimes called Flymphs) imitate the immature insects that are becoming airborne adults. And the trout know that they are easier to catch while they're in the water. Multiple wets are a deadly and classic combination our fly-fishing forefathers frequently employed. Fish them downstream and across, but play around with your technique. Some use a dead-drift swing, casting across and downstream, then mend line and raise the rod tip at the end of the swing (this is sometimes called the Leisenring Lift). We also fish the flies in an upstream dead-drift and have success.

Nymphs, in combinations of different shapes and sizes, are extremely effective, and every serious angler should use them. Most anglers, ourselves included, love to fish dry flies. But nymphs are the flies of choice for serious anglers. And at times, if you want to catch fish instead of just tossing dry flies, you too should be a serious angler. When you fish two nymphs, we suggest trying two strategies: nymphs of the same insect but different developmental stages, such as a caddis emerger and a caddis pupa; or two dissimilar nymphs, such as a mayfly and a caddis, or a large and a small fly. To add weight, you can combine beadheads with normal nymphs, or place split-shot above and/or below the top fly to suit your needs.

Things to Think About When Fishing Multiple Flies

Use as light as tippet as you feel comfortable using. We tend to use tippet a bit stronger than the leader. You will hear that you should keep your tippets as short as possible to avoid tangles, but we don't buy into that. But we do tend to keep our leaders under 10 feet long so they turn over better.

Select a depth at which you want your fly to pass and make the tippet length correspond.

Some anglers use a third fly. We've tried it and it all gets tangled most of time, and when we do hook up, the flies get tangled then and we have to retie the triple-fly rig.

Bring extra tippet and leaders. At first you are going to get tangled up and lose a lot of tippet.

Check your connections for frays, knots, tangles, and wrap-ups.

For fishing multiple-fly rigs, we favor 5- or 6-weight rods with sink-tip lines, and sometimes sinking lines. But if you have a four-weight, you can still fish two nymphs or a dry-dropper rig. If you use split-shot instead of weighted flies, we recommend BB size.

The Dry-Dropper Rig

Fishing with a dry-dropper rig is a productive technique for catching more trout. Here's how to tie and fish one.

A dry-dropper rig is a combination setup utilizing a dry fly that also functions as a strike indicator, and a nymph or beadhead that trails behind the dry fly. Traditional dry-fly fishing is our favorite way to fish. It's a visual endeavor that allows you to see as all the drifting, attacking, and fighting action goes down.

But this visual affair can be even more exciting. If an angler wants to net more trout, fishing with subsurface flies instead of just dry flies is an essential skill. Wet flies are a different method entirely, and some books are devoted to this practice. Not many folks fish traditional wet flies anymore, because of the effectiveness of nymphing. A wet fly is a fly that looks to the fish like a submerged adult or baitfish or leech or something of substance that is swimming or crippled. You can fish one, two, or even three wet flies at one time, but wet flies are a tough way for beginners way to get started. Let's start instead with dropper flies.

Dry flies imitate adult insects floating on the surface, while dry-dropper rigs can imitate insects changing throughout all the various stages of molting, from pupal and larval stages to emergers and spinners. Fishing a dry fly (imitating an adult insect) and a nymph (imitating a larva) simultaneously covers more of the insects' life cycle, and therefore gives you more opportunities to land fish with a single cast. Plus, when fish are finicky, fishing two flies will help you figure out what the trout want, and at what depth.

There are times on the river when a dry fly alone just doesn't seem to work. When trout won't rise to a dry, this typically means they are either down for a nap, or feeding below, and then it's time to tie on a nymph and wake their sleepy heads up.

But leave the dry fly on. Or tie on another one, a bigger one with better floatation qualities. This fly will often catch its own fish, but it mostly will "indicate" when there is a strike on the nymph. If that dry goes under or even twitches a little, it's done its job of letting you know when the trout have changed from surface to subsurface feeding.

Tying a dry-dropper rig takes practice, like most things in life. But keep at it, and you'll find yourself getting better and quicker each time.

1. Choose a large, bushy dry fly that floats high and will hold lots of floatant. Royal Wulffs, Stimulators, and Humpies are all great choices. Tie this fly onto the end of a new leader or the end of your tippet. Use the clinch knot as usual.

2. Next, determine how deep the dropper should trail the dry, and choose a nymph appropriate for that depth. Water speed and depth will help you decide. Red Copper Johns and Hare's Ear nymphs are fine selections—not so heavy as to cause the nymph to hang up on bottom, but still large and heavy enough to drift at an appropriate depth below the dry.

3. Cut an appropriate length of tippet, say 12 to 18 inches for starters. Use tippet of lighter weight than your leader. This way, if it breaks, you lose just the one fly on the lighter line (the nymph) instead of losing both. Dropper flies should trail anywhere between 6 inches to 24 inches or more behind the dry fly, depending upon water depth, current speed, and the size and weight of the nymph.

4. Using another clinch knot, tie your dropper fly onto the tippet. Check that the knot will hold before proceeding.

5. Now, simply feed the tag end of the tippet (the end without the fly) through the eye of the dry fly. This is the trickiest part, so have patience. Next, tie it on with yet another clinch knot. And you're done.

This dry-dropper rig, sometimes called simply a dropper rig, is the most efficient and deadly way to fish (and prospect) for trout.

Tying and casting dry-dropper rigs take practice. Be careful anytime you cast weighted nymphs. Weighted flies track through the air at a lower trajectory than do dry flies, and fly slightly more erratically. Waiting for the line to load on the backcast is critical, and shooting the tightest loop possible will help prevent hang-ups, bird's nests, and tailing loops.

Cover deep pools, seams, and especially cutbanks when using dry-dropper rigs, but don't forget that riffles and long slicks can be full of feeding trout as well. Many anglers fish dry-dropper rigs exclusively, because of their effectiveness. Try this technique for a full day and see if more trout don't end up in the net.

You've fished beaver ponds and you've caught fish. Maybe you caught a lot of fish, probably brook trout, with most of them in the 7- to 9-inch range. What if we showed you how to catch even more fish, and some tips on catching big fish, perhaps even the biggest fish in the pond?

Beaver ponds make it worth the time to hike in to step-across streams. These dammed ponds often show up overnight. Many have the characteristics of small lakes, sort of holding pools with little current. Others have tiny chutes feeding the pond, with multiple braids of current. Still others are a series of beaver ponds laid out like blue pearls on a necklace. But they all call for similar fishing methods.

Most beaver ponds hold brook trout, but many are also home to rainbow, brown, and cutthroat trout, and even grayling. Beaver ponds are also great places to view wildlife: moose, deer, elk, bears, and, of course, beavers.

Kenny uses his skitter technique on a beaver pond.

Chase Medling uses the dam to hide his profile.

Start at the dam itself, and work your way around.

You might have heard some conventional wisdom about how to fish beaver ponds. Fish from the dam side first. Use long leaders, 12 feet or more. Use small flies, the smaller the better. Don't discount these time-honored adages, but be open to other suggestions.

We keep three principles in mind when fishing beaver ponds: stealth, observation, and position. Here's how to put these principles into action

The overriding thought in your head when fishing a beaver pond should be stealth. More than in any other trout-fishing situation, fish in beaver ponds can see you and feel the vibrations you make in the ground when walking.

No false casting, unless you have an open meadow behind you, in which case you can false cast over the meadow, then turn and cast to the pond. Clumsy casts will put down all the fish in an entire beaver pond.

The spongy bog surrounding beaver ponds carries vibrations from your footfalls that spook the trout. Move delicately, slowly, and deliberately. Keep low and stay hidden behind trees and brush.

Fish early and late. High noon sun makes you, your shadow, your line, your tippet, and your offerings easy to spot. If you must fish in the middle of the day, fish to any cover and be even stealthier than normal.

Get on your knees to lower your profile. Observe everything. Watch for cruising trout. Are they little or big? Where are the edges and lies? Where is the best spot to reach the best fish or the most fish? Beaver pond trout typically stay in one smallish area, even if they are in a cruising pattern.

Observe the rising fish. Find the biggest one. Sounds simple, right? Then why do so many anglers cast to the nearest one?

Concentrate on any currents in the beaver pond, especially where the stream enters the pond at its head. Sometimes currents are difficult to detect, but any current carries food and offers shelter.

Concentrate on cover. Beaver ponds are open, and trout will look for any hiding places they can find. Fish to submerged timber, brush, rocks, and anything else that might offer the trout some shelter.

The area below the dam provides a natural shelter from skittish fish, but fishing there presents certain problems. First, your fly line and leader will get tangled with the twigs and sticks, no ifs, ands, or buts. Second, your fly line and leader and the trout you just hooked will get tangled with the twigs and sticks, no ifs, ands, or buts. Keep your rod tip up, maintain line control, and hope for the best. In the hot summer months, hoppers, ants, and beetle imitations will draw vicious strikes. Fish these especially where the stream enters the beaver pond.

If it's windy, move into position using the wind as cover. Choppy water conceals your movements. You'll have difficulty seeing rises, but believe us, the trout are still rising, taking food off the top.

In windy conditions, you can also use a false cast to get your fly to a spot (but that's the only time) you couldn't reach in still conditions. In

BEAVER POND TACTICS

Cast closest to you first, working your way out, fanning from one side to the other. Don't rush your presentations by casting to the first rising trout. If you cast too quickly to a small trout feeding on top, you may cast over a much larger trout between you and the small trout. Bring your bag of trick casts. With willows and other trees and brush usually lining parts of a beaver pond, you'll need to leave the ol' Orvis 30-foot cast at home. You'll be tossing flies to beaver pond brookies with roll casts, sidearm casts, shooting line casts, bow-and-arrow casts, and steeple casts.

*Not even trees devastated by fire can ruin the
natural beauty of a beaver pond complex.*

windy conditions, you ought to think about switching to a wet fly or a weighted nymph.

Try the twitch method: Cast your fly and let it sit on the surface for a few moments. With your off hand, strip in a short amount of line with a jerk, then let the fly sit for another few moments. Try the retrieve method: Cast your fly out, preferably a buggy pattern with rubber legs. Then strip like crazy, with the fly causing all kinds of commotion on the water. I've caught more fish in beaver ponds using this method than any other. Fish nymphs, especially emergers and cripples, if you aren't getting immediate results. Wet flies, if you know how to fish them, are deadly in a beaver pond. Try a big fly: Madame X, Stimulator, Mathews's X-Caddis, Turk's Tarantula, and even a Skater (old-timers will remember these spider/water bug imitators) are all suitable flies. Not even trees devastated by fire can ruin the natural beauty of a beaver pond complex.

FISHING STREAMERS

Casting streamers is about as graceful as Dr. Koop on skates or Cher at afternoon tea. But fishing with streamers is often the most effective method to entice trout (and bass) regardless of how awkward it looks or feels.

Why streamers? We can give you many reasons. In fact, if you seriously want to catch the biggest fish in the river or lake with a fly, then leave the drys and nymphs in the box and fish only streamers. That's how deadly streamers are. Why not use streamers, is the question. Streamers give the fish a change of pace. Trout and bass will almost always take a streamer.

Big fish eat fish. They eat fat swimming creatures. They have to—to maintain their size, they must become piscivorous. That translates into looking for prey that will provide lots of calories. Streamers are big and look like baitfish or other high-calorie snacks.

Ideal Streamer Situations

You probably know the standard situations when streamers work best: in the spring, during high water, if you see no rises, and in the absence of hatches. Here are some others:

1. When temperatures are cold
2. When the water has deep pools, drop-offs, and ledges
3. When fishing undercut banks
4. When you're covering large amounts of water in a short time

5. When searching a lake
6. When you are after big fish
7. On overcast days, rainy days, early and late (low light conditions), dirty water, and right after rains
8. When you need to get down to fish holding deep
9. When you need to reach fish holding under limbs and other obstructions
10. When you are fishing runs, riffles, and trenches
11. When you have long stretches of pocketwater with lots of boulders
12. When fish are feeding on the bottom

So how in the world do you fish a streamer? Start by slowing down your delivery, pace your stroke, open up a bit. Casting streamers all day is going to make your arm drop off by the end of the day, but what the heck? You're all about catching big fish, right? Since streamers take a second to sink, and make a lot of noise when they hit the water, always try to cast about a yard or two above the spot you are eying. In that way, the streamer will be at the proper depth to pass over your fish.

Some anglers think you should always fish streamers downstream, while others believe that doing so spooks the fish. Others believe anglers should always plop streamers across and upstream to get the best drift. Which is best? Both methods work. There is some legitimacy to the idea that downstream fishing leads to pulling the hook out of the fish's mouth, but not often enough to make us worry about it. We have caught plenty of fish—both trout and smallmouths—by casting straight across, or slightly downstream, then swinging the fly through the pool.

We read a few years ago about some anglers who dead-drift streamers. Really? So we had to try it. Cast the streamer like a nymph, letting it sink and go along with the current. Don't be afraid to twitch it a tad here and there, but for the most part let it drift. This works especially when it sinks as deep as possible.

First things first. Stick with a 5-, 6-, or 7-weight outfit because the extra weight of streamers will overpower a lighter rod. Keep your leaders short, from 4 to 7 feet long, 9 feet at most, check it often for frays and nicks. Keep your cast out away from your head; use a flatter swing, and a more open stroke. Cut off your normal tippet and tie on 3X tippet, or a leader tapering down to 2X or 3X.

In big water, you will need to get down deep. You will need a reel or spool loaded with a sink-tip or sinking line. We like a 7-weight or even an 8-weight rod with sinking lines. In big water, your fly should be weighted, and don't be afraid to use a big one, from size 2 to size 6.

What size streamer? What color? What pattern? What flies qualify as streamers, anyway? Favorites include Matukas, Woolly Buggers, leech imitations, Woolly Worms, Muddler Minnows, sculpin, crayfish, and minnow patterns, as well as brook trout and salmon streamers like the Dace, the Spruce Fly, and Mickey Finns and other bucktails. We don't worry so much about specific patterns, but think in terms of shade and color: light and dark, tan or black. Specific patterns just don't seem as important, although a pattern tied with Krystal Flash or Flashabou sure does. Some top streamer-loving anglers swear that streamers tied with lead eyes are the only ones to use.

And size? A matter of choice. From a size 2 as long as your hand to a size 10, streamers will catch fish on any size stream. When we have a fish follow but refuse our streamer, we often tie on a similar pattern in a smaller size and end up catching the finicky fish.

You already know you're supposed to fish streamers in big rivers, right? And you should. But on small streams? You bet. You need to be stealthy and accurate with your casts, but you can finally catch those big trout in those hard-to-get places. Streamers are especially effective in streams holding browns, which tend to hide in hard-to-reach spots, and to be a little more cautious than other species.

Streamers can be fished on any stream with two approaches. Are you after a lot of trout? Or the biggest? If you are after the prince of the pool in a stream, cast upstream to the head of the pool in the most likely look-ing spot, let the fly sink, then strip in line to match the current flow. You may have to try it several times, moving it around, but all at the most likely lies for big fish. We cast only three or four times to the head of a pool before we move to the next pool.

If you are trying to catch a lot of fish in a stream, and you are fishing a pool, position yourself upstream, cast right to left or left to right, closer to you first, maybe 10 to 15 feet out, trying to keep your presentations across and up. Then strip in line, moving upstream 1 to 3 feet with each new cast sequence, making sure to fan out your casts. And you might make 15 to 20 casts to a pool in this sequence. Change things up from time to time by keeping your rod tip high or varying the height, by keeping your rod tip lower, angling off to the side.

Here are a few more tips for fishing streamers:

1. Vary your retrieve speed.
2. Vary the amount of line you strip in on each retrieve.
3. Mend the line from time to time and the streamer will hesitate, or even stop briefly.
4. Most of the time you want the fly to sink, so wait a few seconds after the fly hits the water. But every now and again, if things are slow, strip it immediately when it lands.
5. When you cast with bigger flies, or weighted patterns, remember to open your casting stroke a little bit so you don't hook yourself in the head. A roll cast is effective to get the fly back out to the lie.
6. Sometimes you will see a fish follow the fly. Leave it out there, pick up your rod tip, and let it back down. Strip short at the end, but leave it out there and then pick it up quickly and cast it right back in front of the fish.

FLY FISHING FROM A KAYAK

Purchasing a kayak for fishing is not something that should be done in haste. But it should be done. At first it will require a certain level of bravery, experimentation, patience, balance, and caution. I've been trying to get Williams into one for three years now. He claims he's afraid of water. But I've seen him waist-deep in the San Juan, navel-deep in the Conejos, nipple-deep in the Rio Grande, and he lost his hat in the Animas. (Plus I believe firmly that he partakes in showers. So, what gives?)

Moving on. Choosing the proper vessel is paramount—it took me about two months of research until I felt comfortable making the decision to drop several hundred dollars on a Mini-X, by Malibu Kayaks. But now I have a serious watercraft for getting places few other anglers can access.

But how do you know it's right for you until you actually get in one and try it out? Well, you don't. You'll have to sort of wing it, keeping many things in mind before you actually swipe your card and buy: your height and weight; whether you want an "inny" or a "sit-on-top"; how you will transport it; how coordinated you are; plus versatility, cost, amenities, color, and length.

Kayaks were invented by the Inuit people near the Bering Strait. They created the perfect personal fishing vehicle for traversing their relentless, frigid environment. Anglers should take heed at their ingenuity and sensibility. Kayaks simply get you where no other watercraft can. And with the proper gear, there's no reason why the biggest fish of the season won't find its way into the net.

Purchasing a Kayak

When buying a kayak, an angler must take into account his body weight in proportion to the width and length of the craft. Most websites will list a safe weight range maximum. If the site does not list a weight limit for the kayak, contact the manufacturer or the retailer to find out. Better to be safe than sunk and soppy.

Search for a yak with the fishing add-ons such as rod holders, webbing for your gear, dry boxes, bait tanks (if you choose to fish with other rods besides fly rods), and a platform for standing. This stuff is essential if you want to have fun, comfortable, safe, and rewarding outings.

Mac rigs his kayak for a day's fishing on Hopewell Lake.

Mac in his yak with a stringer in the back.

You might also want to purchase more add-ons. Here is a list of more amenities to make fishing from a kayak safer and more pleasurable.

1. Life vest
2. Padded seat
3. Lightweight paddle
4. Rod leash (so you don't end up just kayaking)
5. Water shoes
6. Small cooler for toting your lunch and beverages

7. Bungee cords for tying down gear
8. Anchor system
9. Chest pack
10. Fishing net
11. Electronic fish finder
12. GPS unit
13. Keel
14. Drift sock

I was yakking a small, private lake in the Texas Panhandle, trolling a weighted Zonker on an outrigged rod about 50 feet behind me. I drifted past an aeration pump close to the dam, when a fish nearly stopped the yak in its tracks.

Thinking I was hung up on the weed beds the whole time, I stripped that thing in believing the heft I felt was only vegetation. Once the fish busted the surface and saw what an ugly mug I had, it went nuts! A few more minutes of fighting and I had netted a 6-pound black bass I have since nicknamed Gatemouth—its mouth was about 5 inches wide!

Types of Kayaks

There are two main designs of kayaks being manufactured these days, with dozens of variations of each. The original design is the cockpit-style, sit-in kayak, or "inny," used most commonly for river running and competitive kayaking. These kayaks are not at all as safe for fishing because:

1. They require a greater sense of balance than sit-on-tops to maneuver safely.
2. They take on water much more readily and are not self-bailing.
3. They lack flat, reachable storage areas for tackle, rods, and gear.
4. They don't typically come with built-in rod holders.

A sit-on-top kayak, however, is the quintessential machine for angling alpine lakes and ponds. These boats are flatter, often wider, more stable, and far more accommodating for anglers and their flotsam and jetsam. A huge array of manufacturers and styles of sit-on-tops add to their allure as well. They are readily affordable and easily customized. Most require little or no help to load up, and no cumbersome trailers, oil, gas, or tags. Plus, kayaks can get anglers into places no other craft can.

Drifting in foot-deep water is possible in many kayaks, which translates into fishing shallow coves as well as the inlets and outlets where

ANGLING KAYAKS

Most angling kayaks are set up for spinning gear, which means there are a few rod holders (basically holes) in which you can drop in a rod with a longer grip. That's a problem for fly rods, since the reel seat is at the very bottom of the grip. Look in some fishing supply catalogs for what's called a fly rod adapter, which will allow you to troll as you paddle with your outrigged fly rods. This is the easiest means of fly fishing, and how I slew the largest bass I've ever caught with a fly rod.

springs and creeks feed into ponds and lakes. Often, bass and trout will sun themselves in these shallows. Without a kayak, many of these places would remain elusive.

KAYAK FISHING METHODS

Trolling

There are several ways to best utilize your kayak. Trolling is the first. I typically strap my outrigged fly rod to one side or the other, and simply troll an assortment of beadheads and streamers about 50 to 75 feet behind as I paddle at a slow, medium, or fast pace. I set the drag so that even a 12-inch fish will take a little line and "buzz" the reel. Once I've hooked a fish, I simply strap down the paddle to the other side and strip the thing in. It's that easy.

Seated Casting

Another mode is casting to structure from a seated position. Paddle up to reed beds, edges, overhanging trees, rocks, and other likely fish-holding spots. Cast your fly toward the structure just as you would if you were wading, and strip in the fly, allowing the excess fly line to gather in your lap. You'll want a longer rod for this, since your line will be only a few feet off the water. You may also wish to have a heavier line weight for this style of fishing, since fish in lakes can grow to enormous sizes. Also, stiffer rods allow for longer, more accurate casts. Vary your strip rate, sometimes letting the weighted flies sink a little between strips.

Standing Casting

If your kayak is stable enough and wide enough, you might even be able to stand up on it and cast from a "platform." I use mine this way if the wind is light and the lake is calm. It allows me to see hidden fish and structure better than sitting at water level. I have caught some hefty bass around lake edges this way, and it's easy to spot those cruising trout as well.

Donning your favorite life jacket, paddle up to the structure you want to fish. Set an anchor if possible. Rise up to a standing position, being careful not to tip over, and cast your usual suspects of flies as if you were Jesus walking on water. But catching fish by this method isn't a miracle, it's a dream. Kayaks simply get you where no other watercraft can.

Jigging

Another not so common way to fly fish from a kayak is by "jigging" with a sinking line and flies such as chironomid imitations that swim in a vertical manner. This often works well when trout are keying in on chironomids headed for the surface. I would have liked to have a sinking or sink-tip line the last time I fished Williams Creek Reservoir north of Pagosa Springs, Colorado. The chironomids were thick, and the trout were leaping out of the water just as the bugs surfaced. I was catching some by dapping a tiny Parachute Adams on the surface, leaving no line at all on the water. But after an hour of that game, my shoulder muscle was burning and I'd had it. I caught a trout that day simply by being in the right place at the right time. A trout leapt directly onto the closed bait well of my kayak. He flopped about, and scared the heck out of me, then flopped back into the drink. I had him for at least the mandatory 8 seconds to consider him "taken." (That's mine and Williams's rule.)

FLOAT TUBES

A float tube, also known as a belly boat or kick boat, is another type of personal watercraft, a one-person floatation device for fly anglers. The first float tubes were doughnut-shaped inner tubes with underwater seats in the "hole," but modern designs include a V-shape with pontoons on either side and the seat raised above the water, so only the angler's legs are submerged. When fishing from a float tube, you'll have to wear a PFD—just as when

Always enter a float tube backwards.

Float tubes can offer great access on smallish stillwaters.

fishing from any other boat—and chest-high waders. But instead of wading boots, when fishing in a float tube you'll wear fins on your feet similar to those used for scuba diving, and use these to propel yourself—hence the term "kick boat."

Float tubes are great for fishing smallish stillwaters, or lakes and ponds with limited wind exposure, or for slow-moving rivers, or stretches of river. They are not recommended for fishing large or fast rivers, or large, windy lakes. In either case, you are all too likely to be swept downstream, or (perhaps somewhat less dangerous but very frustrating) get blown across the lake, with no easy way to get back. Also on large lakes, you'd run the risk of being struck by motorboats, whose pilots might have difficulty spotting you in your float tube, which rides low in the water.

Multiple styles and models of float tubes are available, and as with most aspects of fly fishing, you can also buy various accessories, including anchors and anchor ropes, rod and gear holders and pockets, and even electronic depth sounders and fish finders.

Because you're very low to the water when sitting in a float tube, we recommend a long fly rod, at least 9½ feet, which will allow you to lift your line off the water and cast without difficulty.

There are several obstacles to overcome where float tube fishing is concerned, the trickiest of which is simply entering and exiting the water with this contraption around you. Since Williams gave up on float tubing after a number of years because he's scared of deep water, he often had the pleasure of watching me float from shoreline. I tried being graceful but ending up looking more like a drunken rodeo clown on ice skates about to perform a deep-sea expedition.

I learn pretty fast. Know why? I tried walking forward in flippers once. Don't do it. It's not only a clumsy endeavor, but it's dangerous. I face-planted just once and have never heard the end of it. To walk forward in flippers you gotta walk like a ridiculous duck . . . something you don't want to do in front of Williams, or any fishing buddy. Couple that with holding up an inflated inner tube around your waist, which blocks your view of the ground, and now your insurance agent's face pops into your brain because you know you're about to die while fishing.

After all that, add in that you're carrying an extra-long fly rod and edging up to a body of water typically surrounded by mud or rocks or both. Now, do all that while walking backwards, with a confining safety vest on. Now you see where the debauched ice-skating rodeo clown submarine pilot image comes from?

However, there is a payoff to all this extra work and gear. If you've been a bank fisher your whole life, you've probably always wanted be in the water casting toward the bank, instead of the reverse. And you've also probably always wanted to cover the deep parts of the pond rather than just the edges. Well, with a float tube, you can do just that.

I won't waste the real estate here telling you what type, brand, size, color, or shape of float tube to buy. That's like telling a dude what brand of pickup to purchase. Or how to buy beer. That's your deal. To each his or her own. My concern is what you do once you have the gear. So, here are our First-time Float Tubing Ten Commandments. Please follow them, especially if it's your first time up to the batter's box. And please, when you land your first fish in your belly boat, act like you've been in the end zone before.

1. Gear up as close to the water's edge as possible. This will minimize the number of times you stumble over your flippers and hurt your pride.
2. Know your route to the water—if you do have to walk a ways to the water's edge, you will know where the obstacles are, and how to avoid them.
3. Attach your fly rod to the float tube before entering the water so you have use of both hands. There are typically straps for this, and you can use them to troll while kicking around as well.
4. With flippers on, walk in reverse while on dry ground; this way the flippers won't get caught underneath you and make you trip and fall.

5. Ease yourself into the water backwards until the tube is touching water, then settle in as gently as possible. Kick or "paddle" and fish in reverse, too.

6. Take a net. Lakes and ponds can hold heavy fish, and nets help you land them easier.

7. No matter what, use the restroom before you suit up—#1 and #2. I mean it.

8. Don't float tube with electronics unless they're waterproof, or you're wanting to replace them and you hope to use the excuse, "Honey, it fell in the lake—I needed a new one anyway."

9. Take some snacks and some drinking water.

10. Wear your PFD at all times.

FINDING SECRET FISHING SPOTS

As a group, anglers are a lazy bunch. They (meaning those anglers other than you) choose the path of least resistance, opting to drop a line in the water closest to the road, closest to the trail, nearest the campground, and nearest the parking lot. Even more industrious anglers don't walk far enough away from public access points, giving up to the lure of the water after only a few minutes of walking. This gives you your first few identifiers for a secret trout hot spot.

If you want to get away from the crowds and find your own secret spots, all you need to do is combine a bit of studying with a willingness to explore. It all begins with maps. So get out National Forest maps or topo maps, spread them on the table, and get ready to discover your own secret trout spot.

This summer, we visited the Conejos River, a popular sizable river in southern Colorado. The river fishes well enough even with all the angling pressure it gets. Like most North American coldwater streams of its size (15 to 40 feet wide), the Conejos has many feeder streams that empty into it along its course.

The Conejos is blessed with no fewer than four quality, medium-size tributaries in a 40-mile stretch, and a couple of them aren't much smaller than the main river. Each of them sees a fair number of hikers trekking loop trails. Most of the trails have been constructed to run past alpine lakes and beside the feeder creek. Luckily, few hikers and backpackers fish, and fewer still fish the streams. These loop trails get the most foot and horseback traffic, and that's your clue. Here are some more basic hints for finding secret spots:

1. Don't always assume that heavy hiking pressure means heavy fishing pressure.
2. Even on heavily fished streams, there are sections with less fishing pressure.
3. Find spike trails leading off the loop trails toward lakes and streams.
4. Look for waterfalls. Waterfalls have pools below them that hold big fish. And the water above waterfalls is often difficult to reach.
5. Concentrate on streams flowing into and out of lakes. Many anglers fish lakes and ignore the productive water of the feeder creeks.
6. Look for unnamed lakes. (But check with the appropriate government agency to see if they have been stocked.)
7. Look at the headwaters and feeder streams.

We fished one of these feeder creeks (it is our secret spot, after all, so we can't name it) but did not fish the first meadow where everyone who does hike in chooses to wet a line. Meadows often come out of canyons, and we like fishing canyons. By walking only an hour more upstream, we were able to camp and fish for two days without seeing but one other angler. How did we know about the other meadows and canyons above the famous first meadow? We can read a map.

We can't tell you how many hours we have pored over National Forest maps, Bureau of Land Management (BLM) maps, DeLorme atlases, and topographic maps in search of that one stretch of river that most anglers perceive as either too high up or inaccessible. That chore is easier nowadays, since topo maps for the United States are now on CD-ROM, GPS devices, the Internet, and iPhone apps. Who knows what other technology will hold maps in the future?

On a topo map—whether a real live, hold-in-your-hand map or one on a computer screen or handheld GPS device—green means thick vegetation, blue means bodies of water, and so on. Contour lines are drawn in brown at intervals and give an idea of the shape of the terrain. The closer the contour lines, the steeper the terrain. Either a 7.5-minute or 15-minute map will do.

When you see a blue line (a river) flowing through a tight group of brown lines, the river is moving through a canyon. Study closely, though. Do the lines open up along the way? Do the brown lines go from a straight pattern to a wavy pattern, leaving a greater distance between the contour lines? If so, this could mean the river slows up enough to form some good holding water. Oftentimes, even if the meadow is smallish, beavers can build some amazing dams.

Blue lines can run through V-shaped brown contour lines, and if the lines are fairly close, be assured the water is flowing swiftly down the mountain. So look for where the Vs widen out a bit, and the contour lines are a bit farther apart. That can mean a flatter section of river.

Is the river difficult to access because of the lay of the land? Are those canyon walls really as steep as they look from the road? Sometimes a little legwork will show you another way into those tough spots.

Many lakes are off the trail, and have no established path leading to them. Look hard at the topo map. Often glacially formed lakes will be in groups of several. Most likely, only two or three of them will be large enough and popular enough to merit regular stocking, but at some time in the past, we promise, all those little lakes had fish planted in them. And many of them will be stocked every few years. A tiny alpine tarn can hold some nice fish, especially if the lake is lightly fished. Most anglers would rather toil away at the big-name, larger lake than hike a few hundred yards or a mile to a less-fished lake.

Even fast-flowing streams have sections that hit level ground, where the river slows and widens. Swift streams may also be slowed by beaver ponds. Beaver ponds can hold big fish, even if the impounded stream is tiny. Even if a tiny stream rushes down the mountain, if the beavers have made their homes, the water is frequently deep enough to hold some nice fish. Look for contour lines that open up into a meadow.

Look for springs and incoming streams. The river gets more water and can increase in size and have better water quality. Places that look inaccessible aren't always. Canyons can usually be accessed at some point.

Nontraditional trails, like livestock driveways, can lead to good water. Bushwhacking where there is no trail can lead to surprise trout water.

Government agencies often stock a lake one year and not the next. If the lake didn't endure winterkill, the holdover trout may have grown to bragging sizes. Contact the agency to see if they have stocked the lake in question. And while you're at it, most agencies publish booklets, which list all the available trout water in a state. You'll be amazed to find streams listed that you never knew existed. These are prime candidates for exploration. We found the Dry Cimarron River in New Mexico (formerly a sweet spring creek that has since gone bad) and Lake Dorothey in Colorado this way.

Four-wheel-drive nuts like to drive their vehicles. For them, it's usually all about the four-wheeling, and few take the time to fish while they are in hard-to-access locales. We found another southern Colorado stream this summer (let's call it My New Favorite Stream) where the only accesses were downstream, where the stream hurried down the mountain like it was being poured out of a spout, and the hike up was murderous. And upstream, the only way in was on narrow logging roads with hairpin turns fit only for a small Jeep. No guidebooks ever mention this stream as a viable fishery—too quick, too little, not enough fish. Few locals even knew about My New Favorite Stream. A friend of mine had been studying the map, and we got together when he found that this quick little creek hit a long meadow somewhere in the middle of its downstream course. The Jeep ride took an hour and it was bumpy, but when we reached the meadow, we knew we had found the mother lode.

We caught three species of cutthroats. The trout averaged 12 inches, but we each caught fish bigger than that. And the one that got away was—well, you know the story. So here are a few more words of advice.

Don't always believe what you read or hear about a river or lake. Fisheries have a way of changing over the years. Beaver ponds can be added, river courses altered, fish populations can increase, people lie (yep, it happens), and sections of a river can lie unfished for a long time.

Look for water where the access is by way of lesser-used trails, old logging roads, and four-wheel-drive-only roads. And don't forget that you can always ride horseback on certain trails to make a long trek a lot more endurable.

This is a hit-or-miss science. Sometimes a prospective stretch of stream that has a poor reputation lives up to that reputation. But when you do your homework and you find a secret spot so rich that you won't share the location with anyone but your spouse or your pastor, then it makes all the effort worthwhile.

More Tips for Using Topographic Maps to Locate Trout Streams

Topo maps are excellent resources for locating hidden trout streams. Here's how to use them.

The lay of the land can tell you much about what type of water lies in a given area. A topo map will not only show streams, lakes, small forest roads, county roads, and foot trails other maps won't, but will also illustrate critical vertical elevation changes utilizing gradient lines. The closer together the lines are, the steeper the grade. The farther apart the lines, the flatter the terrain.

Canyon Streams. If canyon pocketwater is in order, look for hidden streams sandwiched between long, closely spaced gradient lines. Since canyon walls are steep, their lines on topo maps are very close together.

Canyon water is often fast-moving and full of boulders and stones that create pockets where trout love to hold. Look for trails that lead to the stream, while making sure to take the elevation change into account. Hiking into and out of canyons can be strenuous and dangerous. Anglers, especially beginners, need to know their limits.

Meadow Streams. Since meadows are by definition flat, wide open areas often hidden at the feet of mountains or hills, they are relatively easy to locate on topographic maps, and can be great places to learn to fly fish. Search for streams that flow between mountains or hills, where the stratified lines are spread far apart. Lines far apart mean flat terrain.

Meadow streams are typically slow, meandering waters with numerous bend pools, overhanging grassy edges, cutbanks, and gravel or silty bottoms. They can be easier to traverse than canyons, but can often be challenging to fish, since the surface can be slick and mirror-like. Slick water might be moving, but since there are no boulders or obstacles to slow or break the water, the surface remains still and flat.

Topography for Safety. It's a good idea to have a topo map of the area at all times when in the wilderness. If the compass or GPS goes awry, a topo map can help identify outstanding landmarks through triangulation and help you regain your bearings. Trust Delorme's Atlas and Gazetteer Series (available for many states; visit www.delorme.com/) for reliability and accuracy. We always have a copy of the area we're visiting reproduced, folded up, and stowed away in our gear so that when we're on the water we know where we are and what to expect just around the bend.

Mark fishing in the canyon

Once, Mac and his brother were fly fishing in the Red River Canyon near Taos, New Mexico. Their plan was simple—hike down the 800-foot La Junta Trail near the Rio Grande junction, fish upstream to the next trail leading out of the canyon, then talk about all the fish they caught that day on the way back to the Jeep.

Instead, things turned sour. They kept fishing upstream, but the trail to get out of the hot-as-an-oven basalt canyon was not as close as they'd thought. The two eventually felt they had no choice but to turn around and hike back—an extra 2 miles of rock crawling and boulder hopping on foot, all with no more water. They barely made it out alive, legs failing, stomachs cramping, and hallucinations of clay frogs in party hats celebrating the moon's birthday. They passed out on the trail multiple times while taking breaks, their skin sizzling in the sun like bacon left too long in a microwave oven. It turned out that, had they packed in a topo of the area, they would have realized that just another few hundred yards past where they'd turned around, the Aguaje Trail was waiting for them.

Tough-to-reach water means that the fish haven't been bothered much with angling pressure and should be bigger and less spooky than trout in high-pressure waters.

You need a fishing buddy.

We all grow up sooner or later. The things we loved so much in childhood somehow faded from our lives as we graduated into real life, got married, had kids. Remember the pleasure of naptime in kindergarten? Remember sharing secrets with your best friend?

Well, most of us have rediscovered the sweet slumber of a nap, only now instead of the cot, we fall asleep in the recliner. And what about best friends? We've still got 'em. It's just that now we just call them fishing buddies.

If you've got a fishing buddy, then you know what we mean. The fishing buddy is the guy or gal who shares their sandwich (you forgot yours), tells you what they're biting, and doesn't complain (much) about horseflies, mosquitoes, and fishing from dusk till dawn.

Like most fishing buddies, we allow ourselves to add inches to any fish we land and reserve the right to lie flat out about the ones we lose. A fishing buddy is not the type to pour salt in your wounds, at least not until you're in a good mood or when you've sheathed your fishing knife. Then it's time to rip you about the fact that you caught more tree limbs than brown trout. A fishing buddy doesn't anger when at dark, two hours past when you agreed to leave, you say "Just one more cast."

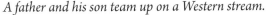

A father and his son team up on a Western stream.

Fishing buddies who have sloshed through streams on fishless days, have slugged down bad camp coffee beside countless campfires, have sat comfortably silent in a bass boat for hours—these are your best friends. Shared experiences, both good and bad, re-create the magic relationships of childhood.

You need someone who can remove hooks from your hand, offer solace when you break your rod, eat a quick lunch in agreed silence on a hanging bluff overlooking the river as the sun sets in myriad colors and both of you, without saying a word, nod at the beauty of it. It might be a corny, knowing nod, one that you'd never share if more guys were around, but with a fishing buddy, implying that the outdoors is a wonderful thing is a-okay. Just don't make too big a deal of it.

My fishing buddy nowadays, for the last decade, over thousands of miles on the road and through countless misadventures is my coauthor, Chad McPhail. For two decades before, it was my brother-in-law, Kenny Medling, who has a head as big as a bison and a brain the size of a brook trout. With both guys, we know certain things about each other, know

One spotter and one angler. Perfect combo.

what to expect from the other after traveling thousands of miles across the country. We know that one of us has surely tied up some extra size 22 Blue-winged Olive patterns; that we will eat Mexican food at some dive at least once on the trip; and that if one of us falls facedown in the river, no photos, never happened. I am very picky about my fishing buddies, but once I get one, they're stuck with me for life. Get a fishing buddy. It's more fun that way.

The rules are easy. We talk fishing until one of us shuts up. We fish all day. We fish together, we give advice willingly, and we take the same without animosity. Ken carries the two-man tent on his shoulders when we backpack (he is short, square, and stout). I carry the food (we don't eat much). Now, if only one of us could cook. Luckily, McPhail is a freakin' gourmet-level chef. I replaced Kenny very well, thank you.

We pack the troutmobile (whichever vehicle Mark is driving at the time is called the troutmobile—for the last few years, it's a four-door Jeep Wrangler) with enough gear to outfit the Mormon Tabernacle Choir. Ken packs the homemade brownies and snickerdoodles his lovely wife Betsy made the night before. McPhail loads us up with energy bars and energy drinks. We eat every last one of whatever it is before we make Raton Pass. Sometimes before we reach the Floating Mesa.

Now, not every angler makes a good fishing buddy. We've hauled some dead weight into the mountains on more than one occasion, people more suited to be bear bait than fishing buddies.

There was the one angler who, as we drove west through New Mexico, surprisingly pulled out a gun and got off two shots at the antelope herd before we wrestled the pistol away.

There was another goober who accompanied us on a daypack trip into the Black Canyon of the Yellowstone River, a day when we happened upon the legendary, elusive Salmonfly hatch. We caught more cutthroat trout than the fishing gods usually allow, but this one wanted to leave early that afternoon and get back to cook dinner. This violates several of the cardinal rules of fishing. First, food is secondary when the fish are rising. Second, you do not leave the river when the fish are still biting. And they were biting, and more than we had ever seen.

His disgruntlement led him to make the unwise decision to chuck rocks at rising trout we were fishing to, and it was all we could do to keep our brother-in-law Dave from tossing his carcass to the maddened, feeding cutts in the cold, swift river.

We've taken the uninitiated on many trips. There was the would-be buddy who only brought ten bucks to last him five days on the road. We ran out of food the second day thanks to that bottomless pit, and he never paid us back the money we loaned him.

We have one friend who shall remain nameless (Coach Randy Denham) whose cigar smoke and overbearing demeanor as captain of our rickety raft on a float trip on the Rio Grande almost caused us to toss him overboard.

And we have this friend whose first trip to the Rockies found him bug-eyed and trembling as we traversed narrow backroads thousands of guardrail-less feet above canyons. We reached the bottom of Wolf Creek Pass at dark, only to find it closed because a tractor-trailer rig had gone off the side. Poor guy still won't go back to Colorado.

And then there was the dude who walked back to camp in the middle of the day to take a nap and set up the tent. We came upon him sleeping peacefully, the tent staked out with our brand new tarp underneath. When we asked him how come he drove eight stakes through the tarp rather than fold the darned thing, he replied that he just figured we had bought too big a tarp. Go figure.

You would think that we would have learned our lesson about fishing with these nincompoops again, but you'd be dead wrong. We understand now that we need to share the fishing buddy rules with new recruits: no guns, no rocks, bring money, and we set up the tent. We consider it part of our job as anglers and outdoorsmen to teach these newbies how a fishing partner is supposed to act. We've introduced Chad Huseman and Drew Perkins and Darrin and Yvonne Murphy and Page McKinney to our fishing buddy waiting list. We brought each one back fairly healthy but certainly better anglers. Each of the candidates is moving up the checklist, but each still has some flaws they need to fix. After all, without a fresh crop of fishing buddies, what would we gripe about?

Two buddies could easily fish successfully from both sides of this still pond.

Outdoor Photo Tips

The art of photography is a complex endeavor, especially when fly fishing and the outdoors are involved. Attempting to do both at once, in the early stages of the learning curve, is cumbersome and comical. Comical, that is, until you drop your brand new camera in the river like Mark did once! We dried that thing out over the rest of the weekend. It still worked!

Try these solutions for taking better fishing pics, and your memories of your adventures in the river will remain just as colorful and vivid as the day you went.

PROPER EQUIPMENT

SLRs

Better cameras take better pictures. Invest in a mid- to high-end SLR (single-lens reflex) camera such as the Nikon D40 or D60, or a Digital Rebel EOS XSi or XTi. Digital SLRs create high-quality, high-resolution shots in a multitude of settings and modes. Many brands are comparable in

We always have a camera around our necks just in case we see a great shot.

price and most in similar price ranges match up well in head-to-head comparisons. Plus, digital SLRs will produce fantastic results.

Point-and-Shoot

Point-and-shoot cameras such as the Nikon Coolpix are very packable, lightweight, and take extraordinarily clear photographs. However, most point-and-shoot cameras limit one's ability to add on lenses and filters that enhance the quality and effects of outdoor picture taking. If a point-and-shoot is the only camera available, experiment with the tips listed below that do not pertain to attaching filters, and fantastic photos can still be achieved.

Tripods and Unipods

Utilize a tripod or unipod with an SLR for super-clear shots when a scenic panorama is involved. Tripods eliminate those out-of-focus shots caused by unsteady hands. Fatigue, hard breathing, and adrenaline jitters are all sporting photography problems that tripods work wonders to solve.

Fly fishing, trail running, kayaking, and many other outdoor activities often take place in very photogenic settings. Utilizing a tripod combined with the proper camera settings can capture crystal clear images, focusing on both the subject and the background if one chooses. Tripods come in various sizes and weights. Get one that's ultra-packable and lightweight, or try a unipod and lugging it around will be nearly unnoticeable.

Polarizers

Circular polarizing filters virtually eliminate the glare and reflection caused by the sun bouncing off water and particles in the atmosphere. Polarizing filters turn ultra-bright rivers into see-through water wonderlands. And when the sky appears hazy and dull on the brightest of days, a polarizing lens will transform the sky into a wonderful, cobalt blue.

Polarizing filters work the same was as polarized sunglasses. The filter on your camera will help you take shots that look exactly as you see the water with your glasses on. For astonishing water pictures, the polarizing filter is a small investment.

The great outdoors can be a great source of inspiration.

How not to take a picture. This was a real "Where's Waldo" composition.

Camera Settings

There are multiple modes to choose from on today's digital cameras. Determining the desired effect of a photograph is the first order of business. Reading the manual that comes with your camera is highly recommended for familiarizing yourself with modes and settings. But to break it down in the simplest of terms, follow our tips below.

For a focused subject in the foreground and a blurred background (this makes the subject stand out dramatically against the background) set the camera dial on "Portrait" (this is often an icon of a female's head), focus the camera on the subject and take the shot.

For a focused background and a blurred subject (this is good for pictures where the background is the star of the show, or for making moving water appear dreamlike and smooth, as well as for certain action shots where the setting is clear but the angler appears to be in fast motion) set the dial to "TV" and set the exposure for 0.3 (1/3 of a second) and focus on the background as the subject passes through the shot. Utilize a tripod for this technique and experiment with the exposure (0.3) time.

For a simultaneously focused subject and background (this is good for capturing a fly fisher in a river in an alpine, mountain setting) set the dial to "Landscape" mode, focus on the angler, and take the shot.

Get some quality camera gear, following these basic tips. Experiment with camera settings, angles, composition, and time of day. Combining these tips and techniques will greatly enhance your future outdoors and fishing pictures.

Tips

Avoid shots that suggest mishandling of fish to be released—avoid jawbreaker shots, gill plate grips, gaffing shots, large stringers of fish, bleeding fish, and similar photos that reflect poorly on anglers.

Shoot from unusual angles when possible—above or below eye level.

Shoot in the morning or afternoon when possible. Side lighting, as opposed to overhead lighting, is preferred. Avoid midday. When you must shoot in strong overhead light, use fill flash.

When shooting large fish, avoid cropping the tail. People want to see the whole fish. But—and there's always a but—if you have a large fish, try different angles, like shooting the head up close, or a shot of the tail being held by the hand as the fish is released, or a shot of the head up front with the back and tail running off into the distance.

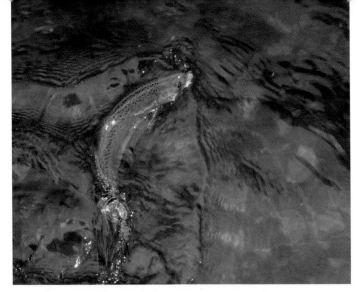

A nice rainbow from Gunnison. Polarized lens creates deeper colors and an unusual close-up creates a cool pic.

Different perspective, not the usual hero shot.

Another way to change perspective.

Avoid crooked horizons.

When submitting photos to accompany an article, shoot with the text in mind—specific lures, backgrounds, tackle, boats. Include scenic, action, and detail shots. Don't submit out-of-focus or poorly exposed pictures. Check slides with at least an 8X loupe to be sure they are tack-sharp.

Take shots of the angler not fishing. Take some of all those things leading up to fishing: changing flies, stringing up the rods, putting on waders, stopping for lunch.

Look for backlit opportunities—an angler silhouette makes a dramatic picture.

Photo Subject Ideas

1. Scenic fishing—all geographic areas and freshwater species
2. Scenic shots of nontypical anglers
3. Scenic shots of shore and boat fishing situations
4. Release shots of all freshwater species
5. GPS and LORAN in use in fishing situations
6. Insect hatches and macro shots of insects
7. Underwater photos of all freshwater species in their natural habitats
8. Weed lines, points, timber, and other structure with an angler in the scene
9. Lures and flies on the surface on the water and in outdoor (other than studio) situations
10. Various shots of fishery management activities: electrofishing (boat and backpack), gillnetting, seining, stocking, creel surveying, public meetings, and more
11. Anglers on and off boats; anglers holding fish with no lure, float, or rod; close-ups of fish being held in and out of water; rod bending shots with no fish, and more

Facing top. Landscape pics enhance your fishing memories.

Facing bottom. Perspective, contrast, shadowing, and timing all play a part in creating a dramatic image.

253

*Fall is a great time to take outdoor shots enhanced
by the natural coloration of the scenery.*

TIPS TO HELP YOU TAKE MORE MEMORABLE IMAGES

Shooting photos outdoors comes with its own set of problems to overcome.

Consider scale or reference when shooting scenics. Mountains are big but
far away, and if you don't have something in the foreground to give them
scale, they pale in the distance. Have your spouse stand off the side and
gaze at the mountains. Use a tree or its limbs or wildflowers in the foreground, off to the side, to make your landscapes seem more majestic.

Don't center your subject. Put your subject to one side or another. Try to
compose a picture, not just take a picture.

Try some shots that are different than the ones you normally take. Instead
of shooting another pic of your grinning fishing buddy holding another
fish, get in close and snap some shots of the fly or lure in the fish's mouth.

Fishing pics don't always have to show you fishing.

Get a picture of him releasing the trout back to the water. How about a photo of your deer blind while standing below it, the trees rising out of it to the sky? Be creative, imaginative. You'll be surprised at the great images you will capture.

Even casual snapshots can bring back nice memories.

Use a flash when you can. Outdoorsmen wear caps and hats and sunglasses, and that means shadows on faces, which are anathema to a good picture. Trying to take a photo of your trophy deep in the woods or early in the morning doesn't allow enough light to frame your subject.

To avoid shadows if you don't have a flash, get your subjects to tilt their caps up, to take off sunglasses, to get out into the light if possible.

If the lighting is poor, the landscape around will look gray and featureless, so shoot closer to the subject, leaving as much of the surroundings as possible out of the photo.

The best way to get a memorable photo is to keep taking pictures. It sounds simple enough but you'd be surprised how many amateur photographers run across a stunning scene and then immortalize it by taking only one shot. The exposure might have been all wrong, the image might be a little blurred, and so on, and all it would have taken to mark the moment would be to take two or three shots and to have bracketed the shot.

Bracket your photos. This means changing your settings up and down on either side of your original photo so you cover your bases.

Movement can be a distraction, ruining a good shot. Yet if used with skill—as seen here and in the image below—can add energy, telling a story.

Mac fishes with his camera uncased and ready to shoot at a moment's notice.

The cheapest way to get a duplicate of a great photo is to do so at the time you take it. By taking several shots of a great photo opportunity, maybe changing up the angle, tightening on the scene, going horizontal and vertical, you get different looks at an incredible setting.

Don't shoot every shot with a horizontal pose. Turn your camera to vertical for a great magazine-style shot.

Keep the horizon square.

Be careful not to have the shot all sky or all land in front of you. Think about breaking each image into horizontal thirds and vertical thirds. Only occasionally will you want to have more than a third of your photo blue sky or grassy meadow.

Be aware of what's in the shot. Don't cut off people's heads; don't have an aspen tree looking like it's coming out of the subject's head, and so on.

Plan shots before you get out in the field or on the water. Think of interesting angles and setups. You might talk your hunting, fishing, or hiking buddies into wearing a red shirt, which shows up great in outdoor scenes, contrasting with all the greens and browns. Thinking ahead will keep you sharp in finding good opportunities when they present themselves.

Don't have too many elements in your photos. Keep them simple and powerful.

Too many photographers want to include a subject's entire body in the photo. This too often means the subjects are too far away, and the result is an uninteresting, distant-looking picture. Tighten in on their upper body, their face, the fish they caught, the rod or the fly they are casting, and so on. What about a close-up of an angler's hands while he or she ties on a fly?

Carry your camera in a cushioned bag. There are a lot of comfortable, cushioned fanny packs on the market, and they will help keep your camera safe and protected from the elements.

The elements can ruin your camera. Heat, cold, moisture, and dirt can all damage your lens and your camera's inner workings. Be conscious of exposing your camera to these elements, and clean it when you get back home. Buy or make a "rain jacket" for your camera. Clean your lens often.

Use filters. The sunlight is harsh at high altitudes. Try warming filters, polarizing filters, and UV filters to get better photos.

Try all your lenses to get outstanding photos. Use a macro lens for a close-up of a feeding squirrel, and a telephoto lens on a grazing mule deer.

Use a tripod every chance you get. This means sharper, cleaner images.

Early and late sun are the best for publishable shots. The high noon sun is usually too harsh.

Try to make a story with each shot or series of shots.

Use a polarizing filter to make great images even better.

BACKPACKING
FLY FISHING

Years ago, we turned to fishing along the back trails initially because we got tired of fishing shoulder to shoulder with so many other fishermen. As the recreational fishing public continues to grow in staggering numbers, and the waters become more and more crowded, the pressure on this country's fisheries will increase. Hiking into the backcountry is one the most obvious ways to get away from all the other anglers.

The combination of backpacking and fishing gets you to places you might not otherwise visit, some of the prettiest places on earth. Fishing for timberline trout amid stands of evergreen forests, under craggy peaks, and standing over verdant meadows is what backpack angling is all about. Backpack angling takes you into the Appalachians, the Rockies, the Cascades, the Sierra Nevada. Around wherever you live, on some weekend, you might be able to visit wilderness areas such as the Pecos Wilderness or Cruces Basin Wilderness to find really primitive settings.

The trout may not be as big as those found in year-round lowland trout lakes and streams, but they are usually wilder and much prettier. What's more, you won't see many people in these places off the beaten path. Casting away the day under azure skies, away from crowds, is indescribably wonderful. "Into the backcountry" doesn't necessarily mean slogging 25 miles through bear-infested forests (even though that kind of adventure is one of our favorites). Most anglers fish public accesses, such as bridges, and don't wander far from these easily accessible spots. So if you can be just a little more adventurous than your average angler, you can find more solitude and get to trout that have rarely seen a fly. There are thousands and thousands of miles of rarely fished streams teeming with wild and stocked trout. Thousands of high country lakes dot the mountains, and many are fished by only a handful of anglers in a decade.

Most backcountry trout are correctly thought to be rather easy prey—though just when you get cocky, you'll run into fussy trout. You rarely see mountain trout refusing attractor patterns in favor of smaller, more hatch-specific patterns. However, backcountry trout are wary of any shadows, footfalls, and bad casts. They spend much of their day hiding from raccoons, ospreys, eagles, mink, larger trout, and other predators, including bumbling anglers. So what's there to lose? Even if you fail to catch a trout, you'll still be in some beautiful country.

How do you begin backpack angling? What kind of backpack fits you best? One of the primary mistakes beginning backpackers make is to pack too much stuff. Another mistake is that many neophytes purchase packs and hiking boots that do not fit their needs or their bodies. Make sure to consult a professional so that your gear matches your requirements. We can attest that ill-fitting equipment can make a backpacking trip a nightmare. Internal frame backpacks are ideal for adults entering the backpack angling craze, so leave behind that circa 1968 external frame pack that's hung on the wall in the garage.

And if you take kids along, remember to integrate them into the trip by allotting them chores. Let the kids set the pace, and keep the trip short, at least on the first few outings. As for gear for kids, purchase a frame pack, since this style easily adjusts to their growing bodies over the years.

As for angling gear, fly rods and spincasting gear are tailor-made for the backpacker. Alpine anglers can now find quality graphite fly rods in multipiece outfits, perfect for lashing onto your backpack. Many seasoned trail hikers prefer the old two-piece rods so that they may employ the rod tube as a walking stick.

It all starts with a good backpack. Go with an internal frame.

A typical alpine lake

Inset: Kenny crossing a feeder creek to Conejos.
Above. Patches of snow remain even into July at Trappers Lake.

Sure, there are some negatives to sleeping under the stars—bears, ticks, lightning, blisters, mosquitoes, getting lost, hypothermia, altitude sickness, and so on. But what the heck, in the big city you can get E. coli poisoning from a burger and paper cuts from file folders. The only negative we run into every time in the backcountry is that we have to eat each other's cooking.

As we walk along the water, do we carry our rods with the rod tips forward or backward? Keep the rod tip up. Secure the fly. Do not walk with the fly in your hands or swinging loosely. Two ways to carry the rod—rod pointed forward, rod pointed behind you. Both work. We carry ours pointed to the sky unless we are going through brush or trees, in which case we carry ours pointing forward.

TOP TIPS FOR BACKPACK ANGLING

1. Keep it light.
2. Make sure your backpack and boots fit well.
3. Don't buy the largest backpack off the rack. You'll only be tempted to fill it up.
4. Buy the best equipment your budget will allow. Buy cheap and you'll regret it.
5. Learn how to read a map and a compass.
6. Learn first aid techniques.
7. Bring warm clothes and layer them for greater warmth.
8. Leave word of your plans with family or friends.
9. Did we mention to keep it light?

These are the types of pristine streams you can reach by backpacking.

ESSENTIAL BACKPACK-ANGLING GEAR

1. Fly rod (go for a three- or four-piece).
2. Only one box of flies or lures—keep it simple.
3. Polarized sunglasses are the most important item. Without them, your eyes are in danger from errant casts. Without them you cannot see beneath the water's surface. And don't forget a brimmed hat or cap.
4. Leaders, tippet, nippers, forceps, floatant. Do not bring a vest. Keep it simple. Try a small fanny pack or chest pack.
5. Waders? Don't bother. Wade wet in lightweight wading boots and neoprene socks. Some friends glue felt to old tennis shoes but they don't drain very fast, and felt can transmit troublesome organisms.

ESSENTIAL BACKPACKING GEAR

1. A backpack that fits your body and pursuits.
2. Top-flight hiking boots—waterproof if you can afford them.
3. Raingear.
4. Warm clothes. We like Polarfleece tops. Remember to layer.
5. First aid kit.
6. Survival kit.

7. Food (lots of calories to replace those you will be burning) and a camp stove. The best on the market is the MSR Whisperlite.

8. Water (the most important item in your pack). Drink plenty of water but make sure to use a quality water filter, the most effective means of combating Giardia.

9. Tent (not one of those cheapies from the big discount stores).

10. Sleeping bag and pad. We like the ThermaRest self-inflating pad for a good night's rest.

11. Bear bag and lightweight but strong rope. You need to store your food away from camp by tethering it above the ground over an appropriate limb.

12. Noncotton socks. Trust us, don't wear your white cotton socks. Buy wick-away socks and your tootsies will be better off.

HIKING FLY BOX

1. One light hiking fly box (which honestly is sometimes two medium-sized boxes)

2. Two dozen #12–#16 attractors (Royal Wulff, Parachute Adams, Irresistible Wulff, Patriot, Royal, or Lime Green Trude)

3. A dozen #12–#18 caddis patterns (Elk-hair Caddis in different colors, plus Henryville and Goddard Caddis)

4. A half dozen Stimulators sizes #12–#16 (orange and yellow)

5. Two big stonefly patterns (Sofa Pillow or similar)

6. Two big rubber-legged patterns (Madame X, Turk's Tarantula, or similar)

7. Two dozen #14–#20 beadhead nymphs (Prince Nymph, Hare's Ear, or similar)

8. A half dozen #16 traditional nymphs

9. A half dozen #16–#20 emergers and spinners

10. Two #8 stonefly nymphs

11. One streamer (I like a Woolly Bugger with a heavy nose)

A stile provides convenient access to this river trail.

Trappers Lake in the high country

FLY-FISHING
ETIQUETTE
(AND WHAT *NOT* TO DO)

Be polite when buying gear in the fly shop. Ask questions, and actually BE the newbie that you are. Don't pretend you're not one. They'll respect and expect this honest behavior far more than the wannabe poser fly fisher attitude who think they know everything. Fly shops have been known to dispose false information to guys like that.

Tip a guide, if you hire one. Especially if you catch fish. Even if you don't, the guide still deserves a tip for all the info he or she dispensed.

Don't make a big scene when you catch trout on a river. Feel free to celebrate. But act like you've been in the end-zone before. We've seen guys do end zone dances after catching a trout and the only purpose it served was to show they'd not caught many.

Don't encroach on other people's water. If you wanna leapfrog around a guy, take a detour through the woods, don't walk just behind him. A good rule of thumb for passing an angler is to go around them and put in on the river in a place where it might take at least half an hour for them to fish upstream to where you put in. By that time, the water you have fished will be "rested" and they can still catch fish without them being spooked. In fly fishing, anglers walk upstream on a river so you don't want to jump in front of someone and make them have to get out and go around. Be aware as you walk behind them—don't get too close. Your footfalls, shadows, and general presence cause problems for fish and anglers.

Just drop in a good ways in front of another angler, estimating that you'll both have hours of fishing before you hit the water the other has fished. And as a long rodder, you'll need plenty of room to backcast and forward cast. Since trout spook so easily, you just can't mix it up in the nearby water. Be nice.

If you stop to talk to an angler to pry info, respect them. Don't invade their space or time. Most fly rodders are eager to share what is working, or not working, but don't assume anything. They may be sitting on the mother lode, working a huge fish, seeing the most prolific hatch ever, that sort of thing. In that case, you can understand their proprietary nature.

Don't walk too quickly along the bank, missing some great fishing spots. Move slowly and watch carefully what's happening in and around the water—you'll greatly improve your chances of success.

Don't urinate or defecate in or near the river or near the trail. Take a hike and do that elsewhere. You run the risk of being seen, for one thing. And two, your bodily waste adds harmful bacteria and ammonia to the riverine environment.

Don't leave trash of any kind behind on the river. Cans, cigarette butts, fish eggs, old leaders, and all other manmade debris needs to be removed. Pack all of that out, please. If you find trash someone else left behind, pack that out, too.

If and when you encounter another angler on the stream, exchange information on what's working and what isn't. If and angler says a #18 Goddard Caddis is working for him, and you don't have one, offer him a fly or two in trade.

When in Rome, fish upstream like everyone else does. Ninety-eight percent of fly fishers fish upstream. Downstream anglers disturb the water up above every other angler on the river. Don't do that unless you're the only angler on the stream. It's okay to let your fly dead-drift downstream, but actually covering water downstream is a breach of etiquette.

Don't bring your dog fly fishing. Dogs jump through the water and scare trout, and also disturb trout redds. Plus, Williams and I both have

been cornered by unpredictable canines whose owners were too aloof or spacey or mean to keep their predators on leashes.

Obey the law! Never try to "stretch" fishing regulations, for example by filling a creel with fish, taking them back to the freezer, then fishing again later in the day. Don't keep fish from a catch-and-release section. Don't violate the slot limits. Know the legal requirements for the water you're fishing, and obey them. Not to do so is poor sportsmanship.

During the spawn, don't fish near the inlets and outlets of lakes—many lakes will have regulations regarding this. Stay legal.

If you catch a female trout and eggs are dribbling from her, get her back into the water as quickly as you possibly can.

Don't park right next to the stream. Fuel and oil leaks can contaminate the water. You can cause bank erosion, too. And your vehicle will be in the way of other fishers.

Don't shuffle your feet and try to stir up insect to cause a feeding frenzy for your buddies downstream. It's the equivalent of chumming water.

Playing a trout too long will kill it. Bring it in quickly and try your best not to handle it too much. Disturbing the protective slime on its body will eventually kill it, too. Be sensitive with trout.

If you know the fish you've landed is not going to make it, kill it quickly. Take a river rock and use it to crush the fish's head. This may seem cruel, but isn't leaving it to suffer more cruel?

Make sure your fly spends less time in the air, and more on the water. No angler ever caught a flying fish—at least not in a trout stream.

On the other hand, don't walk along the bank too slowly, either. Our advice is to "cover water."

Fly fishing isn't like worm dunking. If you have fished with worms, you know that you can sink that baby and let it swirl and have the trout tug at it and they'll keep coming back for it till they get it. Won't happen with flies. Trout feel the sting and they avoid that fly at all costs. Don't waste time going after the trout that hit and missed. A few times back at him and then move on. Pay attention! Be careful when scrambling on rocks or walking along the bank while holding the fly in your fingers. All it takes is for a limb to snag the loose fly line, and the hook will sink right into your hand. Secure the fly to your rod (on the hook keeper or in the cork handle) so you don't have to waste time crying and bleeding all over the bank.

Don't forget to debarb all your hooks. When you hook yourself—for you most certainly will at some point—if you have not debarbed your hook, you will be in for a big surprise. Those barbed flies don't back out easily. You'll lose flesh, or if it's stuck in the right spot, it won't be backing out at all. Rather, it will have to be removed by making it go forward. That's right: You'll have to push the point forward and out through the skin so you can cut it with pliers. Gross, huh? Well, there is a slightly less gross method (see page 177). But all this trouble can be avoided by crushing down the barb with pliers. Many anglers who tie their own flies debarb the hooks right at the tying table.

Watch a stretch of water for a minute before casting. You'll be able to see fish rising or feeding under the water and then you can formulate a plan of attack, how you'll position yourself, how you'll cast, and how you'll drift.

Don't use too much rod for the water and the fish. That's a problem that's hard to fix unless you are willing to drop cash on several rods. A lot of the so-called "beginner" rods are 6-weight, and that's just too thick and stiff for your basic trout stream. The pitch for the 6-weight is that it's versatile, you can fish for big bass and for small trout with the same rod. Truth is you can, but you won't want to. A 4- or 5-weight is better for trout—even a 3. Modern rods can handle heavier fish even though they're slimmer and lighter than their forebears. You'll feel the difference with a lighter rod when you cast and when you feel a take and play the fish.

Don't wade through the fish.

Don't wade where you should be fishing. We know it's fun to wade. That's part of the appeal of fly fishing. But don't wade unless you have to. The more you wade, the greater your chances of spooking trout. Trout can hear and feel your Sasquatch footfalls from a long ways off. Think stealth.

Know where you're stepping before you move. If you can't see the bottom, maybe you're in over your head. Slide your feet, always keeping one on the ground or river bottom. Shuffle. Sashay. Mosey, if you will. But whatever you do, don't beeline rush it.

Wear the newfangled, nonslip "sticky rubber" soles. Soles that incorporate metal studs are even better. A lot of the wading boots are going to sticky rubber because felt can transmit whirling disease and other bad things. We've tried them all, but they just don't hold on slippery rocks as well as felt does. We're hoping that better nonfelt materials become available in the near future.

When—not if—you start to slide down a big rock or the side of a hill, lie back against said rock or said hill. When anglers get top-heavy, they topple over and things get dangerous rather quickly. Keep your rod in your hand farthest away from the hill; keep your other hand close to the rock or hillside so you stay parallel and able to grab hold of something.

Don't set the hook hard on a trout as you would on a bass. Strike too hard and "pop goes the weasel." Lift the rod tip. That is all.

Wear polarized sunglasses or don't fly fish. Period. That said, also have your polarized glasses on a lanyard of some kind so they don't fall off into the wine-dark abyss. Because they will, you know.

Test your knots. Test your leader and tippet. Don't lose the biggest fish of the day because you didn't do a little preventive maintenance. After each catch or snag, test your knots.

Don't be leery of changing flies. If one isn't doing you justice after 15 to 30 minutes, and you're presenting the fly in a righteously drag-free manner, change it.

If you are getting strikes but not hooking up, don't blame the fly first. Look to see what other parts of the cast, drift, and hook-set you might be doing incorrectly.

Don't be fooled by randomness. You may have caught a trout quite by accident or random luck, but that doesn't mean what you did will work again. Sometimes the exception works. Don't get stuck on your favorite fly at the expense of missing fish. Randomness does work every blue moon but you better not count on it. Trout work on instinct.

If a trout takes your fly but you miss the fish, you can try a couple more times, especially if you change flies. Give it a good shot but didn't waste valuable time going after just one fish. You can always let the trout settle back into its routine and go back later in the day.

It's easy to stand so close to the bank that you scare every trout within 10 feet. Don't.

More power on your forward stroke (cast) does not equal more line being cast. It means trouble. Stay smooth and keep things tight, short, and controlled.

Don't wade a deep, dangerous, torrential river your first time out. Keep it manageable, and wet wade a small feeder creek or tributary first. Get your feet wet first (pun intended). As a matter of fact, wade less rather than more. The more you are out of the water, the less chance of you disturbing the good water.

Don't use the little faux lamb's wool patch on your vest for keeping flies. If the barb is bent down, which it should be, you'll spend half a fishing day trying to get it out.

We have broken several rods in our day. Only two were on fish. All the others were broken by leaving a vehicle door open and leaning the rod into the crevice. Dumb move. Your buds don't know you have leaned your rod there. They will unknowingly close the door on them. Great friends, huh? Don't ever lay your rod down on the ground, either. Prop it. Hold it. But don't lay it on the ground.

Also, don't leave your rod lying on the roof of your vehicle while pulling your boots and socks off at the end of the day. Mark and I drove off once without putting his in the Jeep first. Remember that moment in *Raising Arizona* when Hi remembers he left the baby in the middle of the road? That was us when we realized there was only one rod tip between us.

Same goes for leaving your fly box on the hood. Williams lost hundreds of dollars worth of flies in the Jemez Mountains like that once. Not to mention a pricey fly box. He nearly cried. (MDW: I did when you weren't looking, Mac.)

Don't buy expensive fly boxes and then expect to use them. The fancy fly boxes are super for show, for your study or barrister bookcase or shadowbox, and even for a once-in-a-lifetime trip somewhere special, but for the most part, they are not as utilitarian as the cheap floatable foam boxes.

Don't unknowingly pull the rod tip up too far as the fly floats downstream. This causes drag and for the insect/fly to move unnaturally. It also pulls the fly away from a feeding fish.

A good place for beginners is a shallow brook trout stream like this one.

Cell phones on the water are a big no-no. Don't just turn them off. Leave them in the car, unless you have a smartphone and are using it to add photos and info to your angler's journal app or as your GPS. The idea is to use the phone for good and not for chatting or doing office work or that sort of thing.

If you're fishing a roadside, don't slam your vehicle doors and warn all the trout that you're there to catch them. Think stealth.

Never walk behind someone who is fly casting. Or passing gas. Or both.

When flies get snagged on underwater rocks, don't tug on the line to free them. Instead, reel in the slack as you approach the fly where it's submerged in the water, follow the leader down to the fly with your fingers, and free the fly from the obstacle. This will save you tons of flies over the course of a season.

Don't wear your chest waders to fish a shin-deep stream.

A store-bought fly costs 2 bucks. If you get one stuck in the trees, and you will, look at the risk-reward factor. Is it really worth it to cross the dark, deep pool of which you have no idea the depth just to recover that fly that hasn't been working anyway?

Rookies will often cast to the same rising fish over and over without success. They'll change flies, but the ones they select are too similar to the one that's not working. The trick often is drifting a dropper nymph or stripping a Woolly Bugger in front of the trout. Or going with a much bigger or much smaller fly. Summary: change depth or change size.

Bird's nests: It's just easier to cut the line and cut your losses. Start over and tie on a new leader and a new fly.

Bring some snacks and water, even if you parked along the road, because you'll inevitably fish farther and longer than you thought.

Put together the most complete first aid kit you can. Add a smaller version for your vest or fanny pack. Even better, take a first-aid class so you know how to use the kit. At least bring along the first aid handbook so you can read about how to tape your sprained ankle.

Check for frays on your leader and tippets before you start out, and throughout the day.

Brown trout feed voraciously at night if you are inclined to fish at night and local laws and regulations allow. In fact, in some watersheds the largest browns are almost exclusively nocturnal.

Fly fishing is supposed to be fun, a sport. Don't make it unnecessarily serious or too religious or too competitive.

Protect yourself from the sun. More and more anglers are wearing sun gloves to fight the harmful effects of ultraviolet rays.

Under Armour (Cold Gear) is ideal for those cold mornings on the water. Layer for more warmth and the ability to take off layers as the day warms.

In our technological world, many anglers travel by automobile with the luxury of a cellular phone, a convenience many can't do without (though they ought to). Cell phones in the car (and turned off when on the water) are a good way to protect against all the outdoor dangers. You can also carry a CB radio (remember those?) or another kind of handheld radio.

If you are not an accomplished outdoorsperson and you will be venturing deep into the wilderness hiking to a distant lake or stream, make sure you're in the company of someone who is accomplished.

Pack a small survival kit, travel with a compass and the appropriate maps, and learn how to use them properly.

And what about dangers you might encounter? How about hypothermia, altitude sickness, lightning, extreme sunburn, landslides, high water, falling, sharp rocks, slippery rocks, scree slopes, tree limbs and other naturally sharp objects which can poke eyeballs. Dress in layers in the higher elevations, wear sunglasses to protect your eyes, wear shoes with grip soles and ankle support, bring along raingear and warm clothes.

A wide-brimmed hat keeps the sun off your face, ears, and neck.

Pack sunblock, sunscreen, or suntan lotion, even if it's cloudy overhead. You can buy the waterproof kind, but the best idea is to keep applying it throughout the day.

Wear a cap. Better yet, wear a hat so the brim protects your ears (or your balding pate) from sunburn.

Trout don't always face upstream. They face into the current. Current twists and turns, so don't get fooled.

Raingear, anyone? You're going fishing, so the odds that it will downpour just increased significantly. And a cheap rain parka folds up as small as a bandanna and fits nicely in your vest or tackle box. After you decide fly fishing is the sport for you, you'd do yourself a favor to spend $100 to $300 on a quality, breathable fishing jacket made for rain, snow, and wading.

You'll find paths on any fished river. That means that angler after angler tends to cast to the same pools, the same lies, the same water as the previous one. That also means that trout in waters that never see casts are never seeing flies. Cross the river and get yourself to unfished water.

Your leader and tippet will weaken over time and when exposed to light. If you have spools of tippet and packages of leaders from the previous season, toss them. No need to take any chances in case you hook the big one. And while you're at it, take out each of your fly rods and line, cast them in the yard, and inspect the ferrules and guides.

Look in your tackle box or fly vest and check off the basics. Put in an extra spool of tippet because you have no idea how much tippet is left on the spools in your vest pocket. Do you have enough split-shot? You know you'll need extra "strike indicators" since you forgot your six-year-old lost all your bobbers on that tiny pond back in October.

Pack some insect repellent. The mosquitoes probably will be worse than you think, and the no-see-ums can see you.

Did you leave your polarized sunglasses on the dashboard? Double-check before you hike in 2 miles. Polarized glasses cut the glare, and if you're hiking, protect your eyes from branches. Slip your glasses in your vest or fanny pack so you don't run the risk of leaving them behind. (Or do as Williams does, and pack two of everything.)

It's not just having the right gear, but knowing how to use it.

Fishing at altitude? Don't forget how cold it can get in a flash. Set your fleece jacket in the car behind the seat just in case.

Come the start of summer, your fly box doesn't have many flies in it anymore, and your tackle box is lonely. Most of your artificials are in a fish's lip or a low-lying tree limb. Make a shopping list, get online or open a catalog, and fill your order. You deserve it. After all, you haven't fished in months.

Inevitably, you'll have slack in your line after many of your casts. Two things to always keep in mind: First, strip in line with your off hand (your line hand) and it'll pull through the guides. Second, lift your rod tip slowly, in a controlled fashion, as you strip. The slack will collect at your feet so watch that it doesn't get caught up in weeds or limbs.

Beginners get overwhelmed with all the facets of fly fishing, and one common mistake is to clamp down on the fly line with the index finger of the rod hand. If you do that, you won't be able to strip line. Once you start using two hands, which is not a first-day concept, keep a loose but in-contact feel on the line.

If you keep getting drag or microdrag on your line or leader, try to move to a different position. You'll be surprised how often that lessens drag.

Always label fly line spools with their line weight. Label the tag end and reel end of fly line on spools, too.

The most important "rule" of etiquette in fly fishing is the Golden Rule your mother taught you: Treat others as you wish to be treated.

RECOMMENDED READING

BACKPACK ANGLING

Karen Berger. *Hiking and Backpacking: A Complete Guide.*
New York: W.W. Norton, 1995.

Victoria Logue. *Backpacking in the 90s.* Birmingham, AL:
Menasha Ridge Press, 2001.

John Shewey. *Alpine Angler.* Portland, OR: Frank Amato
Publications, 1995.

Mark D. Williams. *The Backpacking Flyfisher.* Birmingham, AL:
Menasha Ridge Press, 2001.

FLY TYING

Charlie Craven. *Charlie Craven's Basic Fly Tying: Modern Techniques for
Flies that Catch Fish.* Harrisburg, PA: Headwater Books, 2008.

Peter Gathercole. *The Fly-Tying Bible: 100 Deadly Trout and Salmon Flies
in Step-by-Step Photographs.* Barron's Educational Series, 2003.

Dave Hughes. *Essential Trout Flies: Step-by-Step Tying Instructions for
31 Indispensable Pattern Styles and their Most Useful Variations.*
Harrisburg, PA: Stackpole Books, 2000.

Dave Hughes. *Trout Flies: The Tier's Reference.* Harrisburg, PA:
Stackpole Books, 1999.

Skip Morris. *Fly Tying Made Clear and Simple.* Portland, OR:
Frank Amato Publications, 2002.

ENTOMOLOGY

Dave Hughes. *Handbook of Hatches: Introductory Guide to the Foods
Trout Eat & the Most Effective Flies to Match Them.* Harrisburg, PA:
Stackpole Books, 2004.

Dave Hughes and Rick Hafele. *Western Mayfly Hatches*. Portland, OR: Frank Amato Publications, 2004.

Gary Lafontaine. *Caddisflies*. New York: The Lyons Press, 1989.

Skip Morris. *Fly Fisher's Guide to Western River Hatches*. Portland, OR: Frank Amato Publications, 2002.

Dick Pobst. *Trout Stream Insects: An Orvis Streamside Guide*. New York: The Lyons Press, 1991.

Dick Pobst. *The Caddisfly Handbook: An Orvis Streamside Guide*. New York: The Lyons Press, 1998.

Carl Richards and Bob Braendle. *Caddis Super Hatches: Hatch Guide for the United States*. Portland, OR: Frank Amato Publications, 1997.

Jim Schollmeyer. *Hatch Guide for Western Streams*. Portland, OR: Frank Amato Publications, 2003.

Jim Schollmeyer. *Hatch Guide for Lakes*. Portland, OR: Frank Amato Publications, 1995.

Shane Stalcup. *Mayflies: Top to Bottom*. Portland, OR: Frank Amato Publications, 2002.

Dave Whitlock. *Dave Whitlock's Guide to Aquatic Trout Foods*, 2nd edition. Guilford, CT: Lyons Press, 1997.

PHILANTHROPY

We at Stonefly Press feel that it's important to view ourselves as a small part of a greater system of balance. We give back to that which nourishes us because it feels natural and right.

Stonefly Press will be donating a portion of our annual profits to conservation groups active in environmental stewardship. We encourage all our readers to learn more about them here, and encourage you to go a step further and get involved.

Bonefish & Tarpon Trust
(www.bonefishtarpontrust.org)

Riverkeeper
(riverkeeper.org)

California Trout
(caltrout.org)

Trout Unlimited
(www.tu.org)

Coastal Conservation Association
(joincca.org)

Western Rivers Conservancy
(westernrivers.org)

Friends of the White River
(friendsofwhiteriver.org)

INDEX

A

Ælian's Natural History, 74
annelids, 71
ants, 71, 183, 184, 185
    fly patterns, 184
Apache trout, 132–33
    See also trout
aquatic insects, 183–84
    See also insects
arbor knot, 62, 97
    See also knots
Asher, 84, 85, 185
    See also dry flies
Atlantic salmon, 134

B

backcast, 102, 103, 104, 106
    See also casting
backhand cast. *See* cross-body cast
backpacking, 261–69
    gear for, 265–66
baitfish, 135, 206, 213, 217, 223
Barr, John, 80
bass, 157
beadhead flies, 163
    Beadhead Princes, 204
    See also flies
beaver ponds, 219–23, 236, 237
beetles, 71, 184
belly boat. *See* float tubes
Berners, Dame Juliana, 74
Best, Thomas, 75
Boke of St Albans (Berners), 74
boots, 199
    wading boots, 18–19, 20, 276
bow-and-arrow cast, 113, 116–17, 194, 222
    See also casting
Brassie, 82, 83
    See also nymphs

breathable waders, 14–16
brook trout, 128–30, 140, 219
    See also trout
brown trout, 122, 127–28, 140, 279
bugs. *See* insects

C

caddisflies, 68, 69, 78, 206, 212, 213, 215
cameras, 247–48, 250
    See also photography, outdoor
casting, 4–5, 98–121, 277
    at beaver ponds, 221, 222, 223
    bow-and-arrow cast, 116–17
    and chest packs, 22
    cross-body cast, 106–7, 108, 113
    in difficult waters, 188–95
    false cast, 101
    high-stick nymphing, 160, 161–64
    from kayaks, 230–31
    from lake shores, 208–10
    one-handed cast, 99–101
    in pocketwater, 211–12
    positioning casts, 147–53
    reading the water, 157–59, 160
    roll and modified roll cast, 102–5
    standard cast, 108–12, 120–21
    steeple cast, *109*, 113–15
    streamers, 223–26
catch-and-release, 173–77
caterpillars, 71
cell phones, 278, 279
char. *See* brook trout; lake trout
chest packs, 22–23, 26
chest waders, 14, 16, 17, 278
chironomids, 71, 83, 206, 231
clinch knot, 63
    See also knots
Compleat Angler, The (Walton), 74–75

Concise Treatise on the Art of Angling, A
    (Best), 75
Conejos River (CO), 234–35
Copper John, 80–81
    Red, 196, 204, 218
    See also nymphs
craneflies, 71, 184, 215
crayfish, 213, 215
crickets, 71, 184
cross-body cast, 106–7, 108, 113
    See also casting
crustaceans, 71, 135
cutthroat trout, 74, 130–31
    See also trout
Czech nymphing, 164, 166
    See also high-stick nymphing

D
damselflies, 71, 82, 206
Damselfly Nymph, 82
    See also nymphs
DeLorme's Atlas and Gazetteer Series,
    235, 238
Denny, John, 74
didymo (*Didymosphenia geminata* algae),
    18
dobsonflies, 71
double-taper line, 36, 37
    See also lines
dragonflies, 71, 82, 206
dry flies, 74, 75–79, 84–85
    choosing one, 86–87
    dropper rigs, 214–15, 217–18
    floatants for, 29–30
    presentation of, 76, 153–57
    in tailwaters, 191
    types of, 76–78
    See also flies

E
Elk-hair Caddis, 78, 84, 86, 87, 214, 268
    See also dry flies

F
ferrules, 53, 95, 96
    See also rods

fiberglass rods, 11
    See also rods
first aid kit, 279
fishing shirt, 12–13
flies, 68, 73, 74–93
    avoiding drag, 156, 164
    for backpacking, 266, 268
    for beaver ponds, 221
    buying, 92–93
    changing, 276, 279
    choosing one and tips for, 86–88
    dry flies, 74, 75–79
    fly boxes, 38–39
    freeing stuck, 185–87, 278–79
    for high-stick nymphing, 163
    inspecting, 196
    matching the hatch, 68, 88–92
    streamers, 223–26
    for tailwaters and small steams,
        191–93
    terrestrial patterns, 184–85
    tying, 91–92
    using multiple, 213–18
    wet flies, 79–84
floatants, 29–30
    and dry flies, 75
floatation devices. *See* personal
        watercraft; personal floatation
        devices (PFDs)
floating lines, 38
    See also lines
float tubes, 231–34
fly boxes, 38–40, 277
    for backpacking, 266, 268
fly fishing
    and backpacking, 261–69
    etiquette and advice for, 271–83
    finding spots, 234–39
    fishing buddies, 241–44
    hiring a guide, 200–204
    packing for/essential gear, 198–200
    popularity of, 1–2, 8–9
    spring to-do list, 195–98
    tying knots, 59–65
    types of waters for, 188–95, 204–12,
        219–23

using a kayak and float tubes, 226–34
   See also casting; gear; tackle; skills
fly shops, 11, 201, 271
forceps, 28
forward cast, 149
   See also casting

G
gear, 11–35
   for backpack-fishing, 262, 265, 266
   essential, 199–200
   fishing shirt, 12–13
   floatants, 29–30
   fly boxes, 38–39, 38–40, 266, 277
   hats, *280*, 281
   hook removers, 28
   inspecting, 195–97
   leader and tippet, 33–34
   leader straightener, 29
   nets, 26–27
   nippers, 27–28
   polarized sunglasses, 30–33, 136, 149,
      265, 276, 282
   raingear, 198, 281
   reels, 34–35
   vests, packs, and lanyards, 21–26
   waders, 14–17
   wading boots and shoes, 18–20
   See also tackle
Giardia lamblia, 198
Gila trout, 133
   See also trout
Gold-Ribbed Hare's Ear, 80, *81*, 83, 86,
      196, 218, 268
   See also nymphs
graphite rods, 43
   See also rods
grasshoppers, *68*, 71, 184
guide pants, 16, 17
guides, hiring, 135, 188, 200–204, 271

H
hammer cast, 106
   See also casting
handshake knot, 63
   See also knots

hats, 198, *280,* 281
high-stick nymphing, 160, 161–64, 212
   See also casting
hip waders, 14, 16
   rubber, 11
hooks
   debarbing, 173, 176, 274
   hook removers, 28
   removing barbed, 177
House and Lot, 68, 84, 85, 91
   See also dry flies
Humpy, 77, 193, 196, 218
   See also dry flies

I
inchworms, 184, 185
insect repellent, 282
insects, 67–73
   aquatic, 183–84
   caddisflies, 69
   chironomids and midges, 71
   mayflies, 70
   in spring creeks, 189
   stoneflies, 70–71
   terrestrials, 183–85
invasive aquatic species. *See* didymo

J
jackets, *13*
jigging. *See* kayaks

K
Kaufmann's Rubber-Legged Stonefly, 82
   See also nymphs
kayaks, 226–31
kick boat. *See* float tubes
knots, 59–65
   overwrapping, 61
   practice tying, 199
   "seating" and wetting, 62
   testing, 276
   types of, 62–65
Kokanee salmon, 134

L
lakes, 204–10, 235

lake trout, 135
   See also trout
lanyards, 25–26
leader, 33–34, 60
   for high-sticking, 163
   replacing, 61, 282
   straightener for, 29
   wind knot in, 187
   See also lines
leeches, 71, 206, 210, 217
Leisenring Lift, 153, 162, 216
   See also casting
lines, 36–38, 60
   bird's nest in, 186
   controlling, 166, 167, 168
   feeling nicks in, 62
   mending, 3, 156, 192
   putting on reel, 97
   replacing, 61
   stripping, 108, 283
   "weights" of, 37–38
   See also knots

M
maps, using, 234, 235–39, 279
mayflies, 68, 70, 184, 213, 215
mending, 3, *102,* 156–57
   in rivers, 192
   See also casting; lines
midges, 71, 155
Murray, Harry, 184
mysis shrimp, 71, 191, 210, 213

N
nail knot, 65, 97
   See also knots
neoprene socks, 20, 195
neoprene waders, 14, 17
nets, 26–27
nippers, 27–28
nylon waders, 14
nymphs, 79–83
   dead-drifting, 164
   dry fly/nymph dropper rig, 214–15, 217
   See also wet flies

O
one-handed cast, 99–101
   See also casting

P
Pacific salmon, 131, 134
packs, chest and waist, 22–24, 26
Parachute Adams, 78, 84, 92, 128, 196, 231
   for dropper rig, 214
   See also dry flies
Parachute Blue-winged Olive, 85
   See also dry flies
Patriot, 85
   See also dry flies
personal floatation devices (PFDs), 181, 206, 231–32, 234
personal watercraft, 206
   float tubes, 231–34
   kayaks, 226–31
Pheasant Tail, 81–82, 215
   See also nymphs
photography, outdoor, 246–59
   cameras, 247–48, 250
   tips for, 250, 252, 254–59
pocketwater, *159,* 161, 162, 190, 211–12, 238
polarized sunglasses, 30–33, 136, 149, 200, 265, 276, 282
ponds. *See* stillwaters
Prince Nymph, 83, 86, 268
   See also nymphs

Q
Quill Gordon, 85
   See also dry flies

R
racks, for rods, 54–57
radios, handheld, 279
rainbow trout, 124–26, 131, 140
   See also trout
raingear, 198, 281
reels, 34–35, 199
   attaching to rod, 96–97
   inspecting, 196
   putting line on, 97

retrieves with, 169
storing, 53, 54
riseforms. *See* trout
rivers, 192
    See also pocketwater
rods, 40–53, 277
    assembling and attaching reels, 95–97
    and backpacking, 262, 264, 265
    best choices, 45, 46–51
    fiberglass, 11
    inspecting, 196
    in kayaks, 230
    for lake fishing, 207
    lifting the tip, 168, 169, 171
    racks and organizers for, 54–57
    storing, 52–53
    for streamers, 224–25
    transporting, 41–42, 51–52, 54–55
    weight/length of, 41, 274
    when using multiple flies, 216–17
roll cast, 3, 113
    forward cast, 149
    freeing fly, 186
    modified roll cast, 102–5
    See also casting
Royal Wulff, 68, 84, 86, 91, 92, 191, 266
    description/photo of, 78, 79
    for dropper rig, 214, 218
    for small streams, 193
    See also dry flies
rubber waders, 14

S
salmon, 134–35
    See also trout
Salmonflies, 70
sandals, wading, 20
Scud, 82–83
    See also nymphs
Secrets of Angling, The (Denny), 74
shirts, fishing, 12–13
shoes
    hiking/fishing, 195
    soles of, 18, 276
    wading, 19–20
shrimp. *See* mysis shrimp

sinking lines, 38, 135
    See also lines
siscowets. *See* lake trout
skills
    catch-and-release, 173–77
    high-stick nymphing, 160, 161–65
    hooking and landing fish, 166–73
    positioning and stealth, 147–53
    presentation of fly, 153–57, 166
    reading the water, 157–59, 161
    wading tips, 178–81
snails, 71
socks, 20, 195, 265, 266
spring creeks, 188–89
standard cast, 108–12, 120–21
    See also casting
steeple cast, *109*, 113–15, 222
    See also casting
stillwaters, 204–10
    float tubes for, 232
    watercraft for, 206
Stimulator, 76, 86, 185, 196, 223, 268
    rubber-legged, 85, 218
    See also dry flies
stoneflies, 68, 70–71, 86, 155, 184
    habitat of, 212, 213, 215
streamers, 83–84, 215, 223–26
    See also wet flies
streams, small, 192–95
    meadow streams, 238
    using streamers, 225
strike indicators, 165–66
sunblock, 198, 281
sunglasses. *See* polarized sunglasses
surgeon loop knot, 64
    See also knots

T
tackle
    flies, 68, 73, 74–93
    inspecting, 196
    leader and tippet, 33–34, 60
    lines, 36–38, 60
    reels, 34–35
    rods, 40–51
    See also gear; specific tackle

tailwaters, 189, 191–92
techniques. *See* casting; skills
terrestrial insects, 71, 79, 155, 183–85
    See also insects
Thompson, Doc, 91
    tips from, 193–95
tippet, 33–34, 60, 282
    for multiple flies, 216, 218
    replacing, 61
    size of, 87
    See also leader; lines
topographic maps, 235, 236, 238–39
Treatyse on Fysshynge with an Angle, The
    (Berners), 74
Trichoptera. *See* caddisflies
Tricos, 71
trolling, 206, 207, *209*
    in kayaks, 230
trout, 122–45
  backcountry, 261
    in beaver ponds, 219
    diet of, 67–72
    habitat of, 140–41, 158–60
    hooking and landing, 166–73
    how to release, 173–77
    in lakes, 206
    riseforms, 141–42, 144
    species of, 123–35
    spotting, 136–39
    in spring creeks, 189
    in tailwaters, 191
    vision of, 12
Trudes, 78, 193, 214, 266
    Royal Trude, 66
    See also dry flies
Turck's Tarantula, 84, 85, 268
    See also dry flies

U
Universal Nymph, 82
    See also nymphs

V
vests, 21–22, 26

W
waders, 14–17, 179–80, 199
    repairing, 195–96
wading, 178–81, 192, 275, 277
wading boots, 18–19, 20, 276
    with felt soles, 18
wading sandals, 20
wading shoes, 19–20
waist packs, 24
Walton, Izaak, 74
water, drinking, 198, 266
watercraft, personal, 206
    floatation devices, 181, 231–32, 234
    float tubes, 231–34
    kayaks, 226–31
wet flies, 79–84, 217
    for beaver ponds, 223
    nymphs, 79–83
    presentation of, 166
    streamers, 83–84
    using multiple, 215–16
women, and fly fishing, 9
    gear for, *13*, 197
Woolly Buggers, 83–84, 225, 268
    See also streamers
worms, 71, 206, 274
Wulff, Lee, 78

Z
Zonker, 84
    See also streamers
Zug Bug, 82, 83
    See also nymphs